Insights
Into
Excellence

Insights
Into
Excellence

Revised Fourth Edition 1992
EXECUTIVE BOOKS
Life Management Services, Inc.
Harrisburg, PA

Printed in the United States of America.
ISBN 0-937539-15-5

ACKNOWLEDGEMENTS

This book is dedicated to the more than 30,000 Corporate and Association Meeting Planners who have entrusted the 22 members of Speakers Roundtable to positively impact their people.

Insights Into Excellence
Contents

"When you turn the pyramid upside down those roles get reversed. Your people become responsible and the job of management is to be responsive to their people."

K.B.

THE ROLE OF A MANAGER

Ken Blanchard
125 State Place
Escondido, CA 92025
(619) 489-5005

Few individuals have impacted the day-to-day management of people and companies as has Ken Blanchard.

A gregarious, sought-after and prominent author, speaker and business consultant, he is universally characterized by friends, colleagues and clients as one of the most insightful, powerful and compassionate men in business today. A multitude of Fortune 500 companies and fast-growing entrepreneurial enterprises have benefited from his unique approach to managing and developing people.

As a writer in the field of management, his impact has been far-reaching. His *One Minute Manager* Library, which includes *The One Minute Manager Meets the Monkey* (1989) has collectively sold more than 7 million copies and has been translated into more than 20 languages. He is also co-author with Dr. Paul Hersey of *Management of Organizational Behavior*, a classic textbook now in its fifth edition, and of *The Power of Ethical Management* (1988) with Dr. Norman Vincent Peale.

Blanchard is chairman of Blanchard Training and Development, Inc., a full-service management consulting and training company which he founded in 1979 with his wife Marjorie. He earned his Ph.D. in educational administration and leadership from Cornell University. He also maintains a faculty position in leadership at the University of Massachusetts, Amherst and a visiting lectureship at Cornell University, where he is also an elected member of the Board of Trustees.

Stories about bad managers abound. In fact, bad managers have been shown to make people sick. My wife Margie wrote a book with Mark Tager entitled *Working Well*. What they were trying to find out was what made a healthy work environment. One of the questions they asked people was: "Can a bad boss make you sick?" What do you think people said? "You're darn right!" People attributed ulcers, migraine headaches, stress and similar ailments to poor managers. You can talk to somebody at one moment and they will tell you how happy they are at work. See them two months later and they might be down in the dumps, depressed, and unmotivated about work. In many cases they have gotten a new boss. And what kind of boss is that? A boss who doesn't appreciate them, jerks them around and treats them as if they were office furniture.

Why do bosses behave like that? Why is the Number 1 style of management in America what I call "seagull management"? Seagull managers fly in, make a lot of noise, dump on everybody and fly out. I think the main reason why managers do this is that they can't understand the purpose of being a manager, that is, the "management paradox" as two of my associates—Rick Tate and Gary Heil—call it.

Most organizations are typically pyramidal in nature. Who's at the top of the organization? The chief executive officer, the chairman, the board of directors. Who's at the bottom? All the employees—the people who do all the work. The people who make the products, sell the products, service the products and the like. Now there is nothing wrong with having a traditional pyramid for certain tasks. The paradox is that the pyramid needs to be right side up and upside down depending on the task.

It's absolutely essential that the pyramid stay upright when it comes to setting major goals, vision, mission, values and the like. Moses did not go up on the mountain with a committee. Direction in organizations has to come from the top. Department chairmen have to set the vision and direction for their people. Where you get in trouble with the pyramid mentality, though, is when it comes to implementation. If you keep the pyramid right side up when it comes to accomplishing goals and visions, now you have a problem. When the pyramid is right side up, who do you work for? The person above you. The minute you think you work for the person above you, you are assuming that person—your boss—is *responsible* and what your job consists of is being *responsive* to that boss and to his or her whims and wishes.

I talk to people all the time, and they tell me the worst thing that can happen to you is to lose a boss, particularly one you have just figured out. Because then you have to go about figuring out a new other boss and how what he or she wants differs from your last boss. People think their career depends solely on the quality of their relationship with their bosses. As a result, the most important people in your organization—those individuals who have contact with your customers—spend all their time looking over their shoulder trying to figure out what their boss is doing rather than focusing their attention on the customer. Why? Because their boss is usually about to hit them. The American way of managing is if you do something right, nobody says anything. If you screw up, they hit you. We call that the "leave alone-zap" style of management.

Nobody objects to vision, direction and values coming from the top of the organization. But when it comes to implementing goals and visions if the pyramid remains right side up all of the energy and attention continues to flow back up the pyramid away from the customers. As a result, you get those people who have customer contact responding to requests by saying things like "I'm sorry. We can't do that. It's against our policy." And the customer says, "What do you mean it's against your policy? It's a stupid policy." And the reply: "I'm sorry. I just work here. They don't pay me to think. I leave the brains at the door and pick them up at the end of the day."

You have all kinds of responses like that. Why does this occur? Because the energy of the organization is going up away from customers. People are defending policies rather than serving customers. Let me give you a couple of specific examples.

One of my colleagues tells a story about a customer relations situation. This associate loves ice cream. One day while he was running errands he got an "ice cream attack" so he pulled into one of the local ice cream shops in San Diego. You know, the kind of place that has 33 flavors. He went in and the young girl behind the counter says, "May I help you?" My friend said, "Let me think about what I want." While he was thinking, an older woman came behind this young girl and whispered in her ear. When he looked up the young girl said, "You'll have to take a number."

Now there was nobody else in the store. My friend said, "you've got to be crazy. Why would I have to take a number? Nobody else is in the store." And sure enough she said: "It's our policy." He said, "Well, it's a stupid policy when there's nobody else in the store. I can see it when you've got a big crowd here, but this is ridiculous." The young girl lowered her voice and went quickly to her last line of defense. "Please don't get me in trouble. She's my boss." The older woman had gone to the other side of the store. He said, "This is so absurd I'm going to have to go along with it." So he took a number, which was 30. Now luckily the number behind the counter was only 27. So here is this poor gal with nobody else in the store shouting "27! 28! 29! 30!" and then finally, "Can I help you?" He said, "I'm no longer hungry."

How do you think the girl felt? What kind of self-esteem did she have? She knew that she was implementing a stupid policy for that particular circumstance. And yet, where was her energy focused? With the customer or with her boss? Clearly, with her boss. My friend went over to the boss as he was leaving the store and said, "That's the most ridiculous thing I've ever seen—having a customer take a number when nobody else is in the store." The boss looked at him with a sarcastic look and said, "If I don't get them to obey the policies when there is nobody in the store, how do you think I'm going to get them to do it when there is a real crowd in here?"

I had a similar experience in Hawaii not long ago. I was there giving a seminar and I called the golf course near our hotel to make a tee off time for after the seminar. I told the man in the pro shop that we would like to tee off at four o'clock. He said, "Fine." I said to him, "How long does it stay light?" He said, "It doesn't matter." I said, "What do you mean it doesn't matter?" He said, "The golf carts have to be in at 6:15." I said, "But how late does it stay light?" He said, "You don't seem to understand. The carts have to be in at 6:15 because they have to be on the battery charger by 6:30." Since it was June, I knew it stayed light until sometime between 8:00 and 9:00. I left confused.

The next day when the seminar was over people wanted to talk to me and my wife, and I didn't get over to the course until 4:30. They would not let us on the course. They said, "The last group goes out at 4:00. It takes about two hours to finish a round and the carts have to be in at 6:15." I said, "Well, can't we just go out and play a few holes?" He said, "We start the sprinklers right after the last group." I said, "Well, is there any way we can go around the sprinklers?" He said, "No. If you do and get wet or something, you're going to sue us." Now my wife, who is much better in these situations, went over to the attendant and, using all of her human relations skills including patting him on the hand, said, "Could we do a little problem solving? We'd like to play just a few holes. How could we do that?" He shouted, "Tomorrow!"

Now the first reaction to this kind of treatment is to blame the attendant. But as we saw in the ice cream example you can't blame the attendant. You have to look at the organization's management. Why do people hold on to silly policies when they don't make any sense for the customer? Because if they don't follow the policies they are going to get beaten up by their boss. The most popular leadership style in America is what we call "bicycle leadership." Bicycle leadership is when you bend your back to those above while you trample those below. I'll never forget that the cover of *The Saturday Evening Post* one time had a beautiful example of bicycle leadership. The first frame showed a guy being chewed out by his boss. The second frame showed him chewing out his wife. In the third frame, the wife was chewing out their little son. In the last frame, the little boy was kicking the family cat.

Blaming of that type occurs when the pyramid is right side up in the traditional sense for the implementation of goals. What do you think the stated goals of most organizations are? It's to serve the customer. And yet, because of the way we organize ourselves, few companies practice effective customer relations. When it comes to implementation and goal accomplishment I feel that we have to turn the pyramid upside down.

When somebody is a guest at a hotel, buying a product or service, as a customer he or she doesn't care who is the top management of the company. The most important person in the whole organization to that customer is the person they are dealing with right then and there. In most organizations the customer contact people are not only paid the least, but they are least appreciated. Why? Because the weight of the whole organization is coming down on top of them forcing them to squish the customers.

You can't expect to mistreat your people and then have them be nice to your guests. In our book *The Power Of Ethical Management*, Norman Vincent Peale and I had a great quote from Benjamin Franklin. He said, "You can't expect an empty bag to stand up straight." What he meant by this is that people with low self-esteem can't be expected to treat others well. If you don't care for your people, how are you going to have them take care of your customers? The only way is if you give your customer contact people some breathing room. How do you so that? By turning the pyramid upside down when it comes to implementation.

When you turn the pyramid upside down, who is at the top of the organization? The customer contact people. Who is *really* at the top of the organization? The customers. Who's at the bottom now? The "top" management. When you turn a pyramid upside down philosophically, who works for whom when it comes to implementation? You work for your people. This one change, while it seems minor, makes a major difference. The difference is between who is *responsible* and who is *responsive*. With the traditional pyramid, the boss is always responsible and his or her people are supposed to be responsive to the boss. When you turn the pyramid upside down those roles get reversed. Your people become responsible and the job of management is to be responsive to their people. That creates a very different environment for implementation. If you work for your people then what is the purpose of being a manager? *To help them accomplish their goals.* Your job is to help them win. Let me give you a few positive examples of customer service in an organization that has the pyramid turned upside down when it comes to implementation.

The first example comes from Nordstrom, a department store chain that started in Seattle and is slowly expanding across the country. It's wiping out competition wherever it goes. In fact, in several areas I understand they are even trying to zone Nordstrom out. Why? Because they are beating everybody to the punch when it comes to customer service. My daughter Debbie, who is 21, worked last summer as a sales cashier in Nordstrom in San Diego.

After about a week on the job, I had dinner with her and asked, "What is it like to work at Nordstrom? Tom Peters and everyone is talking about Nordstrom and their tremendous service." She said, "It's very different." I asked, "What's different about it?" She said, "Well, the first thing that is different is their orientation program. Every employee has to go through an orientation program before they can start work. The whole emphasis in the first part of the program is to teach everyone, all the employees, how to say 'No problem.'" The number one thing they want coming out of your mouth is 'No problem.'

At Nordstrom, they will take anything back that you have a problem with. One of Debbie's jobs as a cashier was taking stuff back. She said, "You wouldn't believe some of the junk

people bring back." At Nordstrom the assumption is the customer is always right. In most cases they give you cash back for
returns. They don't want their customers to go through all kinds
of paper work. The assumption of Nordstrom's top management
is that 90 percent of the people in America are honest and want
good service for being a customer. The other 10 percent will rip
you off. The problem is that most organizations are set up to
stop the 10 percent minority rather than serve the 90 percent
majority of honest customers.

I asked Debbie, "What else is a little different about working at Nordstrom?" She said, "My boss. About three or four
times a day he comes up to me and says, 'Debbie, is there anything I can do for you?' He acts like he works for me." The
reality in the Nordstrom philosophy is that he does. Every manager works for their people.

We had another beautiful example involving Debbie. Her
21st birthday happened to fall during Easter week last year.
That was vacation time for her at the University of Colorado. A
lot of her friends decided to go to Palm Springs. We wanted to
throw a party for Debbie so we decided to have it in Palm
Springs. We went to Rancho Las Palmas Marriott which is a
five-star hotel. It's one of my favorite places to stay. They had
a really nice room for our party, which included a disc jockey
for dancing and a bar. Fairly early in the party the waitress we
had came up to Debbie and asked her what she would like to
drink. Debbie asked for a Cape Cod.

Now I didn't even know what a Cape Cod was. I later
found out it was vodka and cranberry juice. It turns out it's a big
drink at the University of Colorado so four or five of Debbie's
friends asked for one, too. I happened to be standing at the bar
at the time. The waitress came up to the bartender and said, "I
have an order for five Cape Cods." He said, "I don't have any
cranberry juice behind the bar. Check with the kitchen." The
waitress went into the kitchen and came back a few minutes
later and said, "There's no cranberry juice on the property." The
bartender said, "Fine. Send the bellman to a grocery store to get

some." The waitress went over to Debbie and her friends and said, "I'd like to apologize. We don't have any cranberry juice on the property, but a bellman is going to the grocery store, and he'll be back in ten minutes with some cranberry juice."

Ten minutes later, the door of our banquet room opened, and there was the bellman with a case of cranberry juice. At this hotel, they give the bellmen discretionary money to use for the benefit of customers and in customer service situations like this.

Now, what do you think about the self-esteem of those people? Could they solve the guests' problems? Yes! Did they have to go and talk to the supervisor in that type of situation? No! When I sent a praising letter and talked to management about this example they were thrilled. They said that was exactly what they were trying to get their people to do.

When it comes to implementation the purpose of being a manager has got to be service. Serving who? Serving your people so that they can serve your customer. As a manager, if you don't serve your customer or you don't serve somebody who serves a customer you ought to be looking for another job. A customer is anybody who receives the results of your efforts. Customers are not only external to the organization, but can often be internal as well. In accounting, your customers are the different managers and departments that get your reports. In personnel, the customer is every employee.

In organizations, so often we don't make the switch in the direction of the pyramid when it comes to implementation. We set goals, we set dreams, and then we keep the pyramid right side up for implementation. It just doesn't work well that way. What happens when the pyramid remains right side up is that the energy in the organization goes away from the customer and people start thinking that their main avenue to success is their political relationship with those people above them. When it comes to accomplishing goals the role of the manager is to serve your people. It's the leader as follower and servant.

The best way I can illustrate this role and the power of it is when it comes to performance review. When I go around the country and ask people, "How many of you are thrilled with your performance review system? How many of you find it enhances self-esteem?" I hardly ever get anybody to raise their hand and say they feel good about their performance review system except some people in personnel who might have put it together.

Why don't people feel good about performance review? Because performance reviews are usually set up with the traditional pyramid mentality: The job of the manager is to beat people up, to catch people doing things wrong. If you have a performance review system where you have a rating scale from 1 to 10 from poor performance to good if you rated everybody a 10 that reported to you, how do you think you would get rated by your boss? 2 or 3. What would they say to you? "You're too easy. You're giving away the farm." As a result, it doesn't take managers long to realize that if he rates everybody highly, he gets rated low; therefore, the only way he can get rated highly is if he rates some of his people low. Now the toughest job of a manager is determining who they are going to rank on the bottom.

There are three parts to an effective performance review system. *Performance planning* where you set the goals and objectives, *day-to-day coaching* where you help the people accomplish goals, and *performance evaluation* where you sit down and look over a person's performance over time. Which of those three gets done first in most organizations? In most cases performance evaluation. Personnel comes up with some darn form. Then people say, "Well, maybe we ought to have some goals around here." Then they bring in goal writers, and they write goals and job descriptions. They fill notebooks.

What is the only one of the three main parts of a performance review system that never gets done on a systematic basis? Day-to-day coaching. And yet, if we turn the pyramid upside down and make the role of the manager to serve when it comes to implementation, what is the main job of a manager? Day-to-day coaching once goals are set to help people win.

The best analogy I can give to what I am saying goes back to my teaching career. I taught at universities for ten years. I was always in trouble. I was investigated by some of the best faculty committees. One thing that drove the faculty crazy is that on the first day of class I always gave out the final exam. The faculty would say, "What are you doing?" I'd say, "I'm confused." They'd say, "You act it." I'd say, "I thought I was supposed to teach these kids." "You are. But don't give them the questions on the final." I'd say, "Not only am I going to give them the questions on the final, but what do you think I'm going to teach them all semester? I'm going to teach them the answers because when they get to the final exam I want them to get A's." Life is all about getting A's, not some stupid normal distribution curve.

The job of a manager is to help people win. In order to do that you have to philosophically turn the pyramid upside down and recognize that your job when it comes to implementation is to help your people win. When you do that does it mean that you're setting easy goals? No way. In fact, people will set higher goals if they know their manager is committed to helping them win. The reason people don't want to set tough goals is that they think their manager will use those goals to beat them up in a much more systematic way than they did before. My experience is that people will stretch and push themselves if they are in an environment where the manager wants them to win. Life is all about winning and that should be the role of managers. Serve your people and help them win once the goals have been set. Do that, and you'll focus on the most important role of manager!

"...So it is more than willingness to change that sets the true leaders apart. It is seeking out change and wringing every bit of potential out of it that takes you to the next horizon in your own growth."

T.B.

QUICK, BEFORE IT'S GONE: GRABBING HOLD OF TOMORROW

Ty Boyd
The Cullen Center
1727 Garden Terrace
Charlotte, N.C. 28203
(704) 333-9999

Ty Boyd enjoys a multi-faceted career as a businessman, broadcaster, salesman, consultant, and internationally acclaimed professional speaker.

Ty is Chairman of Boyd-Crosby Advertising, Inc., and President of Ty Boyd Enterprises, Inc. Ty Boyd has been seen and heard on nearly every television and radio station in America. He's the host of the syndicated DAWN Show, a daily television series featuring motivational speakers and entrepreneurs. He also hosts a daily sales training program on the Automotive Satellite TV Network called "Making It Happen." He is a popular and in-demand speaker for over 150 audiences each year and has been featured in numerous management and sales films. Ty has been awarded the C.P.A.E. and Cavett Award from the National Speakers Association.

Ty's exceptional experience and research give him an in-depth understanding of many of the challenges facing each of us, both personally and professionally.

When I tell people I'm working on another book, the first question everyone asks is, "What's it about?"

That's not as easy to answer as I thought it would be. When I first started the project, I defined my subject easily. Communications skills. A crucial subject for leaders.

But as I pursued the subject, I realized I needed to do more. I wanted to lead others into new territory in defining their roles as leaders.

So I changed directions. I headed toward uncovering the leadership qualities that will be needed for the next decade—indeed, the next century.

Knowing the best ideas surface through teamwork, I turned to some of today's best leaders to find out what tomorrow's leaders will need. And what I found meant yet another change in direction.

What I found was that, almost to a person, the leaders I interviewed agreed that the most profound change in the business community during the next decade would be just that—change.

Change.

It once happened over decades. It once came upon us gradually, gave us time to adjust, to rearrange our thinking. In those days, you landed a job at the age of 20 and could be pretty certain the same company would be giving you a gold watch at your retirement 45 years later.

In earlier days, you could take a couple of years to make up your mind about career decisions, about new directions for your business.

Today, taking that much time leaves you sitting in the dust.

So the biggest change leaders must adjust to is the rapidity of change, the unrelentingly brisk change that barely allows us to catch our breath before it slips in something new again.

Hugh McColl proved his ability to react to change when his NCNB Corporation grew to be the seventh largest U.S. bank by responding to deregulation in the banking industry in the early 1980's. He says, "Increased competition will put enormous pressures on management to change, be flexible, to turn on a dime."

And most of us in the large companies that have dominated the business world of the '80s aren't equipped to handle that kind of change. Like huge ocean liners, we change directions only slowly. But we would do well to note how quickly and sharply a 25-footer can negotiate a turn in the water. There's a huge lesson there.

Allan Hurst, who's made quite a name for himself as a sales and management consultant (featured in Chapter 11 of this book), pointed out, "Big business gets all the press for screaming and yelling about how they're being strangled by Washington. The small business owner says nothing and just adjusts.

"You can bet five days after a bill is signed in Washington, the small business owner already has a strategy to counteract it."

Big business, on the other hand, spends too much time and too many dollars trying to figure out how to react.

We have to learn from the people who *react by acting*. We have to learn to make decisions quickly, to find ways to put those decisions into operation tomorrow and not at the beginning of the next fiscal year.

But reacting to change with flexibility instead of inertia results in more than business growth. The risk-taking that goes along with riding the crest of change, according to IGA Chairman Dr. Tom Haggai, becomes a trial by fire for leaders.

"Until you risk everything, until you get to that point in life where you face losing everything—and overcome the fear— you're never going to lead," he said. (Read further Tom Haggai thoughts in Chapter 7.)

So it is more than willingness to change that sets the true

leaders apart. It is seeking out change and wringing every bit of potential out of it that takes you to the next horizon in your own growth.

Clearly, *leaders are risk-takers.*
If you aren't pushing the limits, if you aren't making decisions that keep even your staunchest supporters wondering if you've lost your mind, you may not have what it takes to lead into the twenty-first century.
As tough as it is to set ourselves up for that kind of risk-taking, what is even harder is persuading others to make change.
"Change threatens people because it threatens their power," said professional speaker Dr. Jim Tunney (Chapter 20), a former school official who now serves as one of the NFL's top referees. "It threatens their security, it threatens their adjustment. We're going to have to help people understand that change and risk are part of their business."

It's part of our business.
As surely as delivering a quality product, or meeting a deadline or preparing a presentation that shows we're savvy with computer graphics, adapting to change and willingness to run risks are requisites for tomorrow's high-achievers. As leaders, we have to prepare ourselves and our people for that.
And this means, more than anything else, keeping our co-workers, our team, with us as we head toward change.
We do it through communication. We do it by making the challenges fun, by enjoying the process of exploring alternatives and looking for new answers.
We do it by encouraging, expecting, demanding innovation. We do it by allowing our people to be a valued, respected part of the process.
We do it by accepting that risk makes some failure inevitable. In others. In ourselves.

Leaders with whom I've spoken about change have pointed out that one thing we have to change is our attitude about failure. If we actively pursue change, if we are committed to shaking out of it every bit of growth and innovation we can, we are going to fail.

But don't allow yourself—or others—to translate failure into personal defeat.

"I know people who are marvelously creative, but the reason they never lead is they don't have the courage to act upon that which they create," Haggai said. "Leaders have the vision and the courage to act and thus don't even think in terms of success or failure. They believe even failure becomes the stepping stone for the next achievement."

Eddie James, President of Bridgemon, James & Shaver Advertising, Inc., in Louisville, takes an equally pragmatic approach to what many label failure.

"My wife runs a successful company and she'll ask sometimes if I think she should do this or that," James said. "My answer to that is, 'Do it and if it doesn't work, don't do it any longer.'"

Sounds like a simplistic approach; and maybe it is. But the fact of the matter is, both James and Haggai are right. You must have the courage to follow your instincts, to reach for the next goal. You must be willing to overreach yourself sometimes. Willingness to take action is a key ingredient for the real leader.

So my toughest challenge to you, if you want to be one of the change-agents in your company's future, is to be—not just *willing* to face change. But *eager* to seek it out. "Fire-in-the-belly" *hungry* for it. And then so *enthusiastic* about it that you have to make little effort to persuade others—they will be persuaded by your very enthusiasm.

Let's look again, briefly, at a few of the ways we can do that.

1. Face change head-on and quickly.

2. Court change. Anticipate it by remaining a lifelong student of your profession, by keeping your eye on fields that touch the edges of your profession.

3. Encourage your workers to court change by rewarding innovation, by giving them all freedom to dream.

4. See failure as an opportunity offered, not an opportunity missed.

What are some of the changes we must be prepared to face? As you might imagine, they change every day. And will change even more rapidly as the future is upon us. But some of the major ones, mentioned time and again by the leaders I've interviewed, are:

*The changing workforce—Tomorrow's workers may be under-prepared for the work they will be hired to do. Their lack of preparation will challenge us. Other workers who are *overqualified* will be asked to fill the slots of the under-prepared. Keeping them committed to jobs that offer little fulfillment will also challenge us.

As the decade rolls on, the numbers of females in the workforce will increase. These *women* will be drained by the double demands of work and family. We must answer this challenge. *The war on drugs* will move into our companies, our board rooms, our warehouses. Another challenge we must face. And we must be ready to understand and accept the individualized needs of *minorities* of all types.

What each of these changes points out is the leader's growing responsibility for the personal growth and the professional training of his fellow workers. Lifelong learning for all workers will become as necessary as a good benefits package and a liberal vacation plan.

*Making a personal contribution—We're going to measure success in different terms. No longer will it be solely based on the profit margin, the growing customer base, the promotions earned.

We're also going to look at how much leaders contribute to their communities. We need to direct our drive to succeed toward creating a better world—whether it comes down to ecological concerns or improving education or licking the drug problem.

Monetary success won't save any of us from a gradually faltering society and a rapidly disintegrating planet.

*The global economy—We're going to be forced, for the first time in many decades, to earn the standard of living we have taken for granted in this country. We're going to have to earn it with quality. With service. With excellence. And with a return to something we've come to regard as a quaint but outmoded notion.

We're going to have to earn our positions of respect and prestige with a return to...

*Ethics and integrity—The cry for a return to integrity, the warning that Americans aren't going to settle for a lack of accountability any longer, echoed resoundingly as I made my rounds interviewing leaders. If we ignore this cry, if we think we can continue to heap success upon success without regard for values and ethics, we are playing ostrich much more dangerously even than the auto makers in the early '70s, who really believed that Americans would soon abandon their love affair with the small car.

"The number one challenge facing anybody in leadership is integrity," said Bill Foster, former basketball coach of Miami University. "And we'd better hope it filters down. Because if it doesn't, we're all in trouble. Whatever comes in second is a distant second."

We must return values, integrity, to that measuring stick we use to determine when a leader has truly achieved success.

So we face strong challenges as we move toward the twenty-first century. Tougher ones, perhaps, than simply upping our productivity quotas or finding new dollars to invest in state-of-the-art equipment. Challenges that will stretch us as individuals as well as managers of businesses.

And it is that kind of stretching that fosters leadership in each of us.

No one has said it better than the Rev. Jesse Jackson, who recently told an audience of young people, "Every person must have a vision that is greater than his comfort zone. So when I become President of the United States..."

And he's right. If he doesn't have that kind of vision, if he isn't willing to run the risk of falling flat on his face in grabbing for his particular star, he'll be forever earthbound.

And someone else will grab the comet by the tail, someone who:

1. Anticipates change and welcomes it;

2. Feels fire in the belly when facing change;

3. Knows how to persuade others to join the journey to tomorrow;

4. Is willing to risk failure in order to reach success.

This is at least a partial blueprint for facing tomorrow's change. If you follow it, you'll be ready for whatever changes that blueprint requires once tomorrow arrives.

"The new tools of technology are the 'key elements behind change,' and like a deck of cards, you must know the entire deck in order to play the game. Knowing what these tools are and how to apply them creatively, is rapidly becoming a matter of business survival and a key to personal gain."

D.B.

TECHNOLOGY HAS DEALT US A NEW DECK OF CARDS

3

Daniel Burrus
P. O. Box 26413
Milwaukee, WI 53226
414/774-7790
800/827-6770

Daniel Burrus is considered one of the nation's leading technology forecasters, and is the founder and president of Burrus Research Associates, Inc., a research and consulting firm that specializes in researching global innovations in science and technology, their creative application and future impact.

He is the co-editor and writer of four recently published books— *The New Tools of Technology, Medical Advances, Environmental Solutions,* and *Advances in Agriculture,* and is the author of several audio and video learning programs. The company publishes a variety of technology publications, including *Technology Futures Newsletter®.*

He uses cutting-edge information to help corporations, associations and universities creatively apply new technology as they develop both short and long-range plans. His client list includes a wide range of industries, including many companies from the Fortune 500.

Dan's interest in research became apparent in his third year of college when he became one of the first undergraduates in the nation to direct a federal research grant. He went on to found and manage five businesses, one of which was a national leader with over 30 locations.

For the past nine years he has delivered over 100 speeches annually to associations, corporations, and professional organizations.

We are poised on the threshold of the twenty-first century. Life as we know it will change more in the next 15 years than in the previous 100. How will you and I learn, work, and play in the year 2000?

Historical evidence reveals that it is science and technology that create the most predictable permanent changes. After researching global innovations in science and technology, I have been able to identify 20 major new core technologies that will shape the next decade. I like to think of them as 20 new cards to play with.

Picture a deck of playing cards in the palm of your hand. Imagine that I am now handing you 20 new cards, each one having symbols and numbers you haven't seen before. Two very important actions are now required. First, you have to know what *all* of the new cards are if you expect to win the game. Second, the rules have just changed. You can't expect to win unless you know what the new rules are. The old familiar cards still have their power but, in the decade of the 1990s, the game has changed. By showing you the new cards you will have a better chance of winning. Winning is not only a matter of survival, but a key to leadership and entrepreneurship in the 1990s.

Prepared or not, we now must play with all of the new cards. Some of us understand a few of the cards, but many of them are unfamiliar to the population at large. It's difficult to create a better tomorrow when people are playing with a "half deck." To survive and prosper now and in the future, we need to be playing with a "full deck."

These 20 cards are the far-reaching, life-altering innovations and inventions that began to touch our lives in very meaningful ways starting in the mid-'eighties. Many of them are already impacting heavily upon our economy, our educational systems, our governmental structures, and every facet of our personal and corporate lives. Others will have their greatest impact during the last part of the 1990s.

In order to achieve your goals in times of rapid change, it is important to keep the big picture in mind. The 20 new core technologies have changed the big picture! The new tools that you and I will use to build the future will spring from the 20 new core technologies.

The better we understand the individual and collective impact of these cards, the more accurately we see the *new* big picture and take the appropriate actions. What is even more vital is that by understanding that the following 20 core technologies are the fundamental driving forces of permanent changes, we will be well prepared to face the momentous changes that are ahead.

Meet The 20 New Cards We've Been Dealt

1. Genetic Engineering
2. Advanced Biochemistry
3. Bioelectricity
4. Advanced Personal Computers
5. Multi-Sensory Robotics
6. Artificial Intelligence
7. Parallel Processing
8. Digital Electronics
9. Lasers
10. Fiberoptics
11. Optical Data Storage
12. Microwaves
13. Advanced Satellites
14. Photovoltaic Cells
15. Micromechanics
16. Molecular Designing
17. Advanced Polymers
18. High-Tech Ceramics
19. Fiber-Reinforced Composites
20. Superconductors

Creatively Applying Technology

In order to maximize the true potential of the new core technologies, you have to know two things:

Number 1: You have to know what options exist. You can't use a FAX if you don't know it exists. Understanding what options exist is crucial. So many people plan for the future without a clear understanding of what options exist, assuming a future exactly like today but ten years down the road. We will focus on the major new rules that accompany the tools of technology.

Number 2: You have to creatively apply technology. I know people who can pick up a telephone and make a million dollars. I know people who can pick up a telephone and lose a million dollars. What's the difference? It's not the brand of the phone. It's what you did on that phone.

I walked into a small transmission repair store about three or four years ago to get some work done on my car's transmission. I walked in, looked around and said, "You should be using satellites in here." Of course, the guy looked at me a little weirdly and said, "Satellites?" I responded by saying, "What I mean is, you should be using pagers, they work because of satellites. You should be using pagers in here."

And he said, "Pagers? We don't even have a PA system. What are you talking about? We only have six people working here. When I want to page somebody, I just say, 'Hey, Frank!' We don't need satellites in here, fella!"

Then I said, "No, you don't understand, sir. I want you to give the pagers to your customers so they can go shopping in the large shopping center next door. When the car's ready, beep them. Your customers will be able to do two things at once; you'll save them time, and you'll have more customers."

He said, "I think we need satellites in here."

The problem the transmission repair clerk had was that he thought he knew what to do with a pager. Wasn't that a shame? We think we know what to do with a FAX. That's why some of us don't have one. We think we know what to do with a computer. More people are using computers today, but the studies show that we are not experiencing a gain in productivity. We are using basically the same technology and we are all doing the same thing on it. What is the advantage? There is none! We have to do something a little different. We have to creatively apply technology.

How do most business people use a computer? They do what they used to do before having a computer, except now they're computerized. Why is it that recent surveys indicate many of the Fortune 500 CEOs are not using a computer? The CEOs tend to defend themselves by saying, "I have somebody else to do that." You know what I say to them? Great! What *you* need to be doing on the computer is what no one else is doing on it, including your competition's CEOs. You need to use technology in a new creative way. A user-definable way. It's a powerful way to gain an advantage.

Creatively applying technology is a key to your success in the future. The problem we face when trying to creatively apply technology is that we were never taught how to be creative.

It's very likely that you have never had formal training in developing or using your creativity. I'm not saying that you're not creative; I'm just saying you haven't had any training. Why? We tend to think creativity is a gift and that only a few have it.

Some people seem to have creative ideas flowing off the top of their head. This often leads to a big problem. They never seem to do their ideas. Why? They always have a better one.

I was like that. At one point in my life, I was running several different businesses at the same time. Luckily, I remembered something that I had learned when I was a little kid.

When the sun beats down on the blades of grass, it helps the grass to grow and that's a wonderful, beautiful, natural thing. When I take my trusty piece of technology, in this case my magnifying glass, and put it between the sun and the blades of grass, I can make the grass burst into flames. What did I learn? I learned the power of focus. *Creativity has no power if it isn't* _focused._ I believe many of us are out of focus. Do I mean you should try not to have ideas? No! Bring your unrelated ideas into a sharp focus, like the magnifying glass brought the rays of sun into focus. Creative ideas need the power of focus.

What about people who say, "I'm not creative. I can never think of a Halloween costume. I'm an implementer."

Research indicates that every single person is highly creative. Studies were conducted recently to determine what group in American is the most creative. The researchers looked at the Palo Alto research team, NASA researchers, doctors, lawyers, teachers—a wide variety of different groups—to see who is the most creative. The most creative by far were the kindergartners.

What happens as we get older? Does creativity get sucked out of our brain? No, we learned how not to be creative. If you're a third-grade student and you're showing a lot of creativity, what does the teacher typically do? Your parents are called and told, "You've got a problem child."

Let's say that you work in a division of a large company and you are showing a lot of creativity. What typically happens? You're transferred because the manager considers you a hassle. Managers were never taught how to manage someone who's creative. I believe you're either managing creativity or mismanaging it, there's no in between. We all have creativity deep within us, and in this decade of rapid change, it is our challenge to use it.

Time Is the Currency of the 'Nineties

Change has changed! The pace of change will continue to accelerate throughout this decade like a snowball rolling down a hill gathering momentum and speed.

Every now and then I run into someone who believes that the pace of change will once again slow down. They always remind me of a presentation that I delivered to 40 IBM executives several years ago. One of them had invented the bar code reader. The average person first noticed bar code readers in our food stores in 1984. If you bought a gallon of milk, beep, it would tell you how much it cost. The executive who invented the bar code reader said to me, "It took seven years from the time I invented the bar code reader until the time anybody used it. Don't tell me technological changes are fast."

I said, "I understand. There is a time line when it comes to developing new technology." First you have to go through a discovery phase. Then you have to go through an observation phase. Then you have to go through a feasibility phase. Then you have to go through a development phase. Then you have to go through a production phase. And, that takes a lot of time. For example, fluorescent lighting was invented in 1852. It didn't go into production until 1934. It took 82 years and the inventor was dead! If he would have been alive, he might have said, "I've got an illuminating idea; you'll like this." But the idea went right over everybody's head, they missed it. The ballpoint pen was invented in 1888, but you couldn't write with it until 1938. The zipper was invented in 1891; you couldn't zip it up until 1923. Change wasn't that fast when it came to technology. But now something has happened to change itself. Change has changed!

In a time of rapid change you have to move fast. The reason is simple. Everyone else is moving fast trying to keep up, including your competition. It used to be the price that determined what food store you would buy your groceries in. Now, it's the length of the line and how much time you will spend in it.

Every now and then I pull my car into a self-service gas station and I get one of those slow pumps. I become instantly stupid. I won't fill it up. Instead I only pump about $5 in. This is really stupid because I will soon run out of gas again and waste even more time, but I can't help myself. Will I ever go back to the gas station with slow pumps? No, never!

My perception is that I don't have much time, and that perception will intensify for all of us in this decade. Time is the currency of the 'nineties! You need to ask, where are my bottlenecks of time? Or are my clients going somewhere else? I recently changed insurance agents – not because my past agent was not a nice guy; it was because I always spent too much time

with him whenever we got together. I want the human relationship, but every minute counts, and with him I felt it took too
much of my time. He lost a very large policy. Where are your
bottlenecks of time as they relate to the people you serve?

We are all finding ourselves needing to do more with less.
The problem is that there is only so much of us to go around. We
do want to get to know our families. *The solution lies in your
ability to leverage your time with technology.*

Why has the microwave oven been so popular? It allows
the customer to do more in less time. Why is the cellular phone
so popular? You can turn unproductive time, such as being
caught in traffic, into productive time. We need to evaluate all
of our current technologies and ask the question: Am I using this
technology to best leverage my time?

Time is worth more than money! The new Acura all-alu-
minum sports car has a list price of $60,000. The current going-
price at most Acura dealerships is $85,000, if you're lucky. Or,
you can wait a few years to get one at list price. People are willing to pay for time.

In the 1980s, the value was on material wealth; in the 1990s
it will be on free time because you will have less of it. So you
purchased a new Corvette. How often do you get to drive it?

Most sales are based on trust, which means forming a relationship. The problem lies in getting the client to find time to do
it, and then in quickly establishing a trusting relationship. The
answer lies in knowing when to use the human interface and
when to use technology to leverage both your time and your
client's time.

In this era of rapid change, market conditions can make
major shifts overnight. Technologies can either render markets
obsolete or create entirely new ones for our products in a matter
of weeks. Formidable new competitors seem to come out of the
woodwork. *With time-based competition* (using speed as a competitive advantage) becoming more popular than *price-based
competition* (using low prices to gain an advantage), it has never
been more important to take time to focus on the future.

Take Your Biggest Problem And Skip It!

Have you noticed that in times of rapid changes your desk piles ever higher with important problems to solve? Take a minute to think of your biggest problem. The new management principle for the 1990s is: Take your biggest problem and skip it. If you're like most people, your biggest problem was a *current* problem. Your biggest *current* problem is not your biggest problem. Your big problems of the past aren't that big; you already had them. Your problems of the future aren't that big; you haven't had them yet. So you spend all of your time on your current problems, and with the pace of change at such a high rate, your desk keeps piling up with problems.

If I tell you to skip your biggest current problem, what have I just saved you? Time! Time is the currency of the 1990s! That problem was going to drain away so much of your time you would have had to take a stress class—which would have taken even more of your time. What do I want you to do with all that new-found time? I want you to start solving the predictable problems you were just about to have; it's the only way to clear your desk in a time of rapid change.

You *can* predict your future problems. When do people get a burglar alarm? After being robbed. When do people take karate lessons? After being mugged. When do people go to a bank and ask for a loan? When they are hurting for money. What does the bank say? "You should have come when you had money."

If you feel that you can't skip your current problem, then spend far less time on it so you can devote more time to solving tomorrow's predictable problems today.

Focus On The Future

Perhaps the most productive approach to maintaining a future focus is to frequently re-evaluate your corporate mission statement, and to keep it focused on your customers' *future*

needs rather than on *current* needs, functions or products. Some
helpful questions may include:
   (1) Who are my current customers?
   (2) Who are most likely to continue to be customers?
   (3) Who are most likely to be my future customers?
   (4) What new markets are evolving in the direction that
       we are heading?
   (5) What current market could evolve into a new market
       for our products or services?
   (6) Are we working at developing products or services
       that will render our current offerings obsolete?
   With a new higher value being placed on time, it is
imperative to constantly evaluate how you are spending it.

Building Change Into The Plan

   Many people today feel that it is a waste of time to do any
long-range planning because of the tremendous rate of change.
My research indicates that in times of rapid change, it is even
more important to have a specific, long-range plan in writing. It
has been said that failing to plan is planning to fail. You can't
get from point A to point B if you don't know where point B is.
It is, however, equally important to build change into your plan.
   When I climbed my first mountain in the late 1970s, I can
remember looking at the top, my goal, from the bottom and
developing a plan. I could see the path I would take and I knew
my goal.
   A funny thing happened as I started to hike up the mountain.
I had a different view and found a better path, and then another
and then another. Building change into my plan was a good
strategy. My goal was the same, but I now had a better path.
When I reached the top, I saw another top! *It turns out that you
can't see the real top from the bottom. When you get to the top,
there is usually another top. I had to change my goal several
times as I got closer to the top, but I would have never gotten
that far if I hadn't had a goal in the first place.*

The phone company built change into their push button telephones. The push button phone has been around for a long time. Why isn't it obsolete? Because they put two buttons next to the O that did nothing. Why? Someday, they might do something. Good thinking!

Apple Computer first built the Macintosh with no expansion slots because they said it would do everything you'd ever want it to do. What did people do? They got a screwdriver and changed it. What did Apple do? They got rid of the guy who thought that up, and they put slots in it so you can more conveniently make changes.

When you need to buy new office equipment or any new type of technology, ask: how much is change built into it? If change isn't built into it, it will be obsolete far too soon.

A Glimpse Ahead

When planning the future, we must not fail to see the *new* big picture, based on the predictable permanent changes the 20 new core technologies are creating.

Don't be afraid to step away from your *current* problems and take some time to digest some of the changes that are taking place in our society. You have more at stake than just survival. When you take time to understand some of the new cards that we are dealing with, the leverage you gain will easily offset stresses that we are all facing in this decade of enormous change.

What will ultimately determine how well or how poorly we use the 20 cards science and technology have given us will be the way the typical person uses them. The more clearly we understand them, the more we can profit from the benefits they can bring to us. Just as people of the 'fifties could better see the 'sixties and beyond by understanding radio and television, we can see the 'nineties and beyond by understanding this new deck of 20 cards we've been dealt. *By understanding what the new cards are, and how they work together synergistically, we can more accurately visualize where our world is going.*

"Alignment has two parts: (1) the order or sequence in which you arrange your values (in other words, what you value and respect most), and (2) the degree to which your lifestyle is aligned with your values. Real motivation comes from that which we value most."
J.C.

INNER√IEWING: FINDING "THE NATURAL" IN PEOPLE

4

Jim Cathcart
P.O. Box 9075
La Jolla, CA 92038
619/558-8855
800/222-4883

As the owner of a consulting firm in La Jolla, California and a partner in a psychological research firm in Carefree, Arizona, Jim Cathcart spends most of his time helping people understand each other and themselves.

Jim is known for his books on "Relationship Selling," his videos on Customer Service and his successes as President of the National Speakers Association for 1988-89.

With over one thousand professional speeches and seminars to his credit, Jim has become one of the most popular speakers in America. His most popular topics include: Executive Team Alignment; How to attain your Optimum Velocity; and Relationship Marketing and Service.

Jim has been awarded the C.P.A.E. from the National Speakers Association.

There's a story I often use in my speeches about a guy I met on a plane not too long ago. Upon learning that I was the President of the National Speakers Association, he said, "You must be one of those 'motivators'," and then added, "Motivation is no good because it doesn't last." To this, the flight attendant standing nearby replied, "Neither does a bath but it's still a good idea now and then!"

Well, that's true, lots of things don't last—exercise, meals, meditation, relaxation, even hugs—but all of them have their place and are a good idea now and then.

When it comes to motivation, there IS one thing that does last…and that is the source of motivation…our inner values. As a matter of fact, once you learn someone's beliefs, you can accurately predict what will motivate them.

It is possible to discover and understand the central aspects of our personality through a technique called "Inner√iewing," (looking within).

A successful sales leader and mentor of mine, Joe Willard, often reminds me of a favorite saying of his father's: "People change—but seldom." And for our core personality that is true. Outwardly, all of us grow and develop; but on the inside we remain basically the same.

This flies in the face of long-standing assumptions. Let's examine one of them.

JC Penney said, "No man need live a minute longer as he is because the Creator endowed him with the ability to change himself." A lot of people would agree and believe that this means we have the power to change our personalities.

While every person is capable of growth and improvement, virtually no one is capable of an actual change in personality. After all, your personality is the sum total of who you are. Consider the consequences if we really could and did change our core personalities.

Researcher and entrepreneur, Robert Horton, says, "It is a universal human need to be known and understood, but if who you <u>are</u> changes then you can't be known. If you are unknowable, then you can't be loved. If you can't be loved, then there is no hope."

But there <u>is</u> hope because the core of each person is like a seed which has within it the person you were designed to become. If you start with an acorn, no matter how well you train it or how hard you work it, it will <u>never</u> produce a Giant Redwood. But with proper care and attention, it will generate one of the finest OAK trees you've ever seen, but not if you treat it as a Redwood; only if you deal with it as an OAK.

People are the same way. Each of us is designed perfectly for certain environments. Our task, then, is to identify surroundings and people compatible with us. We should do this as early as possible so we may make choices which align us with supporting relationships and environments.

Happiness and success aren't achieved through personal <u>change</u>; they are achieved through personal <u>choice</u>. Once you learn to make choices which will support the person you really are, your life will become more fulfilling.

In 1969 Buckminster Fuller said, "Change the environment; do not try to change man."

Any parent of two or more children will confirm that those children, even though raised in the same home by the same parents, have been <u>very</u> different personalities from day one. These differences were noticeable from the way they took their food to the way they responded to others. You see, just as trees vary from oaks to willows to evergreens, so do people.

Every person is distinct and unique and must be dealt with as such. You've heard the statements: People do things for their reasons, not yours; You must manage different people differently; Different strokes for different folks; To each his own.

OK, if we have a distinct and knowable personality, and the key to our motivation lies within it, then what are the core aspects that define us?

The people who developed the Inner√iewing method and the computerized profile which supports it are the psychological researchers at the Carefree Institute, an Arizona "Think Tank."

They have discovered that there are four primary aspects of personality. They are:

1. Value Alignment
2. Intellectual Capacity
3. Velocity, and
4. Behavioral Style.

Robert Horton, founder of the Carefree Institute, says these aspects are like the gauges on an aircraft instrument panel. If you don't read all the gauges, then you'll never have a clear picture of what is going on or how to respond to it appropriately.

Similarly, if you don't read all of the gauges when dealing with people, you will be forced to guess what their behavior really means and who they really are. There have always been people who have had special abilities which caused them to be respected and valued, like the Indian Scout who could read signs and find significance where others saw nothing. Learning to read the four gauges gives you the special ability to read people. The four gauges again are: Alignment, Capacity, Velocity and Style. Let me define each one:

Alignment has two parts: (1) the order or sequence in which you arrange your values (in other words, what you value and respect most), and (2) the degree to which your lifestyle is aligned with your values. Real motivation comes from that which we value most.

Here's an example: A friend of ours had a successful career as a psychiatrist. He ultimately ended up with a thriving practice in Beverly Hills. As retirement age approached, he became more and more frustrated with his work and finally decided to take early retirement.

With lots of uncommitted time on his hands, he began working with his son in the masonry construction business. In a short time his whole life seemed to improve. Tanned and healthier, he started looking forward to working each day. Importantly, he also became more fun to be around. When I asked him why he had spent all those years in Psychiatry, he explained that his parents had programmed him. He had worked in medicine, not because he loved it, but because it was his parents' dream for him to become a doctor. Being very intelligent and adaptable, he made a success of it on one level, but he was living someone else's dream. Years ago, had he followed his heart instead of his parents' wishes, I'll bet he would have been every bit as financially successful as a Contractor and probably a great deal happier all along.

Some people work all their lives at jobs which don't bring them happiness while others discover their right path early on. Unsatisfying jobs are more stressful, and higher stress levels tend to shorten life spans. The quicker we learn to follow our hearts, the happier we will be and, no doubt, the longer we will live.

Where is your heart? What brings you happiness? Many people don't really know. Here's where to look:

There are seven values and everything we want can be described by them. We each have all seven values. The priority they have for us shapes our beliefs, interests and desires. These values are: **Sensuality, Empathy, Wealth, Power, Aesthetics, Commitment and Knowledge.**

Sensuality represents the relative importance of feeling and sensing. A person with a high sensuality value will seem to always find a way to indulge their hedonistic impulses. For example: Long distance runners are expressing their high sensuality when they run, not for fitness, but for an adrenalin high. Gourmets are highly sensual, as are massage therapists. A man I know set out to buy two sport coats for his travel wardrobe, but at the last minute he settled for one, far more expensive, cashmere coat for the joy of feeling the rich fabric. (That's sensuality at work!) In Manhattan there is a sign which says, "The Lone Star Cafe—where too much ain't enough!" (More Sensuality)

Empathy is the value related to Selflessness or sensitivity to others. Highly empathetic people are humanitarians by instinct. When walking through a crowd they will instinctively notice and respond to the needs of others. They hold doors open, pick up dropped items and cry with joy at someone else's happy moments. You'll consistently find them in nursing, social work, counselling and education. Examples are: Mother Theresa, Albert Schweitzer and, yes, even Mister Rogers.

Wealth as a value is not expressed through the amount of money or number of things one has acquired, but rather through the relative importance he places upon them. It's not wealth for power, but more of the Ebenezer Scrooge approach—wealth just for wealth's sake.

These people seem to aspire for more dollars rather than for the comfort and security money represents to others. For example, it is said that billionaire J. Paul Getty once installed a pay phone in the foyer of his castle for guests to use.

Donald Trump and the late shipping tycoon, Aristotle Onassis, showed strong wealth values by pursuing money long after they controlled more than they could use. For these people wealth is a means of keeping score.

Power comes in many forms, but as a value, it is expressed in the relative importance of authority, influence and gaining the respect and admiration of others. It is the prime mover of politicians, performers and military leaders. When one works for little money but hopes to gain prestige from their position, they are placing a high value on power.

Power oriented people often seek competition in order to show their abilities. But make no mistake, their objective is to win, not merely participate. They agree with former Green Bay Packers football coach, Vince Lombardi: "Winning isn't everything, it is the ONLY thing."

High Power people love being in charge and avoid situations where they play a background role. Two sides of power are personal power, which comes from growing toward one's best, natural self; and position power which is gained through achievement of titles, awards and positions of authority.

Aesthetics or Beauty are most important to some people and they express this value by seeking harmony in their environment. For example, those with a high aesthetic value decorate their homes, vehicles or offices in ways that are visually and audibly pleasing. They'll install a special sound system or color coordinate their environment even when faced with limited financial resources. They will sit facing the best view or install a fountain in their garden area.

Imagine an aesthetic person who just bought a very expensive painting trying to explain the purchase to their high wealth value spouse. One would be describing the look and feel of it, while the other was wondering about its resale value or investment potential.

Commitment is of highest importance to some. Those possessing a high commitment value find it vital to live their philosophy. They sometimes become zealots about their causes and staunch defenders of their beliefs. You'll find them involved in political campaigns, church work, charitable causes, or actively convincing you to adopt their point of view. They are the faithful, hardworking core of every organization or family.

These are dedicated people who take their agreements seriously. They walk their talk. If they say they will do it, they'll

do it. They find it difficult to understand how others can vacil-
late on certain issues, while they feel so committed. Their word
is their bond. A handshake is a contract.

The **Knowledge** value is evident in one's desire to know
HOW things work. My grandfather, upon buying a new car,
would literally take it apart to find out how it operated. Unfortunately, he usually had to hire someone to help him reassemble it.
Knowledge oriented people are curious; they want to know
what your sources are, how you support your ideas, how one
notion will affect other aspects of a problem and so forth. They
tend to be organized and concerned about follow through. To
them, it's not enough to just get off to a good start, they must be
able to see how things will come to completion. Theirs are tidy
minds and they want closure. They tend to be the ones who
take the time to understand and gain mastery in their chosen
field.

One fellow I know with a high knowledge value is an absolute klutz when it comes to mechanical devices, but he is a whiz
in the area of personal finances. That's a combination of
Knowledge and Wealth working simultaneously.

There you have it, the source of motivation, your core values: Sensuality, Empathy, Wealth, Power, Aesthetics, Commitment and Knowledge. To remember them, try to envision a little
sewing kit and use the acronym Sew Pack— S E W P A C K.
Sensuality, Empathy, Wealth (SEW) Power, Aesthetics, Commitment and Knowledge (PACK).

But what if the only thing you knew about a person was his
motivation? Wouldn't you be missing a lot? Sure you would,
because you'd also need to understand one's intellectual capacity, energy levels, background experiences and behavioral tendencies. In other words, Capacity, Velocity and Style.

First, let's examine Capacity. Every person has a certain

amount of what might be called "mental horsepower." For some, it is very high; for others, it is lower. Contrary to popular belief, intellect doesn't determine success—good choices do. Once you know a person's Capacity, you have insight into their intellectual capability and another, major aspect of their personality.

Do you know someone who is clearly over-employed, meaning their job calls for much more intellect than they express naturally? To them, every day is a struggle and their stress levels will likely lead to job burnout. On the other hand, do you know someone who is grossly under-employed? You see, when our job doesn't challenge us to use most of our capacity most of the time, we become bored and disinterested. This also leads to poor performance through lack of attention.

In this respect, true "Alignment" for people is what Buddha called finding your "Right Livelihood," work that is matched to your inner personality. Appropriate capacity is a key.

There is some disagreement as to what constitutes intellect, even among psychologists. But there is no question that styles of thinking vary.

Here is how we define intellectual capacity: It is the ability to make distinctions. Sounds simple, I know, but that's the essence of it. People of high intellect like Albert Einstein would notice the finer points of almost anything they considered. For example, in watching the movie *Star Wars*, one person might say, "Boy, it was exciting, lots of action!" Another might say, "The variety of characters and scenes was tremendous and the visual effects were really impressive." While yet another would see the movie as a metaphor of life and react to the philosophies illustrated and the parallels between the movie characters and our own life situations.

Seeing grey where others see only black and white is noticing more in the same circumstances. This perception of nuance is making distinctions; a sign of high capacity.

A person who makes finer distinctions will see more

options. She'll notice more ways to express an idea or more possible solutions to a problem and consequently will tend to be more flexible and adaptable.

Imagine a Ferrari and a Volkswagen on a highway, both going 90 miles an hour. For the Volkswagen, that would constitute using full capacity, but the Ferrari would be loafing! They are both going 90, but one is really stretching while the other is just warming up. That's because the Ferrari's capacity is greater. At any speed, the Volkswagen is using more of its available capacity than the Ferrari. Capacity must also be aligned with lifestyle, otherwise friction will inevitably result. Volkswagens make better commuter cars than Ferraris, but Ferraris have more success on the race track. Neither is better or worse, they are simply suited to different tasks.

Everyone pretty well knows how bright their own intellectual light is burning and whether they're operating at 40 watts, 60 watts or 100 watts. And as long as their roles match their capacity, that part of their personality contributes to their growth and happiness.

The three major levels of capacity are Operational, Transactional and Conceptual. Operationals see things as they are and deal with what is known and tested. They are typically not risk-takers when it comes to unfamiliar situations. Their orientation is traditional. They focus on the application and operation of things rather than the concepts behind them. Operational thinkers are most comfortable and effective where roles are well defined. Approximately 80% of the population is operational. This is the most common thinking style. These are the folks who cook the food, print the forms, operate the machinery and deliver the goods. They are the public for whom TV is programmed, cars are designed and most advertisements are targeted. What they like determines what is "popular."

Familiar examples include John Wayne, Elvis Presley, and four out of five of the people you see day to day.

A transactional, the second thinking style, seeks out connections or "transactions" between things in order to produce new combinations and better outcomes. For example, Lee Iacocca took proven ideas from a variety of fields and installed them at Chrysler Corporation to achieve one of the great corporate turnarounds in business history. To become the father of fast food, Ray Kroc integrated Henry Ford's concepts of mass production into the kitchen to create what we know today as McDonald's. Most leaders are transactional thinkers who connect the inventions of others to useful applications. Transactionals represent about 18% of the population and are blessed with well above average intellectual capacity.

Transactionals can translate highly complex instructions into generally understandable terms and help bridge the gap between ideas and action.

Conceptual capacity is present in only about 2% of the population. Visionaries like Thomas Jefferson and Walt Disney join people like Buckminster Fuller and Mahatma Gandhi in conceptual capacity. These are the brilliant folks who seem to be always leaning forward in their minds as if they can hardly wait to experience the future. They see with clarity that the future can be improved by actions taken now. This is their focus.

These expansive thinkers often seem out of touch to most of us because they look at today merely as an element to be guided toward the creation of tomorrow.

Can you imagine the motivation level in a company where the conceptuals were working on a production line?

The entire driving force behind the Inner√iewing method is the achievement of Alignment: Helping each person choose the right path and guiding each worker toward their "right livelihood."

Since life is not a practice round, we must get the critical elements right the <u>first</u> time. That requires aligning your natural best self with your circumstances. Inner√iewing gives you a method for understanding the whole person and seeing matches between talents and tasks, values and visions. The beauty of Inner√iewing is that it allows you to see each person as a unique and valuable individual rather than generalizing with observations such as "he's a pretty good guy" or "she's really nice."

The Inner√iewing method is extended by a questionnaire and a computerized profile.* With the assistance of members of the staff of the Educational Testing Service at Arizona State University we have refined the instrument into a questionnaire of about 100 questions. Upon completing the questionnaire, the Inner √iew™produces a 14-16 page computerized summary of the unique aspects of the respondent's personality. This allows the person to make better informed life choices based on a broader and deeper understanding of himself. But you can learn to practice Inner√iewing even without the questionnaire by changing the way you listen to people. The four gauges are the backbone of this listening system.

After Values and Capacity, we look at someone's Velocity. If capacity is "can do," then velocity is "will to do." Velocity is the term we use to describe one's strength of will contrasted with the headstart or handicaps one has experienced.

If, in your background, you were mostly supported and encouraged to follow your heart and develop along the lines of your interests, you had an advantage over those who were not supported or encouraged. Their lack of advantage would mean that they had more to overcome. Example: Two people of equal capacity and matching values are both Harvard graduates pursuing a career on Wall Street. One of them grew up in the generally supportive home of a telephone repairman where very little of a financial nature was discussed. The other grew up in a home where Mom was a banker and Dad was a securities analyst. There was a *Wall Street Journal* on the coffee table every day and frequent family discussions explored the markets, business and banking.

Assuming all other things were equal, who has the advantage? It's obvious that the latter person has had the advantage of better preparation, even though their capacity and alignment for a career in finance is the same.

So background needs to be examined in relation to the field a person is pursuing. This is especially true for predicting future performance, because <u>patterns repeat</u>. If you know the size of the challenges one has had to overcome in order to get to where he is today, then you will know how intensely and effectively he has pursued his goals.

Once you know whether you're beginning with a head start or a handicap, you should factor in Energy. Everyone operates at the speed of their own internal metronome—their natural pace.

Those with high energy are described as working hard and playing hard. They seem to burn the candle at both ends and thoroughly enjoy the warmth of the flames. These are the people who, no matter what the task, seem to pursue it with a vengeance. They seem unable to sit still and need very little sleep to be at their best. They can sometimes work 16-hour days and seem to be having the time of their life.

On the other hand, there are the more laid back, easy paced people who never overreact to urgency. Like wet charcoal, they are very hard to fire up. They accuse their high energy friends of suffering from "hurry-sickness." These even-tempered souls will work a standard 8-hour day and no more, unless it's really necessary. They go by the mottos "enough is enough" and "slow and steady wins the race."

Picture this tortoise and hare team working side by side daily, or married. They might eventually drive each other nuts! But two, similarly paced and otherwise suited people would likely get in step and pull together like a well-matched team of horses. Naturally, tasks and workstyles need to match energy levels.

When you combine one's recurring energy patterns with background, you get a reading on how much velocity they have toward their goals—their angle of attack. The higher the angle, the sooner and more predictably they'll achieve their goals.

The final core aspect of personality measured by Inner√iewing is Style. "Style" is the term used to describe predominant behaviors when people respond automatically or instinctively to various situations.

Inner√iewing draws on the work of William Marston, a conceptual thinker and psychological theorist who developed what he called the "behavioral wheel" to describe four key attributes in determining a person's behavioral style. These attributes are: Dominance, Interaction, Steadiness and Compliance...D-I-S-C.

By assessing how we score on a continuum of high to low in each of these areas, we can draw meaningful conclusions about ourselves and the people who share our careers and personal lives. For example, people who score high in dominance are typically assertive, strong-willed and forceful, while low dominant folks are submissive and acquiescent. That tells you a lot about who can do the better job in a tough negotiation, doesn't it? High Interactive people are bubbly and outgoing, while low-Interactives are stoic and quiet. Which one do you want making sales calls?

High Steadiness people are happy to leave well enough alone and go with the program, while low-Steadiness types are always seeking change. One makes a great file clerk, the other can more quickly find short cuts.

Highly Compliant people stick to the rules and do what is expected. Low-Compliants believe the rules were made to be broken. To them the ends justify the means. So who do you want to be your bookkeeper?

Now imagine if you had never met a person but you knew her tendencies toward Dominance, Interaction, Steadiness and

Compliance. With just that limited information you could guide her toward the jobs and situations that would suit her personality.

But go a step further and imagine that you also knew her background and energy patterns (velocity). Then add a sense of her intellectual capacity and an awareness of the values which motivate her most. At that point you can draw some really meaningful conclusions, even if you have never met this person! In fact, you might actually know this person better than you know many people you are around every day.

You may be asking yourself, how is that possible? I realize this is a bold assertion, but think about it. Don't we often feel we know someone based on a mixed bag of first impressions, one-dimensional situations and inaccurate opinions which we viewed through our own emotional filter?

Up to now, most of us haven't had a more reliable way to know people. We merely formed opinions on limited facts and intuition. But with Inner√iewing we can learn what someone wants (their values), what they are capable of (their intellectual capacity), at what speed they will pursue it (their velocity) and how they will behave along the way (their style).

This not only give us powerful INSIGHT, it also helps us understand people as never before. It allows us to more wisely select team members, predict behaviors of others, and evaluate relationships we are considering. With Inner√iewing we can better understand ourselves, guide and counsel others and, in general, make better choices. Life is a series of choices, each leading to more choices. The better we choose, the happier we live. Our choices are our lives and we are accountable.

Besides, the better we understand ourselves and others, the less we judge them and blame them. The less we judge people the more we support them. The more we support and accept them, the more productive they become.

Inner√iewing accomplishes that, it provides a file for what

you know about people. It gives meaning to formerly random data.

It is easy to imagine a child's closet with all the clothes on the floor. If you were asked to evaluate the variety, style and extent of that child's wardrobe by looking at the pile, you'd be hard-pressed to be very accurate, even though all of the information you need is at your feet. By simply putting all those clothes on hangers and arranging them by style and color, you could quickly evaluate styles, preferences, outfits and more at a glance.

That's what InnerViewing does. It gives you a way to organize information you are already receiving into groupings that have meaning and usefulness.

Doesn't it make sense that since we are forming opinions and making decisions about people every day, that we should take the time to learn how to do it wisely?

Once we take the Inner View™ and understand people as they truly are, we can practice what Robert Horton of the Carefree Institute calls "No fault living:" Being our natural selves, choosing what is best for ourselves and others and living our life as we were originally designed to live it.

In a cartoon show which was popular when I was a child, there was a character, a frog, who constantly pleaded with a magical owl to grant his latest wish. He'd wish to be a rocket astronaut, or a knight in shining armor, or a jet pilot, and in every case he'd get his wish only to end up in some terrible predicament. The owl would always have to step in to rescue him at the last possible moment. And then would end each show with the same sage advice. The owl would say:

> Be just what you are-
> not what you are not-
> for those as they are
> are the Happiest lot.

*Individual *Inner √iew™ profiles*: A computerized narrative (approximately 16 pages) describing your own unique strengths and traits. Based on your responses to a 100 question profile questionnaire. Jim Cathcart, Inc.

"The important thing to remember is that if you don't have that inspired enthusiasm that is contagious—whatever you do have is also contagious."
D.C.

PASSPORT TO POTENTIAL

Danny Cox
17381 Bonner Drive
Tustin, CA 92680
714/838-3030

Danny Cox spent ten years flying supersonic fighters in the U.S. Air Force. During this time he flew on a temporary basis with the Chinese Nationalist Air Force in Taiwan as well as with the Royal Australian Air Force. He was also a test pilot and air show pilot.

Upon leaving the Air Force, Danny joined a nationally known sales company. One year later, he was promoted to manager of one of the company's thirty six branches. Under his guidance, the office accelerated to a record breaking, industry leading pace of doubling, tripling and quadrupling old records.

Three and one half years after joining the company he was promoted to First Vice President and assigned to a district of eight offices. By teaching his sound leadership principles to the eight branch managers, morale and productivity soared and percentage of employee turnover dropped to near zero.

Early in 1977, due to the increasing demands for innovative leadership and teamwork techniques that work, Danny began sharing his successful management approaches with others as a professional speaker. Due to the wide acceptance of both his material and style of presentation he has become one of America's busiest speakers. He has been awarded the C.P.A.E. from the National Speakers Association.

I spent ten years of my life flying supersonic fighters. After ten years, I finally realized that the Air Force was not going to use any of the wonderful suggestions I had made on how to improve their organization. The opportunity came along to shake those people up. I sent in my resignation; they signed it, and overnight I was a civilian again trying to find out what I was going to do with the rest of my life. I had no money saved up and no retirement.

I headed for the west coast to fly with the airlines, believing they would be tickled to death to get hold of me. (As a matter of fact, they did love my qualifications…they just couldn't stand my specifications). Over the phone they'd get all excited about my flying time and all the kinds of flying I'd done. I then had to explain to them that there was one more thing I should ask them about. I said, "What are the height requirements to fly with your airline?" They said, "Five feet, eight," and I said, "That's my goal, to be five feet eight."

And I'm still working on it. I could reach everything in the cockpit, that was no problem, but the airlines didn't want people leaning out in the aisles saying, "That little guy is going to fly this big airplane? You gotta be kidding." I was ready to form an antidiscrimination group. I was going to call it SPOT, which stood for Short People On Top. I was really disappointed.

I had been known as the "Sonic Boom Salesman" in the Air Force. If I could sell sonic booms to an upset, hostile audience, I should be able to sell a product or two.

For a year I was a salesperson for a large sales corporation. After a year I was made a manager. Every day, for about a year, about all I did was show up. And then they made an almost fatal mistake. They gave me the top office out of their 36 offices. I could hardly wait to get back to that top office because that's where I'd been a new salesperson that first year.

You can imagine how those top people in that office, who remembered me as the new salesperson from the year before, welcomed me back as the boss. You can also imagine how they hated me because I tried to turn everybody in that office into a carbon copy of me.

Wasn't that a wonderful plan? I took that office from number one to number 36 in three months time. I knew I was in trouble. You can always tell when you're in trouble as a manager. If you get to the parking lot in the morning and find that your salespeople have arrived early and blocked the entrances with their cars, that's a bad sign. I guess it's the modern day version of circling the wagons. We had not yet had an armed revolt but we were close. I had reached the point where I was afraid to stick the keys in the ignition of my car until I'd checked all the wiring. As a matter of fact, when I got ready to go home at night I used to send my lowest producer out to start my car—just in case. That was the only incentive plan I had.

It was about this time my boss came to see me and said, "Danny, I really made a mistake by making you a manager. I feel it's only fair to let you know that I'm looking for your replacement." I said, "That's not only the shortest but the finest motivational seminar I've ever attended. I'm going to have to learn to do this." He said, "You don't have much time," and I said, "You don't know how motivated I am."

I went to work on me, not them. And I made some discoveries. I found out that salespeople get better right after the manager does. Employees get better right after the supervisor does. Kids get better right after the parents do. Students get better right after the teachers do and customers get better right after salespeople do. It's amazing but it's a universal principle.

I didn't lose my job and, as a matter of fact, after 120 days we were back to number one. We used that momentum and broke office records, company records and industry records. I learned some things along the way. I call them *the Passport to Potential.*

There are three things to do to get ready for your trip:

Learn and visualize clearly how other high achievers think and act. That means you must read and study, listen to tapes and take somebody to lunch before somebody else eats yours, especially in today's business world. It means you're going to have to learn.

Put into practice what you know and how it works. We can learn new things but the tendency is to go back to the office tomorrow and do what I call "repeat yesterday one more time." You've got to break from the old and try the new. You've got to build new habits. You do that with practice.

Develop the characteristics of those high achievers. The key here is develop; you don't have to be born with the characteristics.

These are the characteristics you need for your trip. But what are the things you'll actually need for the official passport?

First, develop a high standard of personal ethics. Now more than ever we need and understand the importance of high standards of personal ethics. We see someone who doesn't have high ethics take off like a skyrocket and say, "Wow, look at that person go. A super star in the making." But later we're saying, "What ever happened to that person we heard so much about last year?" He probably didn't have the high standards or personal ethics that are so important.

Another thing you're going to need for a completed passport is an absence of pettiness. It's so easy to get caught up in petty things in the business world today. There are right things to do and wrong things to do and great people know not only right from wrong, but they also know what is really important to the job...What's really important to their growth. Imagine receiving a memo that says, "From this moment forward, this company will no longer furnish postage. If you want to send out thank you notes to your past customers or potential customers, you now have to buy the stamps." *Isn't that a shame?* You think, "If this company thinks that I'm going to invest 25 cents in a stamp to achieve a $500 commission they have another think coming!"

It's like we said in the fighter pilot business, some die by shrapnel, some go down in flames, but most go inch by inch playing little games. We've got to play the big games. The big games are down one road from the 'Y' we stand at every day. The other road leads to a repeat of yesterday. Those are the games you've already tried. I love that one line in the movie *The Right Stuff*, where one of the pilots says, "You never know how far you can go until you push yourself too far." We've got to understand not only what pettiness is but how to do our best to make it an empty spot in our lives. We've got to understand what is important.

One other characteristic of people I've studied is stability under pressure. I think we have to develop that stability under pressure as we prepare our passports to potential. Stability under pressure allows you to become a tough-minded problem-solver. It all comes back to priorities. Back home we say it this way, "If you've got a frog to swallow, don't look at it too long. If you've got more than one to swallow, swallow the biggest one first."

I told that story one day and a man went out and bought a frog. It was an ugly fake frog that went "RIBBIT" when you pushed on it. It now sits on the desk of whoever is currently having the largest problem in the office. He says it works great because he'll come by and say, "You've got the frog. Hang in there. I've seen you handle problems before, you're good at handling problems." He says his employees are getting little motivational talks all day long.

I thought it was a great idea (we need to help employees understand that everybody is on their team; you're on their team). At the end of the month a recipient for the "Frog Swallower of the Month Award" is selected. The winner stands in front of the rest of the group and says, "Here's how the problem got started; here's how it developed; here are the things I tried that did work; here are the things I tried that didn't work."

What else will you need to complete this passport to potential? I feel that courage is important because it takes courage to prepare a Passport to Potential. We've got to be courageous, not safe plodders. It's easy for people to be careful. They'll say, "I've got to wait till everything is right." That's like waiting with one foot in the air for everything to be just exactly right before we try something new.

That's like saying, "I'm going to drive all the way across the city but I'm going to wait till all the lights are green first." You wouldn't get very far would you? You'd just be sitting in the parking lot saying, "Okay, go ahead and start. They're all green. No, wait a minute, there's one way down the road that turned red. We've got to stop and wait till they're all green." For those people who say, "I've got to wait, I've got to be careful," I say, "if you're too careful nothing bad *or* good will ever happen to you."

You've got to do what you fear. Otherwise, fear is in charge. Fear is not a very rational thing to be calling the shots in your life, is it? That's a good philosophy for anyone, a salesperson, a manager or a parent. You've got to do what you fear, otherwise fear is in charge. It all comes back to courage.

Complete your passport with an inspired enthusiasm that is contagious. Those great people's lives that I studied inspired my enthusiasm. It was like a pilot light on a burner. You've probably got friends who are that way. You can talk to them for two minutes on the phone and for the rest of the day people say, "What's with you today?" You answer, "I talked to a friend this morning. I don't know, he just gave me a lift." What are you describing? You're describing contagious, inspired enthusiasm. I love to be around people who have this quality because they just make you feel good. If you don't have contagious, inspired enthusiasm, beware, because whatever you *do* have is also contagious.

You can develop an enthusiasm for life. I had a woman who, out of 1200 salespeople, was the top salesperson in our company. She broke every single record in the industry. I asked her, "How do you do it?" She said, "God didn't make me with an off switch." What a concept, God didn't make me with an off switch.

I work closely with Dr. Robert Schuller. I do a lot of management and leadership training for the administrative staff at the Crystal Cathedral. Bob Schuller's got it. He wears his clothes out from the inside. He and his wife were over at our house for dinner one night. Half way through that dinner I could hardly wait, I didn't know what for, but I could hardly wait. He's got it. Contagious enthusiasm.

Several years ago I was doing a program in Florida for a room of about 1,000 salespeople. I'd just gotten to the center of the stage when I saw two people walk into the back of the room. I looked back at them and thought, "They've got what I'm going to talk about. They've got inspired enthusiasm. I can see it from the platform." I could see how the crowd was reacting to them. I made a mental note to meet those men. I met them at the break and it was the start of a beautiful friendship. I had lunch with them that day and dinner with them that night.

Any time I go to Florida, which is fairly often, I can always depend on them being there to hear that same program. They've gone through it nine times. They could probably get up and do the program themselves. I'm talking about John and Greg Rice, identical twin brothers, all two feet nine inches of them. That's three inches shorter than a yardstick. You see, they've got it . Of course, at two feet nine, even if they didn't have inspired enthusiasm I'm going to run around with them. As a matter of fact, every time we're together I put one on each side of me like bookends, and then I walk like John Wayne. They're fun to be around.

The important thing to remember is that if you don't have that inspired enthusiasm that is contagious—whatever you do have is *also* contagious.

Let's take a look at four all-important words. The first word is dream. We've got to dream like never before. My dream began on the beach with my boss looking for my replacement. I had to take two days away just to get my thoughts together so I could understand just what potential I had. Dream, that's an important word.

The second word is study. Study everything you can get your hands on to make the dream come true. Study books and tapes. Take people to lunch who are better at their jobs than you are. If someone is better at some phase of the job than you are, take that person to lunch and find out how he does it.

The third word is plan. Plan your time, but time your plan. Give yourself some time pressures. It's like we say back home, "It's okay to have a tiger by the tail if you know what to do next." Or, as Evel Knievel, the great 20th century philosopher, once said, "The worst feeling in the world is to be roaring down that track, hit that ramp and going up off that ramp at 91 mph knowing you should have been at 93 mph." You've got all that time to think, "I'm going to be about two mph short at the other end."

Planning is important, but a plan was not meant to remain a plan. What's that fourth word? Action. Get it into action. Make it happen. Commit yourself to never repeating another yesterday. Don't repeat what you know doesn't work one more time. So I challenge you to never be less than your dreams. I wish you lots of green lights and blue skies.

"In changing times...there are three ingredients you need: ...a good sense of direction...a good, healthy body...(and) a good support system."
P.F.

TAKE CHARGE OF YOUR FUTURE

6

Patricia Fripp
527 Hugo Street
San Francisco, CA 94122
800/634-3035
800/553-6556 (in CA)

Patricia Fripp is Past President of the over 3,000 member National Speakers Association. Patricia is a full time speaker and has received numerous honors and awards for excellence and professionalism in speaking. She is the author of the book, *Get What You Want.*

Patricia started working in England at age 15 as a ladies' hairstylist. She arrived in San Francisco at age twenty with no home or job and only had $500. Three years later she became one of the first women working in the men's hairstyling profession when it was still in its infancy. Before becoming a full time speaker, Patricia successfully ran her own salon and product distribution business. She claims the exposure to top business executives in her salon was her greatest education.

Patricia now addresses approximately 130 groups a year and is featured as a personality on many radio and television shows. She has been awarded the C.P.A.E. from the National Speakers Association.

Have you seen the commercial where Angela Lansbury is talking about her credit card? She says, "I don't want a credit card that impresses; I want a credit card that gives me possibilities." Business today is full of possibilities; therefore, we need to be effective communicators. I am frequently asked if I get nervous before I speak to a large audience. Of course, there are times that I am, but I feel very strongly that our value in the marketplace depends very much on how easy or how difficult it is to replace us. If we learn to stand up and speak eloquently with confidence—in fact, if we can stagger to our feet and say anything at all—we'll be head and shoulders above our competition, no matter what we do. We have to learn to communicate effectively to be successful today.

Professor Albert Mehrabian studied communications at UCLA for 20 years and he wrote a book called *Silent Messages*. He said, "When it comes to developing trust and believability, which is certainly what you need in business, seven percent is what you say, 38% is how you say it, and 55% is how you look." That isn't how you dress; it's body language and facial expressions. No matter what words you use, no matter how eloquent you are, people can tell if you're sincere.

One of my best friends in San Francisco is a man named Bert Decker. He is the founder of Decker Communications, but years ago he was a filmmaker. He once had the opportunity to bid on a job that was worth $250,000 a year to his company. Forty people were given the opportunity to bid on the job with written proposals, but only three were invited in for an interview. Bert had a friend on the committee who said, "Your proposal is the best; don't worry." But after the interview, he didn't get the job. Bert asked, "How come? You told me my proposal was the best." His friend said, "Bert, it was, but in the interview you looked nervous. People will not give a quarter of a million dollar project to a person who looks nervous. People will not believe you if you look nervous; people will not be led by you if you look nervous." Be an effective communicator.

The first time Reagan debated Carter some political consultants gathered high-powered CEO'S and asked them to watch the debate and tell them afterwards how they felt about the issues (they stressed the issues!). When they gathered together again one executive said, "I liked the way Reagan shook hands." Another, "Carter didn't appear to be presidential." And yet another, "I liked the way Reagan chided Carter and said, 'There you go again, Mr. President.'" Nothing to do with the issues —all to do with communication skills.

A young man who worked for me got his dream job in Indianapolis working for a rock-and-roll promoter. While in my employment, I sent him through the Dale Carnegie class, so he really felt comfortable standing up and speaking. As the newest employee of his new firm, he was called in to his boss's office one day. The boss handed him some papers and said, "Read it. Do you understand it? Tell me what you think it says in your own words. Now, get on an airplane at four o'clock this afternoon and fly to West Virginia and give a presentation on our point of view at our industry meeting." Don't you think this young man has a better opportunity to be promoted in his company? The boss had more confidence in sending him to give the speech than anybody else, even himself!

John Molloy in *Live For Success* reports that only 20% of people graduating from college today can give a halfway decent verbal presentation, while leading marriage counselors say that 50% of all divorces are caused by poor communications. Peter Drucker, management expert, says that 60% of all management problems are caused by poor communications. As Ralph Waldo Emerson said, "It's a luxury to be understood."

What Is Your Philosophy?

I started my working career at age 15 as a hairdresser in England. My father paid $250 for me to go to work for $4.50 per week. It wasn't one of the most affluent times in my life! But, at that point, two people were sowing some seeds I fortunately had enough sense to listen to and that I've tried to use all

my business life. I saw my first boss, Mr. Paul, treat every
woman that came in the salon like she was the only one in the
world for the amount of time that she was there. My father, who
became a very successful real estate businessman, always said to
me, "Don't concentrate on making a lot of money; concentrate
on becoming the type of person that people want to do business
with and you most likely *will* make a lot of money."

Isn't that really a key point in business today? As business
becomes more competitive, it should be more fun, more efficient
and more professional to do business with us rather than our
competition.

One of my clients, Fantastic Sam, who owns the haircutting
franchises, told me he has a notice on the wall of his office saying, "God is watching; give Him a good show." He said, "I'm
not a particularly religious person, but having that plaque on my
wall makes it easier to make business decisions." I ask you, if
you had a sign in your office saying, "God is watching; give
Him/Her a good show," would you do anything differently? It's
a good philosophy to take to work. The important thing in having a philosophy is that it helps you through the frustrating times
we all experience, because you know what your purpose is, why
you're turning up every day, and how you want to run your business.

Coping Successfully With Change
Certainly a lot has changed since I went to work well over
20 years ago. The economy is changing; the business climate is
changing; the work force is changing. In the 1950's, 70% of
American families were traditional. That number has now been
reduced to about nine percent. Today 51% of the workforce is
women. According to Roger Blackwell of Ohio State, 52% of
the people in college today are women. The fastest growing
segment in college today is the 25-40 year old woman. Today,
more jobs are being created by entrepreneurial ventures than by
corporations. Fifty-one percent of all the products available by
the year 2000 have not been discovered. Forty-one firms on the

Forbes 100 list in 1945 had disappeared by the year 1977. Many of the companies on today's Fortune 400 list didn't exist in 1920. Even the relationship between men and women is changing. Gloria Steinam said, "Women today are becoming the men they used to want to marry." She added, "Men are not becoming the women they used to want to marry." Who's doing the washing up? I don't know.

Even people's attitudes are changing. Older people are getting more optimistic, younger people more pessimistic. I don't know how you feel about changes that are happening in the world we live in, but many people I talk to are very nervous about change. I would like to suggest to you change is inevitable and there are three things you should think about in terms of change: 1) Change is good and necessary. 2) Cultivate a desire to participate in change. 3) Believe you can make a difference.

There are two ways you can react to change: from intelligence or from necessity. The intelligent way is to think, plan and organize how you want your life and future to look. If you react from necessity, other people are controlling your future. I realize that when I ask you to think, that's easier said than done. Leo Rosten said, "Thinking is harder work than hard work." Surely, our value to ourselves, our families and our organizations is in the fact that we can think. Yet 72% of managers who replied to Alex McKenzie's time survey said they didn't have time to think or plan—surely our number one priority.

I'm not so naive as to think I can give you a simple formula for how you can take charge of your future in changing times. But I will suggest, if you are going to be in charge of that future, there are three ingredients you need: 1) *A good sense of direction.* 2) *A good, healthy body* (it's difficult to be a dynamic success if you don't feel well.) About 80% of diseases today are lifestyle induced. 3) *A good support system.* Leaders get results through people.

A Good Sense of Direction

Let's look at *a good sense of direction*. I think planning is focusing on the preferable future rather than the probable future that comes about if you *don't* plan. It doesn't mean your career or future will work out exactly the way you plan, but it's the process of thinking that's so important. Recently in San Francisco, I addressed an organization called "Women Entrepreneurs." I asked them, "How many of you have had something happen in your career that you considered at the time somewhat devastating?" Everyone put their hand up; some put up two. When you plan, you don't plan for the bad things to happen, but things do go wrong.

I promise you that when you look back at all the setbacks that happened in your career and you take an overall picture of the tapestry of your life, these terrible things will, at most, appear inconvenient.

Not devastating—inconvenient.

I've had several wonderful businesses, a great staff, and yet inconvenient things have happened. I've had staff that quit at inopportune moments. I've had people disappoint me. I have been embezzled. When I look back, at most it was inconvenient. I truly believe that I serve my clients better today, not necessarily because of the successes I've had, but because of my ability to adapt to the inconveniences. I'm sure you'll find the same is true for you.

Think about the way you want things to be. I always wanted to grow up and be successful. When I was a 15-year-old shampoo girl in a chic salon in England, we had many glamorous rich customers. As soon as I got to know them I'd say, "What were you doing when you were my age? How did you make your money? Did you make it yourself or did you marry it?" You may think that was being nosey, but I considered it good market research!

Look After Each Area of Your Life

All my life I figured this was the way to be successful—find out how people planned their futures. One of the most success-ful women I met in my hairstyling salon in San Francisco is a speaker and consultant named Dru Scott who wrote, *How To Put More Time In Your Life.* She always seemed calm and never raced around frantic like me. One day after she'd had her hair done and I'd given her a cup of coffee, I said, "Sit down, Dru. Tell me, how did you get what you want?" She said, "Patricia, it's really rather simple." (I don't know about you, but when I meet people and they say, "Yes, I'm successful, but it was outra-geously complicated," I'm less likely to take notes than if some-body says, "It's very simple.") She said, "All I do actively on a daily basis is look after each area of my life. Every day I do something nice for a friend. I drop a note of appreciation or call and say hello. Every day I do something nice for me, even if it's only soaking in a bubblebath for 15 minutes without feeling guilty. Every day I do something for my mind by reading or lis-tening to cassettes."

I was presenting a series of programs for AT&T in Morris-town, New Jersey. One of their researchers from the company who followed me on the program said, "All the knowledge we have in the world right now is going to double in the next two years." That means if you have the same job in the same com-munity, you would have to change just to stay the same. I chal-lenge you to think about what time you invest, on a regular basis, not only in keeping up with your industry, but keeping up with the world you live in.

Dru said, "Every day I do something for my body. I run or exercise." It's very difficult to be a dynamic success if you don't feel well. A new Gallop Poll survey shows that the num-ber of Americans exercising has jumped to a full 69%. Exercise also seems to be a motivator for people to change their health habits and their diets. In a new survey, 64% of the exercisers have started eating a healthier diet compared to 47% of non-exercisers. And 43% of them have lost weight versus 31% of sedentary people. Another key point is that 19% of the population feel very strongly that they are well satisfied with life. But for the health conscious, that percentage is twice that of the general population—40%!

But life and health consist of more than moving your body and eating vegetables. We are realizing that a positive mental attitude, a feeling of control over life, is essential to mental and physical well-being. The cornerstone of intelligent optimism is the certainty that you have the power to protect your most important resources—a good mind in a fit body. As management expert Peter Drucker says, "We view health as the capacity to manage ourselves to be at our best."

Dru continued, "Every day I do something to keep in touch with the people that now do business with me. Every day I do something to get in touch with somebody who doesn't do business with me now but could in the future. Every day I pray; every day I meditate." What she consciously does, and what I've been aware of since we had this conversation, is to keep balance in her everyday life. We all know that isn't easy because we have pressures. We have time commitments very often beyond our control.

I ask you to think about that every day. Are you leading a balanced life? Are you getting feedback and rewards, not only from business, but your life outside work? A balanced person will make a better leader for the future.

How Do You Know What You Want?

I race around like many speakers and give talks on setting goals, planning and thinking about what you want, and many people say, "Patricia, we understand all that; making challenging goals and writing them down, but how do you know what you want?" If you don't know specifically what you want from your life and your career, don't panic. You're probably like most people. But, what I would encourage you to do is think about everything you don't want and work backwards. It's amazing how clear what you do want will appear. If you looked exactly the way you do right now in one year's time, would you celebrate? If not, what are you going to do? If the quality of your relationships is exactly the same, in and out of business, in one year's time, would that be marvelous? If not, what communication skills are you going to have to learn or use? What time are you going to have to take with the people you think are important to you? If your career took the same natural progression as it's taking right now, is that wonderful? If not, what are you going to have to do? What are you going to have to learn? What will you do to change the future?

There's an old story about a man that was fishing. Every time he caught a fish he'd measure it. The little ones he'd put in the pail and the ones 10 inches or longer would be thrown back in the lake. There was a man further along the bank watching him and he thought that this was rather peculiar. He went up to the old man and said, "Excuse me sir. Why are you throwing away the biggest and best fish?" The old man said, "I only have a nine inch frying pan." Isn't that like life? Very often when we sit down and project the future, we set goals or make plans and then we think, "Oh, that's not possible. I don't have enough help. I'm not smart enough. There's not time enough in the day." Somebody should have told that man all he had to do was cut the 12 inch fish into one inch pieces then they'd fit in his nine inch frying pan. That's what we have to do with the challenging plans we dream about in the future. What "piece" are you committed to each and every day?

What Are You Committed To?

I say to people, "Tell me what you say you want and show me one week of your life. I'll tell you with 98% accuracy whether you'll get it." I have a group of cronies that I get together with for lunch every few months. Now, to me, a crony is one up from a friend. These particular cronies I met in a Dale Carnegie course about 12 years ago. We meet to commit our goals to each other and follow up on each others' progress. One of my friends, Jim, has been saying for several years that he wants to trek through the Himalayas for his health goal. I keep telling him he can't write it down because he doesn't even backpack today. If he writes that as one of his goals, it will totally invalidate everything he wants in his business and life because he's not doing anything *now* to get closer to it.

Speaker Danny Cox says the difference between a goal and a fantasy is that you know something that you can do tomorrow to get closer to a goal. A fantasy is something you just sit in the bubblebath and enjoy. There's an important place in life for both goals and fantasies, but don't confuse the two. As Ken Blanchard, author of *The One Minute Manager,* asks, "Are you interested in or committed to your plans and goals? If you have an interest in what you're doing you do what you have to do. If you have a commitment to your goal, you never ask yourself the questions "Do I feel like doing it today? Am I in the mood?" or "Are the stars aligned?"

What are you committed to every day? More important, you really have to ask yourself "What am I committed to do every day even when I *don't feel like it?*" What happens a week from Thursday when you're dressed for success and racing out the door and your child throws up all over you? How committed are you to your goals and plans for a bright future when real life sets in? The super achievers never ask themselves the question, "Do I feel like it today?" The super achievers concentrate so much on the results they want they don't even ask the question. Whereas, the mediocre people that just get by concentrate on, "How can I get through the day as comfortably as possible?" If you'll look back through your life, you'll note that most of the results you've achieved have come from being uncomfortable rather than comfortable.

So think about what you want. If you don't know exactly what it is, think about everything you don't want and work back-

wards. Think about what you have to do every day to get closer to your goal, even when you don't feel like it.

Good Public Relations

You are responsible not only for motivating yourself, but for motivating other people—selling your company's vision to the whole community. You have to be constantly involved in public relations. I know when Dru Scott was talking about getting in touch with people that could do business with her in the future, she was talking about having high visibility in the business community. In business today we have to encourage our people to keep in touch with the people that now give us business. It seems to me that many sales and business people think it's our customers' and clients' job to remember us. I think it's our responsibility to never give them the opportunity to forget us.

I bought my first building in San Francisco from a realtor friend. I kept it for several years then I called him up and asked him to find me another building. I wanted to trade up because I had a lot of equity in my current one. A couple months went by and I didn't hear from him. I called him again and said, "Al, I'm really serious. I want to trade my building." He said, "Okay, Trish, I'll get back to you." I said, "Al, I need you or someone in your office to call me at least once a week so I know I'm on your mind. I have two people a day I meet that are in the real estate business that would love to do business with me." Three months later, without one phone call from Al, I bought a building through someone else.

I've always been a believer in the value of a handwritten note to thank clients for the opportunity to do business with them. Long time sales trainer, Bill Gove, when he was with the 3M Company, used to write notes. Someone was teasing him one day and said, "All you do is write notes all day long." He said, "No, seven minutes a day. Everyone that does business with me hears from me at least once every three months while my competition is calling on them asking them for their business."

In 1969 I worked for Jay Sebring, who was an innovator in men's hairstyling. He built his reputation by doing the hair of many of the movies stars—Paul Newman, Steve McQueen, and Peter Lawford, to name a few. Jay said a very simple thing that I think about every day in my business life even though I'm in a totally different business, "We only have one gimmick. The best haircut in town." But it wasn't what he said that I found so fascinating—it was who he said it to: *Time, Newsweek,* and *Playboy.* This was in 1965 when no one else was talking about men's hairstyling.

Ralph Waldo Emerson said, "If you build a better mousetrap, even though you may live in the center of a jungle, people will beat a path to your door." Not true. You can be the best speaker, the best hairstylist, the best financial institution, but if the world doesn't know about you, you'll starve to death. I realized in 1969 that:

People do business with people they know.

People do business with people that do business with them.

People do business with people their friends talk about.

People do business with people they read about.

I knew to be successful I had to have high visibility so I went on many radio and television shows. I was interviewed by all the local magazines and newspapers. I was asked to do an article on marriage. Obviously, as a single person, I can't be an expert on marriage, but I'm a great observer of human behavior. Several years ago I was invited to speak at a large "Possibility Thinking" conference at the Crystal Cathedral. I was following Arvella Schuller, a very dynamic speaker, and producer of Dr. Schuller's television show. Arvella told about a conversation she'd had with a marriage counselor who she asked, "Do you hear hundreds of problems in marriages, or does everyone have the same few problems?" He said, "Basically I could sum up all the problems I've heard into two categories: either selfishness or immaturity." He went on to tell her about a couple that came to him for counseling. The wife had told him, "The only thing I ask for in my marriage is to be treated as well as our family poodle. My husband comes home in the evening and pets the dog and talks to him. All I want is a touch and a kind word." Her husband said, "When I come home in the evening the poodle runs to greet me and wags his tail!"

Your Support System

The saddest thing about standing behind a hairstyling chair, which I did for 24 years, is not the varicose veins or sore feet, but the amount of times my customers said to me, "You know, my father died last week (or my sister died last week, or my best friend died last week...) and I never told them I loved them." It has been said that if the end of the world was coming in 10 minutes, every phone booth in America would be full. I say why wait? The feelings we have for other people mean absolutely nothing to them unless they know. That's certainly true of your *support system* at home. It's also true of your *support system* at work—the people that help you accomplish your goals.

How do you get results through people? First of all you have to understand what motivates them. Why do people work? For one thing, people work to make a living. You can't get too motivated if you don't make the house payment. But beyond that I think that people work as an education. The more they understand about how their job fits into the overall schemes and plans of the organization and its future, the more interesting it is to them. People work for the intrinsic pleasure of doing a good job so they've got to know how they're doing. They've got to get feedback. People work to participate in an event with other people. It's nice to be part of a team. It's very nice to be part of a winning team.

People usually start out in a state of excitement with hope that this is going to be a great job with a great future. A job where they're going to learn a lot, work with great people and serve the community. That excitement can last from half a day to forever, depending on their own personal motivation, the environment and the leadership in that job. The next level they go through is reality, and it's important to be in reality. In real life you have to do what you have to do every day—even if you don't feel like it. In real life it doesn't matter how much money you make, the government takes more than you figured. In real life it doesn't matter how much you like that job, some days you'd rather go shopping or fishing. And, in real life it doesn't matter how wonderful those people are that you work with, sometimes they're a pain in the neck.

What we have to do as leaders is not only create an environment where people function in reality, but we have to create enough excitement in that everyday reality so that they don't get into the next stage. It's called looking. That doesn't necessarily mean looking for another job, but it does mean not being committed to the one they have right now. The trouble with life is that reality doesn't live up to expectations. As Oscar Wilde said, "The bride's second disappointment is Niagara Falls."

Learn To Be A Leader

To get results through people you have to learn to be a leader. Six good words to learn are, *"I admit I made a mistake."* Let me tell you why I think that's important. In changing times many of the procedures we use are changing so fast that we're doing them for the first time. It's very difficult for anyone to do something perfectly the first time they do it. If somebody makes a mistake, the important thing is to let them know before it becomes an overwhelming problem. That means they have to realize it's okay to make a mistake, as long as they tell us.

Several years ago I still owned my hairstyling salon while I was promoting myself as a speaker. I needed to hire a new receptionist, someone who was going to manage the shop and greet people, someone who was very high energy. I was looking for the perfect person to give a good first impression of my shop, so I wasn't going to be my usual impatient self. I was going to do the job right this time. I ran an ad in the paper and had 140 calls in a day and a half. I interviewed the best 30 and when it came down to the top four, I had their handwriting analyzed. I had MY handwriting analyzed. I was going to build the perfect team. I made my decision and hired my perfect person. Two weeks later I fired her. I said to her, "I'm not saying you *are* miserable but you look miserable. You can't work for a motivational speaker and *look* miserable. It's bad for business!" I also admit to you that 13 years ago I would have kept her in the wrong job for months and justified why I made that decision. The rest of the staff might have quit, but I would have had the satisfaction that I was right.

Tell the Truth

My friends say to me, "Patricia, you're always so positive, even when you're wrong." It's true. But the difference is, show me I'm wrong and I waste no time defending my former position. It's a waste of time. Why do people NOT tell us the truth? They won't tell us the truth because they think they will be negatively rewarded for giving that information. It starts out when we're little children. "Jimmy, did you knock over the milk?" "Yes mommy." Wham! "Jimmy, did you knock over the cereal?" "Yes mommy." Wham! "Jimmy, did you make a mess in your bedroom?" "No, that was the cat." Jimmy grows up and works with people like you and me.

Imagine if I called one of my suppliers, "Mr. Smith, this is Miss Fripp. Where are my widgets? I expected them yesterday." "Hold on Miss Fripp, I'll check with the warehouse. Jimmy, what happened to Miss Fripp's widgets?" "I put them on the truck myself last Thursday." "Okay. Miss Fripp you should get them by today. They went out last Thursday." Does Jimmy ship them out late or pretend they got lost? Wouldn't it be better if Jimmy felt he worked in an environment where he could say, "Hey boss, I messed up. I forgot to write it down." The boss could then say, "Miss Fripp, you are a valued client and we had a mix-up at the warehouse. What can we do to straighten it out?" It's important to create an environment where people will tell the truth.

We have to learn to tell our clients the truth so we can develop good relationships. I got off an airplane at 11 o'clock at night and called for the hotel limo. They said my client had ordered it, but since my plane was half an hour late, it had returned to the hotel. I said, "Not a problem, can you send me another?" "I'll try," was the reply. I said, "You don't understand, it's two o'clock in the morning on my time clock. I'm very tired, either send me a limo or I'll take a taxi, but I don't want to have to bill my client for a taxi if you'll send a hotel limo for me." The hotel limo had not arrived after 25 minutes so I called back only to be told, "We never send anyone out after 10:30." The next time I stayed at this hotel a couple of years later, at 3:25 in the afternoon, I was guaranteed the limo would be there in 10 minutes. After waiting 20 minutes I called again. "Another 10 minutes." I waited 50 minutes. When talking to the general manager, I explained my problem was not that they don't send limos after 10:30 at night, or not that I had to wait 50 minutes, it was being "10 minuted" to death. The fact that I had fruit, wine and cheese sent to my room did not make up for the fact that I'd have gotten a taxi had I been told I had to wait that long. The note from the general manager did tell me that he absolutely guarantees from now on that every manager, bellperson, and desk clerk in that hotel will know exactly what time the limo will be arriving at the airport so they could tell their guests the truth.

Reward and Listen

The five best words in dealing with people are, "*I am proud of you.*" I'm sure you've read *The One Minute Manager.* It says, "Catch someone doing something right and tell them. And if they don't do it right the first time, catch them doing it partially right and tell them." Thorndyke's Law: "Performance that is rewarded tends to be repeated." I had a young woman work for me about six years ago. Seven years ago she had made the decision "I am an alcoholic. I can't ever drink again." I don't say it was easy living with that resolution, but it was easier, because her support system at home and at work said on a regular basis, "I'm proud of you."

The four best words in dealing with people are, *"What is your opinion?"* I can tell an awful lot about the organizations I work for, not by meeting the executive-type men or women, but by meeting the people in the organizations that might not be perceived as important. Seven years ago I got off an airplane to do a program for what was then the Ohio Bell System. I was looking for an executive man or woman but didn't see anyone that looked like that. So I was walking over to the phone to call my office when I saw a man with a label. He didn't look the way I expected someone that would be greeting me would look. His suit was very shiny, his collar was turned up, his trouser legs were too short. But his label said "Ohio Bell." I thought, "Well, maybe executives dress like this in Ohio!" I said, "Are you looking for me?" He said, "Oh yes, Miss Fripp, I'm looking for you. You're going to love speaking for our people. We have the best group of people who ever worked together anywhere." I replied, "How long have you worked for Ohio Bell?" This enthusiasm sounded like it was his second day. He said, "23 years." I said, "What do you do for Ohio Bell?" He said, "I'm a driver, I drive the executives." For the 45 minutes it took to get to the office he told about his fellow workers. He said, "One man you must meet while you're here is one of our vice presidents. A man named Joe Reed." I asked, "What's so good about Joe Reed?' He replied, "He asks me what I think." That night I was being entertained by two of the secretaries. They said, "Patricia, the way our company is going, we might not have jobs in two years. There might not be secretaries within the Ohio Bell." I said, "That has to make you nervous to think that no matter how hard you work you could end up without a job in two years." They answered, "No, for the experience of working with the quality of people that we're working with, it would be okay if we end up without a job in two years."

Well, I've never had more than 10 or 12 people work for me at once. It's tough making just 12 people feel good all the time. I wanted to find out how on earth this is accomplished in big organizations. I had breakfast with their boss the next day who has been trained by Joe Reed. I said, "What do you do to make the people around here feel this good? "One technique I use," he said, "that seems to work fairly well is that every couple months I sit down with everyone that reports to me and I have a three-on-three session with them. I say, 'What three things do I do in managing you that you like that I should try to do more of?' and 'What three things do I do in managing you that you don't like that I should do less of?'" You understand what that executive was doing was very scary. He was opening himself up for feedback.

If we're open for feedback we are much better as leaders and managers, but it's much better to give it than to get it. I thought this was a great technique; it's not complicated and not only can I talk about it in my seminars, but I can also use it in my own business.

I went back to my staff and said, "I want to be a great leader—one of these people they write books about. If you have any feedback on my almost perfect management style, I want to know." A young woman called Jimmie, who worked for me at the time, said, "Since you asked...Do you realize that when you give me my instructions in the morning you point and I don't like it."

Now, you understand the truth and someone's perception of the truth, might not be exactly the same. After all, I am an energetic, enthusiastic, frankly noisy person. I give speeches and point. It was not my perception that I was shouting and pointing. But at that point in time her perception was more important than mine. So based on that valuable input I never would have received had I not asked, I put my hands behind my back, "Good morning, Jimmie. How are you today? Let's look at your 'to do' pad." And for 10 minutes I would be calm, patient, quiet and "un-Frippy." Would I want to live my entire life calm, patient, quiet and un-Frippy? No. But for 10 minutes a day, if that young woman felt better about herself, better about working in my organization that I had more invested in than she did, I could certainly modify my personality—not change. You don't change a personality without going crazy, but you can modify. You might say, "But, Patricia, you were the boss. Let them modify their behavior to you." Nice, unrealistic, but nice.

Personal Power

Michael Korda in his book *Power* talks about two types of power. The position power says you're the boss, you're the president, you're the teacher, you're the parent. The personal power makes people want to help you accomplish your goals. It's nice to have the position power but it won't take you far if you don't have the personal power to go along with it. If you have a secretary in an office typing at seven o'clock at night when nobody knows that he or she is there, I tell you she is doing that for the personal power of the person she works for, not the position power.

Do you realize that people can smile at you and totally sabotage everything you're doing at the same time? Marilyn Manning, speaking on "conflict resolution," tells about a gentleman in Sacramento, California, who had the opinion that women with children shouldn't work. His assistant, however, was a single parent with two children. She had no choice. This was not self-improvement or luxury, this was survival. One afternoon she raced in and said, "I need to leave immediately, my child is in the hospital." He said, "You know the procedure. Type out a request and I'll sign it." She went to her office, typed out a request and came in again. He was talking on the telephone and rather than initial it while he was on the phone he turned his chair around, put his feet up on the window ledge and continued the conversation obviously longer than necessary. He turned back, signed it and she left, but she set a new goal for herself that night. It took her six months to accomplish that goal, but that gentleman was not in his job anymore. Develop your personal power.

A manager has to get everybody involved. He has to make them think, and think long-term. He has to make them understand that he respects their opinions. A lumber company in the Northwest had a problem. Many of the logs were falling off the assembly line. As a very last resort, the owner of the company said to the men, "Hey guys, you got any ideas on how we can stop these logs from falling off the assembly line?" One quiet little guy spoke up. His name was Charlie and he'd been around for about 20 years. He said, "Well boss, if we tried such and such I bet it would work." They tried it and it worked. It saved the company $1,000 a day.

Well you can imagine that they were rather pleased. They had a banquet to honor Charlie. They gave him a plaque and a check for thinking. All the guys were saying, "Charlie stand up and say a few words." This meek little guy got up, looked around sheepishly and said, "Well, I really appreciate this nice evening, this plaque and the check. It will come in very handy at Christmas. But I don't know why you're making such a big fuss. I thought about the idea five years ago." One thousand dollars a day and he thought about it five years ago! Everyone said, "Well, Charlie, why didn't you tell us?" He said, "I didn't think my job was to tell you what I think. I thought my job was to put the logs back on the assembly line." As leaders, you get results through people. Tap their minds, their creativity and make them feel important. (Thanks to Boo Bue, Dale Carnegie sponsor, for the above story.)

The Illinois Bell Pay Phone Division used to have no competitors. Now they have 200. They had a "Just Imagine" program and I was there when they were three weeks into it. The program was for the regular employees, not the executives, to get together once a week and brainstorm with other people on how they could save money for their company. Two of the groups had already come up with ideas that would save the company a quarter of a million dollars for each idea.

As chairman of Electronic Data Systems, H. Ross Perot said, "Any company that spends a lot of time on internal fighting will lose the battle against the competition. It's always going to be beaten by a company who operates as a team."

Who's Representing Your Company?

One of my former hairstyling customers, Al Stanton, told me an interesting story. Early in his career he worked in the traffic department of the Zellerbach Paper Company. One of his duties was to handle the travel arrangements for Isador Zellerbach, the founder of the company. Mr. Zellerbach was a very personable man who believed in making all of his employees feel important. Stanton appreciated the fact that Mr. Zellerbach would frequently ask his advice on different matters. One day Mr. Zellerbach told him a story from which we can all learn a great deal.

Early in the history of the company a Zellerbach truck was following a man in a rather fancy car on a narrow road. The truck driver was very impatient to pass and kept honking. After about 15 minutes, when he finally did pass, he put his head out the window and yelled, "You ____, you want to take up the whole road?" Meanwhile, the Zellerbach name was all over the truck!

It happened that the gentleman driving the car was the owner of the company that was Zellerbach's best customer in the area. When he returned to work he stormed into his office and told the purchasing agent to cancel all orders with Zellerbach and never buy anything from them again.

It was several months before this lost account came to the attention of Mr. Zellerbach. He tried to get the gentleman on the phone and couldn't, so Mr. Zellerbach went to speak with him in person. When he heard the story he was shocked—shocked that he had overlooked one of the most important factors in his business. That absolutely everyone represented his company. So, from that point on, Zellerbach's truck drivers received lessons in politeness and human relations.

Paul Harvey said, "For a company's advertising strategy to work, it has to be handled not only corporately but also individually." Individually and collectively companies large and small spend a fortune promoting their public image. It only takes one person to ruin that image. Management's biggest problem is to make everyone in the company understand they play a very important part in the overall schemes and plans of the company.

A few years ago the National Speakers Association was in Nashville for a winter workshop. We had a board meeting and we'd been going on for hours. Six of us adjourned to the coffee shop to continue our conversation. We were not trying to be awkward, but being speakers we never stopped talking for a moment while the waitress was taking the order. Nobody wanted anything exactly as it was presented on the menu and nobody wanted the same as anybody else, but the waitress was nice and patient. At the end of ordering I said, "My dear, this is going to be worth your while. These guys are big tippers." She said something I've never forgotten. She said, "I'm not being nice for a tip. I don't care if you don't give me a tip. I just feel if we give you good service, your group will come back to our hotel next year." I was impressed. This was a waitress talking about "our" hotel. I went back to my office and sent a letter to the manager. "Dear Sir: I am a motivational speaker. I travel nationwide talking about good and bad service. I would like to commend you. Your staff was superb but especially this waitress..." I related the tale. I continued, "I don't know what you do to motivate your people, but keep doing it, it works." I never had a reply. I think maybe the waitress and the manager should change places for a couple of weeks! She knows more about public relations than the manager.

Working together as a team is not easy. Working together if the team does not have a good leader is practically impossible.

The three best words in dealing with people are "*If you please.*" The two best words, "*Thank you.*" And the one best word is "*We.*" How can WE improve service for our clients together?

In changing times you need *a good sense of direction.* Think about what you want to do. *If you don't know exactly what you want, think about everything you don't want.* Remember, your number one priority is to think and plan and, at the same time, to get results through people. Appreciate *your support system* at home and at work. Get them involved. Ask them what they think. Make sure they know it's okay to make a mistake as long as they tell you about it.

Albert Einstein said, "Let us not strive to be people of success, but people of value." Surely, when we are of value to our staff, community, industry, families, and each other, then we really will be a success.

> *"If I were to grow, I was going to have to come to grips with my belief system—made up of everything that I've ever seen, heard and experienced."*
> *B.G.*

YOU DO IT
TO YOU!

Bill Gove
250 JFK Drive, Suite 101
Atlantis, Florida 33462
407/964-5225

Bill Gove had a long and successful career with the 3-M Company. Bill had extensive experience in sales, sales management and ultimately became marketing manager.

Since leaving 3-M in 1950, Bill has given over five thousand speeches at corporate sales meetings, sales rallies and association conventions. These presentations have been for profit as well as nonprofit organizations.

His presentations always offer an exciting blend of humor and practical content. His presentations focus on communication skills and ideas for getting more out of life.

Bill was elected as the first President of the National Speakers Association, spearheading, along with Cavett Robert, the formative stages of this professional organization.

If I had it to do again, I'd spend less time trying to inspire and motivate my audiences and more time sharing skills and information. Because I'm absolutely persuaded that if a person wants to bring about any fundamental changes in his life, it's going to take more than speeches and slogans to get it done.

I attended a so-called "Success Rally" out on the West Coast some time ago. Heavy duty program—three of the top inspirational speakers in the country. Even though it was in all respects a business get-together, they opened with a salute to the Flag, followed by the National Anthem, and an invocation by a minister from a local Evangelical Church.

Now, I can handle this. But when a speaker looks me in the eye and says, *"Whatever you set your mind to—you can do!"*—and forgets to mention the part that hard work, dedication and commitment play—he's holding something back.

I've been in the speaking business for over forty years. John Palmer, my agent in Chicago, figures that I have made over 5,000 speeches. Now, wouldn't you think that over the years, I would receive at least one letter from someone who had heard me speak that said, "Mr. Gove, years ago, I was in your audience at San Luis Obispo, California. You said something, and I had an 'out-of-body' experience—a 'spiritual transformation.' Thanks! Thanks! Thanks!" Want to know something? The next letter I get will be *number one!*

Now, I've received thousands of letters and calls that had to do with skills. You know—like "Bill, I heard you speak in 1955. You were still with the 3M Company. You were talking about 'The Sounds of Selling—What the Professional Salesperson is Saying.' You were talking about value added in those days. You said, for example, 'Mr. Prospect, when you buy from 3M, you have to take me with the package. I go with the deal. Sure, you could buy from someone else, but you wouldn't get me. And if you don't think I can make a difference—try me!'"

Someone else wrote, "Bill, you used to talk about how the salesperson should establish trust when calling on a new account by saying, 'Mr. Prospect, if at any time during this interview I give you the impression that I'm more interested in what I get out of this than I am in what you get—throw me out! I deserve it!'"

Oh, someone might come up to me in an airport and say, "Mr. Gove, are you still speaking about 'non-manipulative' closes like, 'Mr. Prospect, if this makes sense, can we get started right now?' or, 'If you're comfortable with this, is there any reason why we can't get going?' I used that stuff for years. It really works."

Like I said, lots of kind words regarding specific skills—not too much feedback on the motivation side. How does "Red" Buttons put it —"I never got a letter!"

Maybe I've become hardened, and if I have, it's only because it took me such a long time to realize that if I were to make any substantial changes in my own life, then reading books, attending seminars, and yelling out positive affirmations wasn't going to hack it.

If I were to grow, I was going to have to come to grips with my belief system—made up of everything that I've ever seen, heard and experienced. A belief system, like yours, that was put together by others: parents, teachers, coaches, ministers, priests, peer groups, etc.

I realized, too, that I had to change some habits. And that isn't easy, believe me. Habits are like old friends. We hold on to them with unbelievable tenacity.

I can almost hear someone saying, "Okay, okay, I'll unclutter. I'll even work on some of my habits. But this will take time. If I want to take a bigger bite out of life—what do I do in the meantime?"

I'm going to share with you what I believe to be the most powerful of all psychological and metaphysical truths:

It is not what happens to us that does us in—that burns a hole in our bellies—that keeps our lives from working—it is how we perceive it—react to it—respond to it...

And the only way we can improve the quality of our lives is to TRANSFORM THE QUALITY OF OUR PERCEPTIONS!

"Just common sense," you say. Sure it is. But common sense, because of its simplicity, is a very elusive truth. Something happens, okay. The car breaks down on the Interstate— IRS calls to invite us in for an audit—we win a trip to Mexico City and we're still down there trying to win a trip back—or whatever.

Now, we mistakenly believe that those things caused us to be upset. They didn't. They can't. Only *we* can upset us! How easy to understand. How difficult to put into practice. See, perception is what the mind tells us about what just happened. It is not necessarily what just happened. Let me give you some examples:

I'm a much better salesperson today than at any time during my career. Is it because I'm older, more knowledgeable, more comfortable? Not really. I'm better because I *see* selling differently. I used to think that selling was something you do to people. Now I know that selling is something you do *with* people. I used to think that customers were there to dazzle with my verbal skills. Now I see customers as part of my very own *support system*. See, a writer can write alone. A painter can paint alone. A sculptor can sculpt alone. But a salesperson can't sell alone. I like to use the word "partnership" to describe the perfect seller-buyer relationship because a partnership assumes that what is good for one is good for the other.

Yes, I'm a more effective salesperson—not because I've undergone any dramatic changes in my life—but because I *see* selling differently. It's simply a matter of perception. Here's an example of what we're getting at that Larry Wilson uses in his seminars at his Conference Center in Santa Fe:

He selects three people from the audience.

"You," he says to one of them, "are from the Bronx."

"You're from Tampa," he says to another.

"And you're from the Everglades," he says to the third.

He then throws a fake snake on a table in front of them and says, "If this snake were for real, I think I could predict just what the reactions would be. You, from the *Bronx*, would probably fly back to La Guardia without a plane. You, from *Tampa*, would probably move out of the snake's path—give it plenty of space. You've been around snakes all your life." Then he looks at the audience and points to the person from the Everglades. "This guy," he says, "never met a snake he didn't like. He'll probably pick it up and fondle it."

The message: The snake couldn't care less. It was not its appearance that caused the problem. It was—and here we go again—how it was *perceived!*

One more time. It is not what happens that causes stress— it's how we perceive it! And so the only way we can improve the quality of our lives is to transform the quality of our *perceptions!*

"Okay, Okay," you say, "maybe you're on to something but what's my next move?"

Well, if you're really serious, you can get started right now! Pick up a notebook or ledger and tonight at bed-time, try to remember the things that happened during the day that upset you —caused pain—used up your energy. Everything you can remember—write it down. Now it's on record!

Thumbing through my own ledger—and I've been using this technique for years—some of the things I've recorded are: "I had a bad day playing golf today—hit 'em with my knuckles—but I didn't need Phil to say, 'Gove, I've seen better swings on a condemned playground!'"

"Got caught in traffic on I-95—guy behind me kept blowing his horn. Could have strangled him."…"My secretary got an obscene phone call—collect. And accepted it!"…"The Red Sox lost again in extra innings—bums!"…"Kermit recommended a new restaurant—the food was lousy. I called him and told him the catch of the day was hepatitis!"

Now, if you don't believe this strategy works—try it for a couple of weeks. Just for a couple of weeks—just try it. At the end of the second week—turn back to day *one.* I guarantee you that after you stop laughing, you'll agree that most of the things that distracted you weren't worth the time that it took to write 'em down! Then you'll find out—as I did—that it is not what happens—etc. etc. etc.—

—And that you are finally in control of your own life.

"Leadership is not being nice to people. Leadership is recognizing that people need an environment where they can be nice to themselves."
T.H.

TAKIN' UP THE SLACK*

Tom Haggai
209 N. Main St.
Suite 203
High Point, NC 27260
919/889-8962

Tom Haggai's message is timeless, but his language is flavored with contemporary phrases; his warmth, humor and understanding indicate a very human guy. So he is! Tom has been a public speaker since age 12. He communicates comfortably with the curious teenager …the college idealist…the young executive and conservative business person.

Tom's stewardship of time is evidenced in his multi-faceted careers. He serves as Chairman of the Board/CEO of IGA (Independent Grocers Alliance), that is owned by 16 wholesale food corporations serving 3,000 stores in 48 states, Japan and Australia at this time.

Although Tom has many corporate responsibilities, he is able to carve out time to average at least two major addresses a week nationally and internationally. Throughout the nation, Tom Haggai is heard daily on his radio show—One Minute, Please. Dr. Haggai is a recipient of the C.P.A.E. from the National Speakers Association.

The high-water mark of western migration occurred in 1850 when 55,000 pilgrims left the United States at Kansas City to seek the promised land in Oregon.

In the early 1840s, wagon trains of twenty to thirty wagons could negotiate the plains without much organization, but when the trains grew to fifty and sixty wagons, the wagon masters had to come up with some new methods of safety and control.

So the trains were split into segments of five wagons each. The members of those parties left in the morning together; shared lunch and evening meal together; helped each other with ox and wagon problems; cheered and comforted each other at their own campfires. So the line of wagons would be five wagons, then a gap, then five more wagons and a gap, and so on.

As evening drew near, the wagon master would send his pilot forward on horseback to scout out a suitable plain where all of the segments would rejoin in one huge circle. So proficient were these pilots in marking out the needed diameter of their circle that the last wagon neatly closed the loop without any wagon in the circle before them having to move.

After the oxen were unhitched they could be left in the circle or led to another guarded area. The tongue of each wagon was inserted into the rear axle assembly of the one before it and secured there by chains. Guards were then posted around the perimeter. So formidable was this tactic that no Indian war party ever attacked any western travelers employing it.

What the wagon master really worried about were the straggler wagons, those that because of breakdown or pilgrim illness had to pull out of the segment and drift in when they could. These were the ones that were vulnerable to Indian raids and injury.

Physical strength and mental ingenuity were needed to cajole, encourage, help, and rebuild—to get the troubled wagon back to the safety of the train.

* * *

*The Great Leader Guides Different People in Pursuit of a
Common Goal*

We have become accustomed to painting our leaders somewhat larger than life—way out in front of their corporations—
dragging the corporate team forward by the sheer magnetism of
personality. The leader is seen as the dominating suitor overwhelming the reluctant damsel. Such ego drive may for a short
time be mistaken as leadership, but it evaporates in the first crisis.

The leader exerts special influence over a number of people
for their mutual benefit. His personality in action molds the
group together. His leadership traits are authenticated by the
group's willing followership. In most instances, misunderstood
leaders are not ahead of their time as much as they have sepa-
rated themselves from their time. Conceptual thinking, creative
genius, and expansive vision may mark their individualities, but
progress depends on complementing those talents with an empathy that seeks to understand one's followers, sense their needs,
and suggest ways that both the leader and the follower can be
satisfied with the end result.

Leadership, as we have seen in people like Roger Milliken
and Dick Harrison, is mental contact leading to a social process
that subdues dominance and heightens delegation. An attitude
of "give and take" transforms a dissatisfying job to a satisfying
mission.

The person who views himself as a hero in his own time
feels "center stage" is his due. Such self-anointed leaders, rising
on the shoulders of their own press releases, are actually indiffer-
ent, narrow, fickle, duplicitous, cowardly, stubborn, and isolated.
They attempt to overcompensate, lest they be found out for what
they are. My selected leaders have praise, vitality, enthusiasm,
positiveness, friendliness, trustworthiness, and sympathy.

So in each chapter I have taken a bifocal approach to leadership. The emphasis on the leader is matched by the effect on
the led.

To be sure, raw survival may cause the autocratic, personality-cult leader to have a following. There is a lot of truth in the perversion of the Golden Rule to "He who has the gold, sets the rules." With calculated smiles and measured pleasantness, the personality-cult leader charms his way; but gradually his failure to build an infrastructure reveals to his followers that he succeeds at their expense. No hatred is as severe as when love is followed blindly, only to find the so-called leader absent when the dead end is reached. The extreme was cited by Emil Ludwig in his biography, *Napoleon:* "But the crowd must be learning to hate him; for, in that darkling hour, hundreds of unarmed citizens, idle spectators, women have perished. What is that to him? It is not his aim to be loved."

Even if the autocratic personality-cult leader is warm and paternalistic, he is unveiled as cruel if he has not developed individual initiative in his followers. Wanting to be all things to all people, he may well leave them nothing. This leader fails to let people loose and encourage their development so they might take his place and even overshadow him. No matter how kind, he flunks the test of serving his followers.

The wagon master earned respect and control by understanding that stimulation and energy derive from guiding different people in pursuit of a common goal.

The Leaders of a Worldwide Success Story—Coca-Cola

Such a twentieth-century wagon master resides at the world headquarters of Coca-Cola in Atlanta, Georgia. Yes, I mean *world* headquarters! How do you keep the wagons together when they reach into over 150 countries of the world? It is one thing to leave your office and wander through an adjacent plant or store, quite a different thing when the employees circle the world—with different cultures and different tongues sharing the same truth, integrity, value, character, consistency, clarity, confidence, pride, and purpose. All of this energy is directed toward selling people 250 million times a day to add a simple moment of pleasure—"the Pause that Refreshes"—to their often prosaic daily lives. Such a cajoling and complimenting leader is Donald R. Keough, president and chief operating officer of The Coca-Cola Company.

Few would question that Roberto C. Goizueta, chairman and CEO, has one of the fine-tuned conceptual minds of world business. The Cuban-born, U.S.-educated executive had built-in excuses to be mediocre at worst and timid at best but, instead, has honored the legacy of the late Robert Woodruff by believing simple refreshment can stimulate otherwise drab moments, whether it be a Coke, a glass of OJ, a cup of coffee, or a movie. Handpicked by Mr. Woodruff in 1980, Goizueta changed Coke from the starchiness of his predecessor to "...an enthusiasm akin to that of schoolboys released from a long detention period."

Up to his recent retirement, Lebanese-born but Egyptian-raised, Sam Ayoub was chief financial officer and the steward of Coca-Cola's abnormally large resources. In fact, Coke had such an international flavor in its executives—including Brian Dyson from Argentina and Tony Amon from Middle Europe—that Roberto Goizueta had a belly laugh at a Los Angeles analysis meeting when Don Keough, following him and Sam Ayoub to the podium, opened his remarks in his perfect Midwestern diction: "At the outside I'd like to apologize for my accent. I hope it doesn't detract from the international flavor of the company."

Coca-Cola had its territory staked out. It possessed the most recognized English label in the world from its colloquial world headquarters in Atlanta, Georgia. But new frontiers remain the dream of its leadership.

Yes, a few years ago Coke was lulled to sleep, tranquilized by its own successes and excesses; but its main rival, Pepsi, forgot the old legend that says if you finally get a giant to nap, be sure to tiptoe around him. Enter the Goizueta era, turning the operational reins over to Don Keough. If Coke was blinking, as a somewhat suspect author suggests, it was the reaction of looking into the brilliant light of its 100th birthday cake that celebrated its record-setting year.

Don Keough looks the part of a wagon master. Nebraska-born, rising through the experiences of each aspect of the company, Don possesses a robust Irish wit; is devoted to church and family; is chairman of trustees at Notre Dame University; is quick to laugh and instinctively gregarious; is firm but friendly. He has innate sound judgment. Former Omaha Mayor Bob Cunningham, a Creighton classmate of Don's, described him like this: "He's a big, warm teddy bear type of Irishman, a very funny man."

Don Keough is the personification of the United Technologies advertisement editorial in the *The Wall Street Journal:*

> Let's get rid of management.
> People don't want to be managed.
> They want to be led.
> Whoever heard of a world manager? World leader, yes.
> Educational leader. Political leader. Religious leader.
>   Scout leader. Community leader. Labor leader.
>   Business leader. They lead.
> They don't manage…if you want to manage somebody,
>   manage yourself.
> Do that well, and you will be ready to stop managing,
> And start leading.

This may have been on Teddy Roosevelt's mind when he wrote: "People ask the difference between a leader and a boss. The leader works in the open, the boss in the covert. The leader leads, the boss drives."

Don Keough is the consummate leader possessed by the ultimate virtue—great loves. If love doesn't carry a man beyond himself, it is not love. Love that is always discreet, always wise, always sensible and calculating, never reaching beyond itself, is synthetic. Love makes the leader magnetically vulnerable. Of course, I'm not writing of weakness but strength. Love without courage and wisdom is mere sentimentality. Strength without love usually becomes egotism that leads to suspicion, distrust, and jealousy. Such strength tends to take the form of grandiose ideas and overestimation of one's power and control, giving a false sense of omnipotence.

Leadership built on devotion cannot be passive. We can expect to get action from Don. He defies the observation of Paul Vilandre of Convergent Technologies who marveled, "Smokestack industry gets hung up on the elegance of the decision vs. the substance" (*The Wall Street Journal*, Jan. 10, 1985). Don is willing to be assertive but realistic enough to encourage assertiveness from others and humble enough to acknowledge the superiority of ideas presented by others. *The effort is not to make people feel that they are of use to Coca-Cola but that they are of value to Coca-Cola.*

Picture with me a significant gathering of Don's associates. Here their president is preparing to speak. You can imagine an international executive standing behind a lectern reading in *ex cathedra* tones the address carefully homogenized by his writers. Not Don Keough! He speaks informally from his heart and with a touch of humor on winning. He tells his audience he can recognize a winner once a gold medal is hung around his neck or the profits of the corporation have sky-rocketed or a new product has been successfully introduced. "Winners," he has said, "come in every size and shape; they are introverts and extroverts. They are educated, uneducated; some of them are charismatic and articulate, and others are dull as dishwater."

He then refers to a sociology professor from one of the country's major universities who spent his life studying leadership by tracing the careers of five thousand former students: "I have come to the conclusion that the only way one can determine a leader is to look at the person and see if anybody is following him."

After democratizing the audiences with such comments, Don Keough then stimulates them upward by sharing "Keough's Commandments for Losing":

1. Quit taking risks.
2. Be content.
3. Before you make any move, always ask yourself, "What will my investors think?"
4. Avoid change.
5. Be totally inflexible—stay on the course, no matter what.
6. Rely totally on research and experts to make decisions for you.
7. Be more concerned with status than service.
8. Concentrate on your competitor instead of your customer.
9. Put yourself first in everything you do, ahead of your customers and suppliers.
10. Memorize the formula "TGE...That's Good Enough" to set a ceiling on quality.

Then add a bonus rule:

11. Find a way to rationalize the slowing of growth.

Go back and read these eleven "Commandments for Losing" and again see yourself sitting in the sizable audience of Coca-Cola peers. Even without knowing Don Keough, you can see the smile with which each point was developed and the compliment implied therein. Absent are the placating empty words designed to be warm but cold when spoken by a president either wanting to be quoted correctly by the press or fearing being quoted at all. Don is actually complimenting his associates' abilities. He knows that none of them would knowingly do these things, though any of us can get careless. What he is really doing is praising the group into constructive performance.

There is nothing new about his approach really, for it was verbalized by Dr. Elton Mayo of Harvard Graduate School of Business Administration. The testing ground was the Hawthorne Plant of Western Electric in suburban Chicago. The testing time was 1927-1932. The theory that Dr. Mayo proved was that workers tend to cluster together into informal groups in order to fill a void in their lives. *The void is a person's need for companionship and cooperation.* The Industrial Revolution depersonalized man. If that was true in 1930, think about our automated age now beginning to utilize robotic technology. At least in 1930 the worker might be reinforced at home while, today, fewer than 25 percent of our homes are traditional, meaning both parents in the home.

So Dr. Mayo's prescription was to cultivate communication between employer and employee and to put supervision in the hands of people to whom respect for other persons came naturally. Supervisors were to be trained in the skills of listening, understanding, and eliciting cooperation which was quite a departure from the image of the straw boss of the day. Dr. Mayo literally became an industrial evangelist. He had a simple message: Productivity declines when work deteriorates into an impersonal exchange of money for labor. He called it *Anomie,* which left workers feeling rootless, unimportant, and confused by the indifference to their environment. The only other place I have seen this word used was in James Michener's novel *Texas* when the settlers were lost in the expanse. If people became docile, they didn't have to be angry; they just became woeful, inefficient producers. The Siamese twins of productivity and quality died simultaneously.

Now let's bring Dr. Mayo and Don Keough together in these last years of the twentieth century and join them with Daniel Webster who defined labor as, "One of the great elements of society...the great substantial interest on which we all stand. No feudal service or the irksome drudgery of one race subjected to another but labor...intelligent, manly, independent, thinking and acting for one's self, earning one's own wages, educating childhood, maintaining worship, claiming the right to the elective franchise and helping to uphold the great fabric of the state. That is labor, and all my sympathies are with it."

Dr. Mayo has said it and Don Keough is shouting, "Amen." People work effectively where people feel warm. Can you imagine a simpler word than "warm?" Yet isn't that true?

Where we feel a sense of belonging and a sense of worth, we respond productively. We need that sense of achievement, self-esteem, recognition, and security even more than we need the money, for as the University of Michigan found in a 1977 study, three out of four Americans would prefer to be working even if they could live comfortably without working for the rest of their lives. This desire to make people feel "warm" worked for Dr. Mayo a half century ago and works for Don Keough today.

Don said on one occasion, "I have a calling card. It says, 'Donald R. Keough, President of The Coca-Cola Company.' Now in the last analysis, the only thing that is really mine is the 'Donald R. Keough.' I am a temporary president. I am a temporary resident of this fancy office. I hope that when I have to tear that card up and when I carry one that says just, 'Donald R. Keough,' I will be enough of a total person that I will be considered worthwhile. I think about that...a lot."

How does this attitude translate into actuality with Don Keough's corporate team? Ask him: "A lot of managers focus on weaknesses. And we all have them. I think that is a fundamental mistake. You have to look at the beauty spots. We all have those, too. When you do that, and let the person sense it, then you get all the best that's in them. And they are not demeaned or destroyed by your constantly reaching in to find their weaknesses."

When you make people feel good about themselves, you are helping them say, "God, you didn't waste your creative power on me."

What does Don mean by "beauty spots"? It's the climate he has created. Whether in Houston or Singapore, his call begins: "You have to be proud of increased sales in Classic Coke. The public sure shouted their loyalty when we introduced our new formula, and I'm proud we could respond so quickly. Now I notice you still have that nagging problem with your division.

What's your game plan? You do feel it's solvable? Well, here's the best thinking from our end. Are we a help to you, and how can we better assist you?"

The entire tone promotes a successful conclusion with the person nearest the problem receiving the credit. The tone is neither false praise nor destructive flattery. Victor Frankl, the veteran of the Holocaust, a psychologist and teacher, taught us in *Man's Search for Meaning* that unreal optimism can be more damaging than criticism or pessimism. By comparison, candor can be upbeat.

Don Keough joins other admired leaders in addressing issues with the attitude of helping, not condemning. Exploratory surgery is an act of desperation. You desire to cut in with the idea of where you'll come out. I hear you talking back to me as you read these pages: "Tom, business is hard and harsh; you can't always be pleasant." Wrong! You can be pleasant. The more pleasant you are, the firmer you can be. Pleasantness helps you to look without apology for the silver lining of each cloud. You look for opportunity to celebrate. You hope, *by praise*, to turn any little progress into momentum.

Again you talk back: "Whenever I'm critical, it is constructive criticism." Constructive criticism is never identified by the mouth speaking, but by the ears listening. Praise is the rite of passage that allows you to be constructively helpful. Going through the heartaches of scouting, as well as the repositioning of IGA, I have found I can face the tough decisions and still be pleasant. Pleasantness may test whether you are rightfully objective or wrongly subjective.

Leadership is not being nice to people. Leadership is recognizing that people need an environment where they can be nice to themselves.

In each of us are sterling strengths and woeful weaknesses. The leader's role is to create the atmosphere where the person's

strengths outweigh his weaknesses. It's much like the missionary asking a recent convert how he was enjoying his newfound
faith. The convert quietly replied, "Ah, Mr. Missionary, I find I
have within me two dogs. I have a good dog and I have a bad
dog. They're always fighting."

"And which dog wins?" queried the missionary.

"That's easy," replied the convert, "whichever one I say
'Sic 'em' to."

Leadership is warmly encouraging your associates to whis-
per, "Sic 'em," to their strengths. To put it another way, when
you help associates to appreciate expressed appreciation, you're
watching them move in the right direction.

Refining Your Employee Appraisal System

Employees properly expect reassurance. A worldwide corporation sets the example for each of its facilities by keeping an
open-door policy at the corporate headquarters. Communication
is every leader's responsibility. Pruning the grapevines that
strangle best intentions is a necessity. Don Keough makes a
practice of meeting new Coke people wherever he travels and is
blessed with an incredibly retentive mind for names and faces.
He is aware that even the international success of Coca-Cola
doesn't erase the twin questions that have a way of popping up:
"How sound is our business in the face of our competition?
How secure is my job?"

Here's where an effective appraisal system should be "a
given." One of my first corporate responsibilities was to review
the organization's appraisal system. "Appraisal" has never been
an attractive word to me. It presumes a role that makes me
uncomfortable. *Random House Dictionary* defines appraisal as
"the act of estimating the value of an asset..." We agree our
greatest asset is "people," but calling them assets is dehumaniz-
ing. The appraiser who views himself as an amateur psychologist compounds this problem. A chill sweeps over me when I
hear appraisers use "buzz words" to classify employees. They

adopt that nagging tendency to solve a new problem by giving it a new name!

With the responsibility to perfect the appraisal system, I studied ten corporations, beginning at the Pentagon with the highly structured system of the U.S. Air Force and ending at Hughes Aircraft where my late brother Ted was senior scientist.

Not one of the ten was satisfied with the way they appraised. That was encouraging! Any time we are satisfied with our judgmental procedures toward our fellowman, we are in trouble. We should always be refining our efforts to be fairer and more insightful. Also, most appraisals are downward or, at best parallel, but never upward. Those who report to us seldom, if ever, have the opportunity to appraise us. One of the many reasons I admire Colonel Frank Borman was his decision to encourage a team of union and nonunion employees to run a report card on him. It was a team effort so no subordinates would feel threatened. Frank felt that because they owned 25 percent of the nonnegotiable stock and couldn't sell if dissatisfied like public investors, they should be able to appraise him to help the Eastern Air Lines.

I reached several conclusions about appraisals.

1. *Even if the form is structured, the actual appraisal should be done in an informal setting.* Don't even begin unless you have time and hope to be free from interruptions. Never should the two people be across a desk from each other. A desk lends itself to an adversarial relationship. I usually sit beside the person, possibly making a few informal notes, and then filling out the necessary form later. After filling out the form and writing a summary essay, I sit with the person again to go over my observations. Hopefully, he or she will be comfortable signing off on it.

2. *My goal is to dwell more on the future opportunities than on the past performance.*

3. *My desire is to lead the person to self-appraisal, giving me the privilege to be the listener and catalyst.* Whenever people are free to set their own standards, they are more stringent

on themselves than you would have been. Leaders in effective corporations gladly grant employees more rights than the average company, but the employees are challenged to accept greater responsibilities enthusiastically. The proper balance of rights and responsibilities equals effectiveness.

Rights don't democratize the corporation but underscore caring leadership. People want leaders to lead—make no mistake about it.

Everyone Needs A Leader

In January of 1986 I sat at Food Marketing Institute's Mid-Year Convention listening to Professor D. Quinn Mills of Harvard University. Although I respect him, I found myself shaking my head negatively. Though it seemed out of character, I felt Dr. Mills was bordering on insulting his audience. He was using People Express Airline to teach us the "new wave of corporate climate." First, I felt it was a poor choice to hype any company that had been in existence less than a half dozen years. Continuity is a basic factor in leadership. Secondly, Dr. Mills was making the case for a democratic work place where the officers sold tickets and pilots loaded luggage. Thank goodness flight attendants didn't fly planes!

From the first year of operation, I had predicted the demise of People Express. How people like Dr. Mills could get "carried away" I'll never understand. People want a hierarchy; otherwise, they feel insecure about privileges. As Dr. Mayo had found, people tend to cluster and, not given leadership, will designate their own. People Express is now history, and the only people more embarrassed than the creditors are the professors.

There is no question who leads Coca-Cola. In the uncertain moments before they turned Classic Coke into a bonanza guaranteeing more shelf space in the food store, Roberto Goizueta and Don Keough, not a surrogate, met the press and bit the bullet. People rally around people, not philosophy.

With all the opportunities at Coca-Cola, lifetime employment is not a consideration. They don't roll heads carelessly nor move people indiscriminately, but they also won't allow good employees to be undermined nor the company to become hostage to bungling.

Coke had gone through a period before the Goizueta-Keough era where all of us in the business community were hearing their squeaky revolving door too often. Don Keough puts determination far ahead of termination unless behavior is flagrant. He challenges his personnel people to work diligently to place the right person in the right job.

Good people can be lost through misplacement, especially when the company stretches around the world. I am old enough to remember that Jimmy Tabor flunked out as a pitcher but became a star third baseman with the Boston Red Sox in an infield that included York, Doerr, Pesky, and Tebbetts. I recall that Bob Lemon couldn't hit his weight as a centerfielder but led the Cleveland Indians into the World Series as an All-Star pitcher. As someone who has had to do more than his quota of firing, I believe firing is as important a role as hiring and is necessary for a healthy corporation, but each instance must be tested and justified.

A bottom line is operative in this chapter. The pilgrims and the wagon master were pushing together for the reward of a promised land. The pragmatic side of your praising and cajoling in a corporation is the financial reward. A worldwide corporation like Coke has to have salary management but flexibility to make exceptions. The exceptions actually legitimize the rules. You can be rewarded with more than normal increments and you can merit jumping several positions. For years I have quarreled with surveys that place salary somewhere between fifth and sixth of the ten things a person wants from a job. Not for a minute do I believe there are many people who will say, "Just pay me enough and I'm your boy." At the same time, most people probably value salary second or third, but in a false search for nobility, they feel it crass to put it there. Anticipating good returns for your efforts is proper.

Motivating People the W. H. Belk Way

One man who had native sense about people was the late William Henry Belk, one of the unsung geniuses of the Southeast. The four-hundred-store company that bears his name is one hundred years old and is consistently the most prosperous department store chain of our nation, a fact not generally known because of the unique and totally private structure of the company. In a century the stores have had just two leaders: Mr. Belk and his second-eldest son, John M. Belk.

Mr. Belk came out of modest beginnings in Union County, North Carolina, with a large Presbyterian faith incorporating the Puritan work ethic and Calvinistic optimism, but he had few dollars. To accelerate growth, William Henry Belk handpicked managers that he made partners. In most instances they brought no money to the table; but they shared his vision, ambition, and integrity. Their stores were to offer better values and be the retail anchor of each city or town where they were located. The managers were to work hard, take an interest in civic and political affairs, and be recognized as regular attenders at the churches of their choice. Folklore has it that an entry interview with Mr. Belk included such a personal question as: "Are you a Christian...and a Presbyterian?" which most felt he considered synonymous! When Arthur Tyler responded, "I'm an Episcopalian," Mr. Belk mustered up all of his ecumenical grace and observed, "I knew *one* good one once, Arthur. You better be like him."

The driving force was that Mr. Belk made these early managers partners. He gave them the ownership of at least one-third of the store while he kept each store a separate corporation with a central buying service.

One of the last original partners is one of the greatest influences in my life, so beloved by our family that Edwin Colin Lindsey is simply "Uncle Colin." Born in Pelzer, South Carolina, over eight decades ago and raised in Mackintosh, Florida, so far "behind" the post office that when he flew to London on the *Concorde,* it took him the same amount of time as it once took him as a lad to hitch his mule to the wagon and go to town to fetch the mail. It is his Lindsey name that is hyphenated with Belk in Florida and Puerto Rico at thirty-five sites with the best volume and net return of various groups.

Mr. Belk early recognized Uncle Colin's ability to read people from an experience they shared outside of retailing. I witnessed this ability at a Board of Governors meeting of our THA Foundation (a foundation whose purpose is the giving of lucrative scholarships nationwide to financially needy young people who, upon graduation, will serve professionally in the educational field (grades K-5) or in non-profit youth organizations such as Scouting, YMCA/YWCA, Boys'/Girls' Clubs, Big Brothers/Big Sisters, etc. Colin Lindsey and John Belk were part of the original twelve designers of the foundation).

Before this board of governors came a young man from Boston who showed great promise except for his obvious obesity which created a poor impression. While others held back, Uncle Colin quickly spoke up, "Poor chap, raised so poor on a steady starch diet that's all gone to his stomach. He sure needs our encouragement, and at college they'll give him a balanced diet." Unc was right. The young man trimmed down to become more attractive to interview committees and has written quite a chapter with Big Brother/Big Sisters.

Such judgment isn't new for "Unc." At the close of World War II, in Winter Haven, where he opened his record-making store, "Unc" hired Del Funari, using the GI Bill offering split-dollars employment. "Every time I turned around, I bumped into Del," said Uncle Colin, "he was always at my shoulder learning everything I knew and much more. I figured he had just what I needed because he had ambition and 'guts.'" Here Del Funari was, a "minority"; an Italian in a small Anglo-Saxon town; a Catholic in an 85 percent Protestant county; a fast-talking Yankee in the heart of Florida's "cracker country." Today, upon Uncle Colin's retirement, Del heads the Belk-Lindsey group.

There is a great contrast between worldwide Coca-Cola and Florida's Belk-Lindsey stores, but there is also a great commonality of attitude. Mr. Lindsey's managers possess an almost religious loyalty toward him, although I have never heard him use the word or consider it a part of his measuring system. He not only paid them sound salaries but also large bonuses. His appraisal system wasn't annual, semi-annual, quarterly, or monthly. It was constant updates.

Here's the "grabber." As E. C. Lindsey gave them their sizable bonuses, often equaling or exceeding their salaries, he *never, never* allowed them to thank him. He told me, "If they thank me, they'd have felt obligated to me. Instead, it was satisfying for me to say, 'I'm not giving you a gift. I'm proud to present you with what you've earned this year based on your fulfilling your commitment and much, much more. Thank you.'"

It was Unc's conviction that if he let them feel obligated, they might despise him. He wanted them to know he was only giving them *their* money which he felt didn't cost him a thing. What pragmatic praise! What a way for "Takin' Up The Slack."

How wise is this approach! Unable to thank Mr. Lindsey, the managers were motivated to do a better job the next year. If they didn't receive bonuses, the managers literally resigned themselves. Without bonuses they knew, without a word from Unc, that they lacked competence or had self-doubts or didn't like what they were doing or were bored or stagnant. The bonus told them and Uncle Colin how excited they were, what good planners they were, how strong they were in climbing over obstacles, how much inner drive they possessed, and how much proper pride they had.

What leverage Uncle Colin had! He threw all his weight behind helping them look good. From their humble beginnings they were grateful to Mr. Belk for giving them a chance to gain identity and wealth. Unc's integrity demanded he pass the opportunity on. He built them up, raised his voice seldom, ranted never, but used the bonus as a pitch pipe to help his managers find the right note. Never have I witnessed such a dissimilar group of managers harmonizing on the same song.

Whether Coca-Cola or Belk, Don Keough or E. C. Lindsey, the underlining motive is the same. Goodness and fairness are not "carrot stick" mentality appealing to survival instincts. They are not "feathering their own nests" at the exclusion of their associates. It is a case of sharing the spirit. Literally blood, sweat, and tears are expended by those caught up in the drive, dynamism, and dedication of the leader's dream. They are immune to corporate narcissism that allows chewing up people to promote the leader's image.

They are moving among the wagons in the train, balancing the tangible and the intangible to fulfill different dreams with common endings.

---

* Taken from Dr. Thomas Haggai's book, *How the Best Is Won.*

"'It is almost impossible not to become more successful or happy if we really want to be.' Success, whatever it may be defined as for each of us, is simply the natural outcome of our directed intentions and actions."
I.H.

STOP HOPING AND START COPING

9

Ira Hayes
326 Meadowlark Ct.
Marco Island, FL 33937
813/394-0830

Ira Hayes is recognized throughout the United States as the electrifying "Ambassador of Enthusiasm." He is one of the country's foremost authorities on positive thinking and motivational behavior.

Ira has been awarded the C.P.A.E. and is past President of the National Speakers Association. He has given speeches before over four thousand audiences, including Positive Thinking Rallies attended by up to 18,000 people.

To get to where he is today, Ira began many years ago as a sales trainee for the NCR Corporation. He created ideas and techniques and caused these management skills to evolve because of his own unique positive motivational attitudes and abilities. In the process of a brilliant career that ultimately saw Ira become head of NCR's Advertising Department and organizer of NCR's speaker's bureau, Ira continued developing and purifying his marketing and management skills.

The huge cat's explosive roar split the calm twilight, and was immediately joined by the man's shriek as the two tumbled onto the dusty plain. The two sounds blended into one chilling chord of struggle; the killer beast rumbling its deadly growl of slaughter, and the man screaming in the terrified determination of defense and survival.

The weight of the massive cat slammed the man onto his back, stunning him and knocking his stone club out of his grip. The beast crouched low over the victim and dropped its jaw for the crushing bite that would snap the man's neck.

From behind the boulders that framed the opening of the man's subterranean dwelling, the women and tiny children stared in silent resignation. Beyond hope, beyond thinking, the trembling figures in the rocks could only leave the man to cope with his fate. To succumb or survive the prehistoric tiger's attack was up to him alone.

The beast lunged at the man's neck and shoulder, but the wiry victim rocked forward and hugged the tiger's throat against his chest. Beneath the cat's fiercely working jaws, the man held on with a death grip. The gleaming yellow fangs slashed at the empty air and the roaring beast's hot breath poured down the man's naked back. The struggle continued from heartbeat to heartbeat, the caveman taking in every move the tiger made and countering with his own defenses. The big cat and the man tumbled and scrambled together, claws matched against hands, fangs matched against cunning.

Methodical in his panic, resolute in the deadly significance of the match, the caveman's awareness kept up with the split second timing of each movement. The claws continued to shift and slash as the man managed to move the struggle closer and closer to the spot where he was originally seized by the ravenous beast.

One hand left the conflict to dart out to the side and then return immediately to the clash. Again the hand flew out, but this time the fingers felt the familiar worn wooden grip of the stone ax that had saved the man's life so many times. The hand curled around the handle, the arm pulled up and inward, and the stone club sailed up, over, and down onto the back of the tiger's skull. The jolt rocked through the beast's body. Again the club came up and back down onto the sagging head. With a rasping groan, the big cat slumped to the dusty surface of the plain, sliding off the man beneath it.

Staggering to his feet in a daze, the man looked past the limp form of the tiger to the rocks surrounding the entrance to his underground cave. The human forms there raised their arms as though to salute his success. The man turned and moved away as the people from the cave came forward to claim the slain beast. As his breathing pace returned to normal, the man began to forget about the tiger and direct his attention forward, as he had always done before.

Just like the caveman in the story, all of us today find ourselves in situations where we are confronted with a problem that is our own responsibility to take care of. The problem doesn't always threaten to eat us alive if we fail to jump immediately into vigorous action that guarantees a successful outcome, but whether gobbled up whole or merely nibbled into frustration or failure, it is still the classic struggle of the man against the tigers of the world that would overcome him.

My own story does not at first seem quite as dramatic as that of the caveman who resisted becoming the tiger's dinner. But as a young man just starting out in business in the early 50's with a growing family to support, I realized that success or failure was all up to me. I felt I was looking out at the new tigers of a modern age.

In the decades of activity that made up my life from those earlier days, it became increasingly clear to me that "It is almost impossible not to become more successful or happy if we really want to be." Success, whatever it may be defined as for each of us, is simply the natural outcome of our directed intentions and actions. We can count on success if we really want it. And we can recognize and combat today's tigers in their new guises, waiting to catch us and keep us from our goals.

What I may not have realized as a young man starting out was that the contemporary tigers lying in wait to pull people off the path to success are those subtle, insidious character traits that appear to be so harmless, that many of us do not even think to be on guard against their attack. Though some of us may not see them, those tigers are crouched there every day of our lives. Once we can open our eyes and recognize these tigers as the destroyers they are, we are then prepared to design our own weapons to combat and destroy their all-consuming power over us.

In almost all cases, we would have whatever we really want, if it were not for our tendency to succumb to the negative forces of Carelessness, Laziness, Indifference, Forgetfulness and Temptation.

Carelessness	Being inattentive, incautious, unwary, indiscreet, reckless, inaccurate, negligent, thoughtless or inconsiderate.
Laziness	Having an aversion to work or effort, slow moving, sluggish or inactive.
Indifference	Without concern, not caring, apathetic, a "so what" attitude.
Forgetfulness	Unable to remember or recall, to omit, inability to think of things.
Temptation	Being attracted by the possibility of gratification or advantage, lured into doing something unwise, being led astray from something that needs attention.

Over eons, since the first caveman discovered that the tigers were out to get him, man has faced a continuously evolving series of threats that have adopted ever-more subtle manifestations. Today, the weapons of old are no longer suitable for coping with modern attackers.

The rock, club, hatchet and spear have given way to a new and more powerful set of weapons designed specifically for the tigers of this age. The road to success is made up of single steps, each taken one at a time. Forming and shaping each of the new weapons is likewise a step by step procedure.

In my own life, I discovered eight crucial points that are the counterforces for coping with the five weaknesses that work to destroy our dreams and keep us from our desired success. I found these eight admonitions to be such powerful tools that I had them printed out on individual cards and hung them from the dashboard of my car. Every morning as I look at the card on display, it reminds me to be alert for those weaknesses that would grab me and drag me down. Every Monday morning I flip to the next card and work on the next counteracting force. After eight weeks, it's time to start over again from the beginning.

The eight weapons to counter and cope with the five weaknesses are:

1. DO IT NOW

If the caveman took too long to complete his powerful ax or stone club, he might be destroyed by the first tiger he meets.

Nothing can be accomplished until you begin. So this first card reminds us of the average person's most serious weakness—the great temptation to put things off until later. When embarking on a new and exciting program of self-improvement, this is a most important card. Sit down right now and write down all those things you know you should have done or have promised yourself or someone else you would do. Whenever this card comes up, let it remind you of one of the greatest and most refreshing qualities a person can have, to be able to cope with things as quickly as possible.

2. ORGANIZATION AND APPEARANCE

If the caveman could not find his club when he needed it, it was too late. And just maybe if the wild beast saw the man walking by with his death-dealing ax, they would learn not to attack.

It is my belief from observing hundreds of people that their inability or lack of desire to get organized is responsible for a great majority of failures. It is why otherwise bright people turn out to be mediocre performers and achieve only a small degree of the success they rightfully could achieve. A disorganized desk, car, or way of life leads to confusion, rushing around, agitation, and a poor attitude. Your appearance is also very important. Each time this card comes up, concentrate that week on straightening up your personal things. Take a good look at your clothes, your hair, your self. Remember how you looked the first day on the job? How do you look today?

3.   BE CHEERFUL AND OPTIMISTIC

The caveman who is cheerful and happy over last night's victory conveys an important message to other tigers who may have been watching the death of one of their own pack.

No one wants to hear your problems. They have enough of their own to cope with. In every thought you have, every act you perform, everything you say, you have the choice of being either cheerful and optimistic—or negative and doubtful. I assure you, success is much more quickly attained when you expect it. It indicates to those around you that you are prepared and confident. Your cheerfulness and optimism will usually be returned to you by the other person. This very important card helps set you off from the crowd because today most of the people you meet are not cheerful and optimistic. In fact, it has become almost unfashionable to smile anymore. You will stand out like a star. Few people can say no when they're smiling.

4.   MODERATION

One strong well-built ax on the caveman's shoulder is far more effective than a dozen makeshift sticks in a bundle somewhere in the cave.

You may be greatly tempted to rush into new ideas and programs at the expense of other things you should be doing. "Moderation" reminds us that great accomplishments are made, objectives are reached, by a well thought out program of activities that can comfortably be done day by day. Moderation—one of the foundation stones in the life of almost every great person.

5.   SAY SOMETHING NICE TO EVERYONE YOU MEET
The roar of the savage beast is terrifying. The purr of the cat by the hearth is comforting.

Sincere flattery can go a long way. I'm sure you have experienced the glow of satisfaction that comes when others say something nice about you. Share the feeling! What better way to start a meeting or any other contact than by saying something nice. "You have a beautiful office here, Mr. Jones." "That's a beautiful tie you're wearing." Or even, "How very nice to see you!"

6.   DRIVE CAREFULLY
When travelling, the smart caveman would be keenly aware of his surroundings lest a tiger catch him unprepared or unarmed.

Generally speaking, most salespeople drive considerable distances to cover their sales territories. Accidents are always waiting for you. Especially when you are rushing or mentally reworking an unhappy situation or trying to beat the clock. Every eight weeks when this card comes up, it reminds you: Put on your seat belt! Drive within speed limit! If you're drinking, don't drive!

7.   ENTHUSIASM
The caveman could stand over the vanquished tiger and beat his chest with a shout of victory so all would know of his personal triumph.

Here is one of the most important of all the cards. Millions of words have been written about it. People spend their lives seeking it or asking how to find it. In my own life, I found that you don't just reach out and grab it. You don't get up some morning and say, "I think I'll start being enthusiastic." I believe enthusiasm is attained through personal experience. As you get better organized, things will go more smoothly. You will be more successful and you will experience that wonderful feeling of accomplishment. You'll find you have a better attitude. As this continues, you discover some bright day you really are enthusiastic—about your job, your family, your success. You are coping, not merely hoping.

8.   KEEP GOING

Today the stone ax and the fallen tiger. Tomorrow the bow and arrow and the delicious roasted birds. The next day, new and exciting triumphs in the search for a better life.

There are very few people in the world who couldn't be more successful, make more money, or be happier if they really wanted to. Why are so many unable to accomplish this? They can't keep up a program of self-improvement long enough. Anyone can be efficient and do things for seven weeks. Anyone can stay organized and neat in appearance for seven weeks. Anyone can be cheerful and optimistic for seven weeks or say something nice to everyone they meet, anyone can be enthusiastic for seven weeks. But, the eighth week is when you separate yourself from the great mass of people you compete against. Card number eight is "Keep Going." It reminds you to start over again with number one, *"Do It Now!"*

As our society and technology moved forward from the days of cavemen facing tigers, the complexity of coping with daily life continued to multiply. Man against beast is a recognizable conflict in which the only hope is to cope. In modern life, however, confrontations and conflicts are not always so clear-cut. Many times we can be caught in confusion and the hopeless feeling that life is too much to handle and end up relying solely on hope—waiting helplessly for someone to come along and bail us out. We give up our capability to cope, to deal with difficulties in a direct and positive manner, and begin to cling to hope alone.

 **DO IT NOW!**

 **ORGANIZATION AND APPEARANCE!**

 BE CHEERFUL AND OPTIMISTIC!

 MODERATION!

 **SAY SOMETHING NICE TO EVERYONE YOU MEET!**

 **DRIVE CAREFULLY!**

 ENTHUSIASM!

 KEEP GOING!

Do It Now!

Nothing can be accomplished until you begin. So, our first card reminds us of one of the average individual's most serious weaknesses--the great temptation to put things off until later. When embarking on a new and exciting program of self-improvement, this is a most important card. Sit down right now, and write down all those things you know you should have done or have promised yourself or someone else you would do, or something you want to accomplish. Whenever this No. 1 card comes up, let it remind you that one of the greatest and most refreshing qualities of a person, especially in selling, is the realization by the prospect that you are "on the ball." And when you tell him you're going to do something, you really do it.

 Organization and Appearance

It is my belief from observing hundreds of people that their inability or lack of desire to get organized is responsible for a great majority of failures. It's why otherwise bright people turn out to be mediocre performers and achieve only a small degree of the success they rightfully could achieve. A disorganized desk, car, or a way of life lead to confusion, rushing around, agitation, a poor attitude, and, most of all, reflects to customers that you're a pretty poor businessman. They question the advisability of doing business with you. Your appearance, your briefcase, your working tools are very important. Each time this card comes up, concentrate during that week in straightening up your personal things. Take a good look at your clothes, your hair, yourself. Remember, how you looked the first day on the job. How do you look today?

 Be Cheerful and Optimistic

No one wants to hear your problems. They have enough of their own. In every thought you have, every act you perform, everything you say, you have the choice of being either cheerful and optimistic--or negative and doubtful. I assure you success is much more quickly attained when you expect it. It indicates to those around you that you are prepared and confident. Your cheerfulness and optimism will usually be returned to you by the other person. This very important card helps set you off from the crowd, because, today, most of the people you meet are not cheerful and optimistic. In fact, it has become almost unfashionable to smile anymore. You'll stand out like a star. Few people can say "No!" while they're smiling.

 Moderation

You will be greatly tempted to rush into your new ideas and programs maybe at the expense of other things you should be doing. "Moderation" reminds us that great accomplishments are made, and objectives reached, by a well thought out program of activities that can comfortably be done quietly, day by day. If you take only two photographs of users each day, you'll have nearly sixty the first month! If you send only two pieces of mail to customers each week, in one year more than one hundred customers will hear from you and know you better.

Moderation: one of the foundation stones in the life of almost every great person.

 Say Something Nice to Everyone You Meet

Sincere flattery can go a long way. I'm sure you have experienced the glow of satisfaction that comes when others say something nice about you. Share that feeling! What better way of starting a meeting, opening a sales call, or any other contact than by saying something nice.--"You have a beautiful office here, Mr. Jones." "That's a beautiful tie you're wearing."--Or even, "How very nice to see you!" Your objective is to get the order, and I can tell you from my own experience, I've never lost an order complimenting the customer.

 Drive Carefully

Generally speaking, most salesmen drive considerable distances to cover their sales territories. Accidents are always waiting for you. Especially when you are rushing or mentally reworking an unhappy situation or trying to beat the clock. Every eight weeks when this card comes up, it reminds you: Put on your seat belt! Drive within speed limit! If you're drinking, don't drive! You can't find success in the hospital!

 Enthusiasm

Here is one of the most important of all the cards. Millions of words have been written about it. People spend their lives seeking it or asking how to find it. In my own life, I found you don't just reach out and grab it. You don't get up some morning and say, "I think I'll start being enthusiastic." I believe Enthusiasm is attained through personal experience. As you get better organized, things will go more smoothly. You will be more successful and you will experience that wonderful feeling of accomplishment. You will find you have a better attitude. As this contines, you discover some bright day that you really are enthusiastic...about your job, your family, your success.

 Keep Going

There are very few people knocking around the business world who couldn't be more successful, make more money, or be happier if they really wanted to. Why are so many unable to accomplish this? My personal opinion is they can't keep up a program of self-improvement long enough.

Anyone can be efficient and do things for 7 weeks. Anyone can stay organized and neat in appearance for 7 weeks. Anyone can be cheerful and optimistic for 7 weeks--or say something nice to everyone they meet--or drive carefully--or be enthusiastic. But the 8th week is where you separate yourself from the great mass of people you compete with. Card No. 8 --"Keep Going"--reminds you to start again. Here comes No. 1--"Do It Now."

It is not always easy to cope. Sometimes retreating to hope seems the most comfortable thing to do. I've found, however, that recognizing the tigers and being armed with appropriate weapons to combat them is one positive step towards making daily life an enjoyable experience. Once I discovered this effective eight point system, I was that much closer to being able to stop hoping and start coping. I am sure you will too. Why not start right now with the message on card number #1!

> *"The Consistently Exceptional Leader fosters action, independence, and interdependence in subordinates, not dependence. People are developed to stand on their own and rise, in a competent, decisive way, to the day-to-day challenge facing them. They are taught to be autonomous so they achieve for their own reasons."*
> *C.H.*

Christopher Hegarty
P.O. Box 1152
Novato, CA 94948
415/892-2858 USA

Christopher J. Hegarty is a successful entrepreneur as well as an international award winning public speaker. He has been awarded the C.P.A.E. from the National Speakers Association. More than 400 of the Fortune 500 companies, numerous trade and professional associations, and many other large and small organizations in 27 countries have used him as a speaker/trainer.

As a consultant and advisor, he has had a variety of assignments including: member of the President's Council at the American Institute of Management, Strategic Consultant at Stanford Research Institute (SRI), and advisor to the Governor of California.

Nation's Business identifies him as one of the top management consultants in North America...*U.S. News and World Report* considers him an expert on work and workaholism. Additionally, references and articles about his work have appeared in more than 500 publications including *Forbes, Dun's Review, Industry Week, Government Executive* and *Entrepreneur*.

He earned a Doctorate in Management Education from CDI International and has served on the faculty of the University of Southern California. He is the author of the book on "upward management," *How to Manage Your Boss.*

Leadership today is more challenging than ever. Organizations face entirely new challenges attracting and holding top people .

There are a number of reasons for this. The two most prominent ones are:

1) The personal values revolution** that causes people to identify with work differently.

2) The fact that organizations can no longer guarantee lifetime or even long term employment and individuals fully realize there is no traditional job security.

To attract and keep high quality individuals who already are or have the potential to be winners requires exceptional leaders who know how to appeal in new ways to the people who are able to perform well.

THE AUTOCRATIC AND BUREAUCRATIC FORMS OF LEADERSHIP ARE NO LONGER EFFECTIVE

What is needed are exceptional leaders who are capable of attracting and selecting the right people and dealing with them in a way that causes them to commit to the overall performance of the group as well as to the specific measurable job they are each required to do.

People who work for exceptional leaders learn to be individually competitive and simultaneously cooperative with all the other people in their group. Their motto might well be:

THE PRIMARY FUNCTION OF EACH PERSON IN OUR GROUP IS TO BE AS VALUABLE AS POSSIBLE TO THE PEOPLE OUR GROUP SERVES...THE SECONDARY FUNCTION OF EACH PERSON IN OUR GROUP IS TO DO THE SPECIFIC MEASURABLE JOB HE OR SHE IS PAID TO DO

IS THERE A SECRET TO LEADERSHIP?...YES!

"A LEADER GETS THE RESULTS THE LEADER HAS THE RIGHT TO EXPECT"

The above statement illustrates the secret of leadership. To the degree that a leader knows the following steps in dealing with people will the leader have the right to expect high levels of performance from them.

Take S.T.O.C.K. of your people.

There are five separate areas that need to be clearly understood and implemented for a Leader to get high levels of performance from the vast majority of his or her people. These areas are Selecting, Training, Organizing, Communicating with, and Keeping people.

A Leader seeking high levels of performance is required to:

1. **Thoroughly understand how to precisely select the right person for each job.** *Many people are selected for wrong reasons.* The key criteria to be used in selection are a person's emotional dynamics, personal values, and an understanding of their talents as opposed to their skills.

2. **Keep in place a creative relentless *training* and *development* program to expand the skills of everyone in the group, including the leader, on a permanent basis.** *Exceptional Leaders keep their people in a state of "Creative Discomfort" by acting as a role model for change and innovation. They model the behavior they want to create in others.*

    The single biggest concern of people at work today, even more vital than whether they will lose their job, is the deterioration of working conditions. Proper training keeps people motivated, makes them feel relevant and expands their skills to match ever increasing job performance requirements in this time of downsizing, restructuring and rapidly accelerating competition.

3. **Execute a master system of *organization* that directs and assists the efforts of the leader and all of his people.** Many organizations have improved their performance dramatically by competent organization. It requires clarity, good listening, priority setting and relentless evaluation. Vital Tasks Management* has enabled individuals and groups both large and small to execute and maintain an organizational plan that has increased productivity dramatically.

4. **Develop the *communication* skill necessary to develop and maintain high levels of rapport with each individual in the group, as well as with the group itself.** *A major reason why good people leave an organization is because of lack of rapport with the boss.* Exceptional Leaders are genuinely interested in establishing rapport with the people in their group and continuously work at it. Public speaking is a skill needed by leaders, yet a recent national poll found that only 6% of CEO's believe they are competent public speakers. The most important skill is how to listen *to* people not *against* them.

5. **_Keep_ people at their jobs interested in high levels of performance on a long term basis.** If people are *precisely selected* and *continuously* trained properly they will remain in their jobs longer. A bigger challenge is to *keep* them learning, growing and innovating.

***

SIX KEY DIMENSIONS OF LEADERSHIP

"THE GOAL OF MOST LEADERS IS TO CAUSE PEOPLE TO FEEL REVERENCE FOR THE LEADER...THE GOAL OF THE EXCEPTIONAL LEADER IS TO CAUSE PEOPLE TO FEEL REVERENCE FOR THEMSELVES"

Consistently Exceptional Leaders operate from vision, inspire, create commitment, act as role models, and evoke the highest level of commitment and competence possible from subordinates.

There are six key dimensions of Leadership that Consistently Exceptional Leaders seem to share. As Leaders you do not need to rank very high in all six but you must evaluate yourself and back yourself up with the appropriate people in your organization.

UNDERSTANDING THE KEY DIMENSIONS OF LEADERSHIP

VISION

The force of a leader's convictions and scope of vision are more vital than a position of power or authority. It is strategically important for a leader to "put the cart before the horse" when preparing to define objectives. The end result must be identified before starting the process. Many people only extrapolate from the past rather than identifying what they would like to have happen and then plan back to the present. Now, more than ever, it is critically important to have a sound vision before stepping into the future. The vision must be based on input incorporating all the latest changes, but must not be restricted by

that input. Every industry and profession today is the process
of continuous change, and the leaders who succeed will be the
ones who understand and capitalize on change rather than fight
it.

> The microwave oven has permanently changed food
> packaging and preparation, and yet many food companies
> lost a significant opportunity because of their lack of vision
> on how to capitalize on the major innovation (the company
> that developed the microwave also had no vision about how
> to use it, and instead of dominating a massive worldwide
> market, it played almost no role in the microwave's future).
>
> The fax machine is currently changing the way letters
> and documents are transported, and yet many communica-
> tion companies who could have readily capitalized on this
> innovation have not done so.

"Vision" is a competence that has been identified and associated with leadership for centuries. All of the great leaders of
the world from early Roman Emperors to Napoleon and from
Karl Marx to modern leaders of the capitalist world have shared
this competence. They had a burning vision in their minds of
how they wanted things to be and didn't allow the day-to-day,
more mundane issues to cloud their view. They knew what they
wanted and they were obsessed with achieving it.

Several current authors have elaborated on the concept of
vision. Joe Batten, author of *Tough Minded Leadership* empha-
sizes the need for vision, not only in top leaders but down
through the management ranks. A production manager, in order
to be consistently effective, must have a clear "picture" of how
the organization should look and function. He/she must be able
not only to "see" it now, but also "see" it in the future. The
effective marketing executive must not only deal with current
trends, but also must be able to "see," identify, and capitalize
on future changes that are happening at ever greater rates of
speed.

The future is not pre-determined: it doesn't already exist. The future only exists in our minds and what we are able to conceive in regards to how we what it to be. It has been said, "the best way to manage the future is to create it." The exceptional leader keeps one eye on the present and one eye on the future. This leader recognizes the importance of "writing the last chapter first" and knows that a clear understanding of where you are headed is necessary in order to carve out the shortest path to that destination.

"Vision" is an intuitive process. Everyone has intuition but many of us are not really in touch with our intuition nor do we understand how to use it. Much has been written on the right and left hemispheres of the brain. Current research indicates that intuition tends to be more of a right brained process, whereas the left brain is more concerned with facts, figures, details and logic. The integration of both left and right brain are necessary for competent thinking, but vision comes from being able to better understand and capitalize on our intuitive right brain process.

Action is a critical factor in achieving success but ACTION WITHOUT VISION IS RANDOM ACTIVITY. We almost always get what we expect, not what we want. Vision, more than any other single factor, helps to raise expectations of both individuals and groups.

When JFK announced in 1961 that the U.S. would send a person to the moon and return him safely, the media ridiculed him and his own advisors admonished him because he had no answers on how it would be done. The response of JFK was, "Now that the vision is in place, the answers will be found." The rest is history. Even if you are in a small organization and do not have major responsibilities, vision will aid and assist you in reaching your goals.

VISION MUST ALWAYS BE TIMELY AND CURRENT

EXECUTION

VISION WITHOUT ACTION IS SIMPLY HALLUCINA-TION. A major reason for continuous procrastination on the part of most people is some combination of the fear of failure and/or the fear of success. Both are powerful deterrents to taking intelligent risks and executing plans. A great motto might be **"risk taking is not only a requirement it is also a privilege."** As soon as a CONSISTENTLY EXCEPTIONAL LEADER defines the ultimate vision for the organization, he/she then creates a master battle plan that breaks down all components into measurable tasks and clearly communicates them to the individuals who must complete the work.

> If you were building a major resort complex, it would be wise to plan the opening date first and then plan back from that so that you know what you have to achieve as you make your way toward the final goal. For example, if you were building a complex over a five year period, and started from the opening date and planned backwards to the present, you'd know exactly what date all the carpeting had to be through the loom at the factory in order to reach your project in time. (Late arrival of carpeting is one of the most frequent reasons for major real estate complexes not opening on time.) If it's not through the loom on time, you could then very early take the steps to correct the problem. Operating back from your vision rather than waiting to get the bad news will help prevent delays in opening on schedule.

There is nothing more common than unsuccessful talented people. Many people can "vision" the future, but lack the competence necessary to capitalize on what they see. Without execution, all else can be a waste of time.

Numerous ideas have gone by the wayside because of a leader's inability to translate visions into action. The CONSIS-

TENTLY EXCEPTIONAL LEADER recognizes that having the vision is only the start and that real success entails establishing the structure and having the irrevocable commitment necessary to do whatever it takes to make the vision a reality. Execution involves turning the creative into practical and doing the planning and organizing to create a vehicle for action. There are numerous examples of mediocre ideas, products, and services that have been quite successful because of a well disciplined, executed strategy. There are also many examples of superb ideas, products and services that did not become successful because of the lack of disciplined execution.

Another major factor that is encompassed within the category of execution is judgement. The core of judgement lies in one's willingness to spend time intelligently analyzing the data and then making thoughtful decisions. Many CONSISTENTLY EXCEPTIONAL LEADERS are convinced it is better to make a mediocre decision than no decision at all. Indecisiveness is a major factor in the downfall of many leaders.

Exceptional leaders use superior judgement to minimize situations that may require superior skills. Superior judgement is developed by watching what works and eliminating what doesn't. In decision making, it's all right to change a decision as soon as you have evidence it won't work. Your vision and your approach to execution cannot remain static but rather must continuously evolve as conditions warrant.

VISION WITHOUT ACTION IS HALLUCINATION
ACTION WITHOUT VISION IS RANDOM ACTIVITY

INSPIRATION

All inspirational leaders "suffer" from their own self-made magnificent obsession and they are so resolute, so clear in their values and their value that they obsess others to join them.

When Donald Petersen of Ford Motor Company had the vision to turn the company around in the early 1980's, his vision was to identify, "What are the characteristics that would enable us to build the most superb car customers would value?" He inspired people in every department to make their contributions so that both union and nonunion workers, finance, design, marketing, engineering, R & D, all people in the various departments were inspired to do what they could to help determine the ultimate car that might be built. Ford Motor Company's turnaround is one of the greatest successes of the late twentieth century in American industry. An exceptional vision was inspired and executed with drive and empathy and propelled Ford to the top of their industry.

Rarely is it the case when one individual single handedly can translate ideas into reality. What is required is pulling other people into the "vision" and rallying them behind it. The leader must be able to present ideas in a convincing manner and generate enthusiasm in others. Helping people buy into a "picture" that may seem a bit far out or beyond their imagination requires skill and the ability to effectively communicate complex ideas in simple terms.

Integrity and charisma emanate from people who are fully focused on what they want to achieve, clear about their value (what they are capable of) and their values (what they believe in) and who demonstrate it to others. They may not always be the most articulate public speakers, and they may or may not always appear overtly enthusiastic but they have a deep passion to turn their vision into reality, which in turn generates excitement in others. Charisma is often thought of as something people are born with, but many people who would be considered introverts have acquired the skills to inspire and motivate large groups of people. Charisma emanates from a person who is obsessed to achieve and obsessed to include other people in a vision. Integrity allows a leader to be aligned with internal values and consistent in inspiring others.

DRIVE

For CONSISTENTLY EXCEPTIONAL LEADERS the primary drive is not to personally achieve or affiliate but to organize and execute plans that cause others to achieve and affiliate. Drive is the internal force that propels people to meet their goals. CONSISTENTLY EXCEPTIONAL LEADERS see themselves as responsible for organizing, communicating with and causing others to get the job done. These leaders may or may not stand out in a crowd, but they are always willing to stand apart from any individual or crowd that will hold them back from what they are after. They are able to eliminate the "trivial pursuits" and not get mired in the "obscurely relevant." They are very clear about what they want to achieve and invest no time in people, events or activities that do not contribute to the goals they have established. They are willing to be disliked and misunderstood when it is required to get the job done. CONSISTENTLY EXCEPTIONAL LEADERS never pursue being popular although it may ensue. They are totally committed and while they are tough they can be fair as well.

Drive can originate from lack of self-esteem. Many people are driven to be successful because of underlying feelings of inadequacy. While this is a major contributing factor in many success stories, it is much more exciting and enjoyable to be driven to succeed from a passion to participate in something that's important and valuable to you and other people. It is easier to accomplish something if it is valuable to all the people involved.

It's important to recognize that CONSISTENTLY EXCEPTIONAL LEADERS are not just workaholics, but rather work from a sense of joy and passion. The workaholic is driven by a high state of anxiety to accomplish something or perhaps to avoid a sense of failure, whereas a person of high self-esteem is participating in a passion for achievement. The joy is both in the process itself and in the anticipated result.

History has emphasized the importance of drive in the success of a leader. There is story upon story of individuals who had ideas which were turned down but who kept coming back until they succeeded. The "driven" leader does not allow obstacles to deter desire or actions but merely looks at them as additional challenges to overcome. The drive we refer to here is not just a desire for monetary success but an internal desire for achievement; a restless striving to fulfill one's potential and to accomplish what one is capable of accomplishing. The "driven" leader doesn't give up but continues to change strategies until he/she finds the way to attain the goals and objectives set for the organization. CONSISTENTLY EXCEPTIONAL LEADERS dramatically increase the drive of people through the example they set.

OWNERSHIP

The CONSISTENTLY EXCEPTIONAL LEADER approaches work, and life in general, with what can be identified as 100/0 responsibility and tends to teach others the same attitude. The leader accepts that he or she is always, without exception, the one responsible, totally responsible for the output of the group. If every person in the organization accepts the same 100/0 responsibility, full acceptance of responsibility for the output of the group, they will all eagerly participate in the ownership and execution of the goals and objectives of the organization.

Most people can be evaluated as either an External or Internal. Externals are people who believe that the direction much of their life takes is really out of their control. They feel they are a victim of fate and circumstance, a product of destiny. Their career success depends more on what company they happen to land in and what type of boss they happen to draw. They are quick to pass blame. That blame may be directed toward parents who weren't intelligent and didn't provide enough direction or foster enough independence or may be directed towards inanimate objects; "If I'd just gone to the right school." Most commonly however, it's directed toward co-workers. An "external" production manager might blame failures in the production department on poor research and development. Sales people who are "external" may blame manufacturing for poor quality products and, in turn, slacking sales. Externals are quick to blame and pass accountability off, thereby creating for themselves a sense of blamelessness, deceiving themselves and believing that they are not responsible for their life or performance.

CONSISTENTLY EXCEPTIONAL LEADERS, on the other hand, are "internals." They look internally for solutions to problems and know if an answer is to be found they will find it. They know they will determine whether or not a project is to be a success or a failure. It is this "total ownership," this remarkable sense of personal accountability that enables them to cut through many of the obstacles that others might see as impossible to surmount. They know there is a way to solve the problems, and even though they might not currently see the way, they persist until they find it. The pathway to CONSISTENTLY EXCEPTIONAL LEADERSHIP requires a 100/0 responsibility. The leaders' value is determined by faith in themselves and others to develop the confidence and competence necessary to achieve the vision. Any obstacle or setback is seen only as an inconvenience and does not deter the CONSISTENTLY EXCEPTIONAL LEADER from moving forward.

EMPATHY

Before a leader can move people to higher levels of performance it is necessary to understand where they now are in terms of competence and the impact of their values and interest on that competence. A leader must be able to size up the group as a whole and each person in it individually. Leaders who lack the skill, or interest to do this tend to create a communication cycle of resistance, resentment, and revenge. On the other hand, when you deal with others in an empathetic way, you build a communication cycle based on clarity, cooperation, and commitment. Exceptional leaders are the ones who develop high levels of rapport with people. They are willing to be disliked and misunderstood if necessary to get the job done. The CONSISTENTLY EXCEPTIONAL LEADER not only has the ability to communicate the vision clearly, but is successful in understanding people and building and maintaining a team effort through integrity and true compassion. People respond to empathetic leadership by becoming more competitive and cooperative simultaneously. That is, they strive to do their jobs better while, at the same time, reaching out to help others in the group.

Building a team requires accurately assessing the skills and talents of others and then knowing how to effectively utilize those talents along side the talents of other team members. John Kotter, in *The Leadership Factor*, emphasized the importance of selecting the right players and then creating an intelligent action plan to develop them. The CONSISTENTLY EXCEPTIONAL LEADER fosters action, independence, and interdependence in subordinates, not dependence. People are developed to stand on their own and rise, in a competent, decisive way, to the day-to-day challenge facing them. They are taught to be autonomous so they achieve for their own reasons.

To know your customer and to know your co-workers today is more challenging than ever, because the world is undergoing a personal values revolution and reintegration much more significant than most people realize. This will require leaders to understand and deal effectively with very diverse groups of people.

*LEADERSHIP IS NOT DEFINED BY HOW YOU BEGIN
BUT RATHER BY HOW YOU FINISH*

*IT IS AN EXCITING AND REWARDING ADVENTURE TO
BE AN EXCEPTIONAL LEADER. THE ISSUE IS NOT
CAN YOU BE ONE...IT IS WILL YOU...WILL YOU?*

---

* Much of the material used in this chapter was excerpted from *Consistently Exceptional Leadership Profile* by Hegarty & Nelson (Institute For Exceptional Performance)
** *The Nine American Life Styles* by Arnold Mitchell

"...Human beings are creatures of habit. We like to do it the same today as we did it yesterday so we can do it the same tomorrow. Because the rut gets comfortable. But, the only difference between a rut and a grave is it's length, depth and how long you're in it!"
A.H.

Art Holst
2001 W. Willow Knolls Rd.,
Suite 206
Peoria, IL 61614
800/926-9339
309/691-9339

Art Holst began his early career as a salesman after completing his formal education in marketing. As a successful professional salesperson, Art opened his own company.

For fifteen years, Art was an official for the National Football League. As a line judge in the NFL, he officiated four championship games and both Super Bowl VI and Super Bowl XII. He is now a League observer, responsible for rating the other officials each week.

Art has received much recognition and many honors for his professional speaking. He has spoken to a wide variety of audiences. In addition to being a recipient of the C.P.A.E., Art has received an award from the National Speakers Association for his use of humor in his presentations.

In addition to his extensive speaking engagements, Art finds time to be actively involved with community affairs and has authored the book, *Sunday Zebras*.

My first year as a line judge in the National Football League was 1964. I was working a game in Cleveland and the fullback was Jim Brown. Six foot two inches and ran the 100 in about 9.5—tough to bring down. Cleveland was playing Dallas. Brown came through the line with a ball and a big middle line-backer for Dallas went to tackle him. When he did he grabbed Brown's face mask. That isn't fair and that's why we're out there. I threw the flag, stopped the clock and told the referee, "I've got number 55 on the defense pulling the face mask! Personal foul! 15 yards!" About that time, this guy jumped up; all 6'6", 260 pounds of him. He looked down at me and said, "What?" I said, "Get back in there and play football before I bite your head off." They're all real good guys. He very politely said, "If you do, sir, you'll have more brains in your stomach than you have in your head."

So I'm not an expert on any intellectual subject. But when you're out there you're a little like Raquel Welch's elbows, everybody knows they're there, but nobody cares. My last game in the National Football League was in 1979 at the championship game in Pittsburgh in the freezing rain between Pittsburgh and Houston. Four weeks before that I had been in Pittsburgh for a late afternoon, nationally televised game between Pittsburgh and the Dallas Cowboys. The score was 21-17 in favor of Pittsburgh. In the third quarter Roger Staubach, who was quarterbacking Dallas, got hit in the head and went down.

Now, a time-out for an injured player prior to the last two minutes of the half does not count against the three that they guard so carefully; it's a referee's time-out. But, unbeknownst to us the scoreboard operator in Pittsburgh, a guy I'll never meet who probably thinks his job doesn't account for anything, put one time-out on the board for Dallas when there were really none. We don't look at the scoreboard. We can't even see the scoreboard!

That's one of the criteria for working in this league, if you can see the scoreboard you don't qualify! At least that's what a lot of fans think! So we've got one time-out up on the board for

Dallas when there were really none. Staubach comes back in and two or three plays later he's hit again and down he goes. We signal a time-out, still no charged time-outs against Dallas. The scoreboard operator puts "two" up on the scoreboard. Now, with a minute and 50 seconds left to go in the football game, Dallas' ball, on the Pittsburgh 25, Dallas is still down by four points. Staubach calls his first time-out. We mark one on the card and the scoreboard operator puts "three" up on the scoreboard.

Now we have a developing problem in communications. When things are not what they are, they are what? What people think they are! And 55,000 people in Pittsburgh thought there were three time-outs against Dallas. Now with a minute and 20 seconds to go in the ball game, it's Dallas' ball on the Pittsburgh 20. Staubach called his second time-out, Dallas. We marked it down and the scorekeeper put a "four" up on the scoreboard! Immediately Chuck Noll, the coach for the Pittsburgh Steelers, began to holler at me, "Pardon me," or words to that effect. I couldn't figure out what this great coach was so upset about. I didn't even turn around.

With 20 seconds left in the ball game, Dallas' ball on the Pittsburgh 18, fourth down, Staubach called his third and last time-out for Dallas. The scorekeeper puts a "five" up on the scoreboard and Chuck Noll hollered out, "Turn around and talk to me you dirty Framisamis Peppaloomer!" I turned around and said, "What do you want to talk about coach?" He said, "I want to talk about how many time-outs you're giving Dallas!" Now he was standing in that six-foot wide white stripe he was not supposed to be in. I said, "We're giving them three, and you get back out of the white." The coach said, "You've already given them five!" As he said this he took two steps across the white onto the field right in front of my nose. I said, "No, coach. We've given them three, but I'm going to give you 15 yards!"

I threw the flag in the air. Oh, was that popular in Pittsburgh! They were going to name me Steel Queen. Bob Fredric, the referee, had just told Landry that he'd used his last time-out. He turned around just in time to see my yellow rag hit the ground. Fifty-five thousand people started to boo me. He ran all the way across the field and said, "Artie, what have you done?" I said, "I have just stuck the Pittsburgh coach half the distance of the goal for unsportsmanlike conduct. Put that ball on the nine yard line and give Dallas a first down!" He said, "Yes, and I have to walk it off!" I said, "That's the penalty of leadership—walk."

Then, the greatest thing that ever happened to me in my 15 year career of professional football happened. On the next play, Staubach went back to pass, hit Drew Pearson in the end zone right on the numbers and he dropped it. If he hadn't dropped that ball I wouldn't be writing this today. I'd be pushing up marble in some cemetery!

Why do I tell you this story? I tell you that story because four weeks later the National Football League sent me back to Pittsburgh to work that championship game between Pittsburgh and Houston. Nobody decides who's going to work where in this league, except the league office in New York. The officials are rated every week. They're rated by a man in the press box. That's what I do now. They're rated off the films in the New York office as well as by both coaches. Four ratings a week are made and at the end of the year they add up those ratings. If you're rated number one in your position, you work the Super Bowl and wear one of these rings that I proudly wear. If you're rated second or third you work the championship game and so on down the line. You see, we in the National Football League, like you in business and in life, pay off on excellence!

We pay off on excellence. So, back I went to Pittsburgh to work that championship game. I had worked the Super Bowl the year before when Dallas beat Denver and I guess I was rated second or third my last year. So, I went back to Pittsburgh to work that championship game and I haven't been there since I stuck Mr. Noll with the only unsportsmanlike conduct call he's ever had.

I got out to the ball park about eleven o'clock in the morning, two hours before the game. I was dressed in a business suit.

I walked into his office and he got up from behind his desk, walked around, stuck his hand out, smiled and said, "Art, congratulations." I said, "Thanks, coach. The same to you." He asked, "What do you want?" I said, "I gotta get my legs taped." He said, "Come on, I'll take you over to the training room."

We walked over and talked about our families, the weather, the game and never once did that great coach mention that call. He was able to take it, wrap it up in a box, put it on a shelf, learn from it, and forget about it. We walked into the training room. Some big lineman was laying there getting taped, two or three other big guys were waiting and Noll said to the trainer, "Get this guy off of here. Art's got some pre-game duties to do." I got up and they started to tape my legs. Coach Noll started to leave, I said, "Coach, wait a minute. You're the head coach of a championship team in a championship game and you take the time, the attention to detail to see that I get my legs taped. I just want you to know that I appreciate it." He said, "Art, I want to tell you something, When you're the head man, you got to be a detail man, an organizer, a communicator and a delegator. By the way, Mean Joe Greene wants to talk with you about that call in the Dallas game!"

He walked out and standing right beside me was Big Jack Lambert, the big red bearded linebacker for the Pittsburgh Steelers. He's retired now. I don't know Lambert off the field, he may be a great guy. But, I'm going to tell you one thing, when Lambert put on pads he had no friends. I've had a lot of fouls against Lambert. So he took one look at me and said, "It's you again!" I said, "That's right, Lambert." He said, "Every time we get a big football game we get you and your yellow flag against the Pittsburgh Steelers." I said, "Lambert, just knock it off, I'll see you out on the field in two hours. Get out of here!" You've got to take command—foolish as it was. He turned around, walked about two steps, turned around again, and with a big grin on his face said, "I'll say one thing, Art, you're the second best football official in the National Football League." I felt good. I said, "Who's first?" He said, "The other 98 are tied!"

What I'm saying to you is if you're in second place don't get too smug. Everybody else might be tied for first and that makes you last. There's only one place to finish in this world and that's on top! That's what the challenge of professionalism is all about—to be on the top—all of the time.

Vince Lombardi, who coached the Green Bay Packers, said, "It takes *talent* to become a champion, but it takes *character* to stay there." I want to paraphrase a quote from the immortal Vince Lombardi. He said, "Being a pro is not a sometime thing. It's an all the time thing. You're not a pro once in a while, you don't do things right once in a while, you do them right all of the time. Being a pro, a winner, is a habit. Every time a football player goes out on the field to ply his trade he's got to play from the ground up; he's got to play from the soles of his feet right up to his head. Every inch of him has to play." It's the same in business and in life. *If you're a pro, you're a pro 24 hours a day.*

So what's this challenge all about? Number one, *respond to change*. People say to me, "I can't change." I tell them, "Baloney!" The Lord gave us the power of choice. When we get up in the morning, we can be happy or sad, productive or unproductive; it's up to us. I was talking the other day to a group of young bankers. I asked one of the young men, "How long have you worked for the bank?" He said, "Ever since the day they threatened to fire me." He didn't know how fast he could change!

Football is a game of change. If the quarterback calls a "49 sweep" in the huddle (that's the fullback wide right), comes up to the line of scrimmage and sees the defense set against the play, does he buck his head against a stone wall? Of course not. He uses his individual God-given power of choice and calls an audible. He reaches down, tickles the center (that's what they do, that's why they all want to be centers, it feels so good) and says, "48 blue, tax reform." I don't know what that means, I don't think Congress does either. He says, "48 blue, tax reform." When 10 other offensive guys hear those words, "tax reform," they say, "Hey, that's not a 49 sweep anymore that's a square out pass." The split end out there says, "I don't block the linebacker anymore, I go down four steps, turn to the left, the quarterback throws me the ball, I catch it and go for a first down or a touchdown." Why? Because he had *the ability to change.*

A few years ago we had a game in San Diego between San Diego and the former Oakland Raiders. John Madden was the coach of the Oakland Raiders. I was the line judge. I was on the line of scrimmage opposite the head linesman. The head linesman and the line judge keep track of the line of scrimmage. That's our territory. Tony Veteri was the head linesman, positioned in front of the Oakland bench, while I was opposite him in front of the San Diego bench.

Now the question is, how many men do you have to have on a line of scrimmage in football? Answer? Seven. If you have six it's a foul. Why is that important? If you catch a team like Dallas, they'll take the slot man over on the right, bring him up from the line of scrimmage and drop the wide receiver off. Or, they'll take the tight end over on the left, drop him back and bring the flanker up. Sometimes somebody forgets a signal and you end up with six guys on a line then you throw the flag. The question further arises, "can you legally have eight men on the line?" Answer, "yes." "Nine?" "Sure." "Ten?" "Absolutely." You only have to have one man in the backfield. But, what do you see play after play, game after game? You see seven men on the line of scrimmage.

Human beings are creatures of habit. We like to do it the same today as we did it yesterday so we can do it the same tomorrow. Because the rut gets comfortable. But, the only difference between a rut and a grave is it's length, depth and how long you're in it!!

Tony and I had worked more than 200 football games in the NFL, but we had never seen an eight man line. In the second quarter the game was scoreless. It was Oakland's ball, third and eight on their own 40. Out of the huddle they come. Stabler brings them up to the line and I count eight guys on the line. Not trusting myself when I get over five, I counted them again. I still got eight. They set for a second, which the offense must do on every play. After they had set for a second, 88 out there on the end of the line turned and went in motion, diagonally into his own backfield.

My wheels are turning. I know that one man for the offense may be in motion, parallel to or away from his line of scrimmage. But can he come from the line of scrimmage? I don't think so. That's not good enough! Oakland snapped the ball, I threw the flag—not too high!! Ben Tompkins, our back judge, yelled out, "Great call, Art." My confidence level went up. Stabler completed a pass for 25 yards and a first down. I came running in, "No, bring it back, illegal motion." Veteri came running over from the other side, "What is it?" I said, "Illegal motion." He said, "Art, he's going backwards." I said, "Tony, he came from the end of the line." He said, "So." And he shrugged.

A shrug is not a signal in football. It's also not a good sales tool. He said, "So." I said, "So, it's illegal. Go tell him!" I don't want to talk to Madden. I'm smarter than that! I'm over on the San Diego side and they think it's a great call! They don't know why, they just think it's great! Well, we bring the ball back. Oakland has to punt. Five minutes later Oakland has the ball again.

Now they've got third and 13, back on their own 30. Out of the huddle they came—up to the line of scrimmage—and I counted eight men on the line with 88 out on the end again. They set for a second. Now 88 knows he fouled last time because he heard his number over the PA system. But he doesn't know why. So, this time he's taking no chances. He turns around, goes in motion straight backwards, he's going out of the ball park! They snapped the ball, I threw the flag a mile in the air. Stabler completed a 50 yard bomb to Cliff Branch—a leaping catch down on the other 25 yard line! I came running in, "No, bring it back—illegal motion." Veteri comes running over from the other side and says, "Art, what in the world are you doing?" I said, "Tony, it's illegal for that guy to go in motion from the end of that line." He said, "Well, you go tell him!!"

Now Madden's over there going, "Boidflklk, jsuiofg;l." He's selling Lite Beer. I went over and he said, "Art, what in the world are you doing to us?" I said, "John, it's illegal for that player to go in motion from the end of that line." And this is what he said, "Art, this is our secret play! It's the only thing we've practiced all week!" I said, "You run that thing 10 times today, I'm gonna throw 10 flags." We went into the half. What was the first thing I did before I did anything else? I grabbed the rule book. You can't carry that thing on the field, it's bulky and it looks funny to say, "Just a second and I'll look that up."

Here's what it says football fans. "After all 11 players for the offense come to a full one second stop, one offensive player may be in motion, parallel to, or away from his line of scrimmage and he must be a backfield player." A backfield player is defined as one who has set for at least one second at least one yard off the ball." Great call! Naturally! But somewhere, sometime, somebody had said to me, "In order to legally be in motion you have to set for one second in that backfield," and that tiny piece of information had stuck with me and prepared me for change.

What will you take from this chapter to help you *respond to change*, to anticipate change in this time of the most rapidly changing society the world has ever known? Microtechnology, computers, robotics, all kinds of changes are happening all around us. Can you respond to it—and even more importantly —can you be a cause of change!

As you talk about excellence and professionalism, do you know where *discipline* fits into a successful operation? I'm the symbol of discipline on the football field. Somebody has to make the rules, somebody else has to enforce them. There's also the *discipline of self-discipline*—the toughest discipline in the world—doing what I'm supposed to do, when I'm supposed to do it, where I'm supposed to do it as the line judge in the National Football League.

Let me tell you a true story. I worked the only professional football game played at the University of Michigan Stadium in Ann Arbor. It was a pre-season game between the Detroit Lions and the Baltimore Colts. It was 93 degrees with 80 percent relative humidity. The temperature of the artificial turf was 148 degrees. Standing on the sideline before the game was the referee. He was about to referee his first game in the National Football League. He had been a line judge and been moved to referee. He turned to me and said, "Art, are you scared?" I said, "No, I'm up, I'm not scared." He said, "I've got a little knot in my stomach." I said, "Let me ask you a question. There are 93,000 people here, over 90 ball players, all the coaching staffs and the other five officials in this game. Can you name one that is more competent to referee this game than you?" He said, "No." I said, "You're it baby—and I've got one more question to ask you. Do you think that you can referee one play right in the National Football League?" He said, "Of course." I said, *"I've got a secret to tell you. That's the only way they'll ever play this game, one play at a time."*

You see it's one customer at a time, one chance to reflect the advertising of a company. One chance at a time and that's where it's at. If you work one play right and then the next one and then the next one, pretty soon it's a game. Then it's a season. Then it's the Super Bowl. Don't you see? And, you do that in a teamwork environment—football is very much a team sport, there's a sense of loyalty. I'd like to talk about the *discipline of loyalty.*

The most severe criticism a football official ever receives is when seven football officials, alone on a Saturday night, look at 10 rolls of slow motion film of the game they worked the previous week, along with a critique sheet from New York. That's when you hear the most severe criticism. I remember a game in Chicago between the Bears and Green Bay Packers. I called a clip against the Bears that took the winning touchdown away from them. Clipping is blocking from the rear; blocking from the side is not a clip and this was one of those "iffy" ones. The next week, we're in New Orleans on a Saturday night at the Marriott Hotel. There were six officials at that time watching five rolls of slow motion film with a play by play critique sheet of the game and they had a big red question mark by that play with a comment, "check this, we don't think it's a clip!" We ran it four times, four of the guys on the crew were "iffy" on the thing, but the head linesman with whom I differed occasionally, jumped up and said, "Art, that wasn't a clip." I said, "Tony, it was a clip." I was on a short fuse and we ended up toe to toe and had to be pulled apart!

I've seen that many times. But, I'm going to tell you something. I've never seen one football official in the National Football League show up another one on the field. If that Back Judge calls some little bump pass interference, and the guy couldn't have caught the ball with a butterfly net, you don't see the field judge come running over and saying, "My God, Burt, how could you have called that?" He'll come over, nod, smile, and say, "Burt—dummy, pick up your flag. He couldn't have caught it with a net!" That's loyalty—working together.

What I'm saying is that a part of excellence, a part of professionalism, is *loyalty* to your organization. Loyalty to the people who work around you, for you, under you or over you. Loyalty to your products, to your people and to your friends.

Number three. Are you a *problem solver*? We've got a lot of problem finders today. We've got a Ralph Nader syndrome: find something wrong with everything. Sure you've got problems. Interest rates yo-yoing all over the place, economy soft, economy hard, gold prices down, gold prices up, too much competition, all of that. You could have it worse. Football is a problem solving game.

I went to Knox College in Galesburg, Illinois. Most of you never heard of it. I enrolled during 1939. We were famous athletically for one thing—28 consecutive football losses. We led the world in football losses. When I was a freshman we broke that record, and I'm proud of it. I'm going to tell you how it was. We were getting beat as usual in the fourth quarter. We were down, 21-20 with four minutes to go in the ball game when somebody in the stands threw a firecracker. The other team ran off the field! Eight plays later we scored—on a field goal that was partially blocked.

The problem in football is, how are you going to get the ball from one end of the field to the other and in your possession? And if you're on defense, how are you going to stop the other team? How are you going to relate features to benefits to sell better than the other salesperson? How are you going to make a product better? How are you going to deliver it better? How are you going to help solve the problems of your customers? How are you going to not only respond to them, but anticipate them?

That's why God gave us this ability to think creatively—to solve our own problems and others. That's how we earn our keep for the space that we take up on earth.

There are problems everywhere. They even have problems in church. I used to go to a little Lutheran Church in Minnesota. It had one of those high choir lofts. It also had one of those women who sing soprano—who could hit high C. They always reach for it like it's an orange on a tree! They go right up after it! One Sunday, she went after that high C and head first she went right out of the choir loft. On the way down, her foot caught in the chandelier and there she was, swinging in front of the congregation with her dress hanging down over her head. The minister was equal to the occasion. He leapt to his feet and said, "The first man that looks at her will be struck blind." Ollie and Sven, two old Swedes, were sitting right down on the front row. Ollie poked Sven and said, "You know Sven, I think I'm gonna risk one eye."

Risk in business, risk in our free way of life. But I'll tell you one fundamental truth. *You can't have reward in one hand without being willing to take risks in the other.* And sometimes after you leave the collective society of a team, you reach the point as a pro where you have to make an individual decision.

Let me tell you a story. I worked the game in Chicago when Gale Sayers ran for six touchdowns against the San Francisco 49er's in 1965. It was the greatest performance I've ever seen by a running back. Everybody will remember that—it's in the Hall of Fame. My only claim to fame, my only appearance in the Hall of Fame was on film following Sayers down the field at quite a distance.

But something else happened in that game that only four of us will remember. In the late third quarter San Francisco had the ball and ran a running play around the strong side, around the tight end. They made about eight yards. I was the back judge. I blew the whistle, put my foot down and as I lifted my head and blew the whistle the tight end from San Francisco blocked Mike Reilly, number 65, the outside linebacker for the Chicago Bears—265 pounds, 26 years old, fully armored with helmet and shoulder pads. He knocked Reilly off balance and as I looked up I saw this football player coming at me. I'm five feet nine—170 pounds—knit shirt—lovable. I had a problem and I couldn't call the office!

I had to make a decision and I made it. I reached up instinctively and grabbed Reilly by the face mask, I know why that's a foul because the face mask is a great lever. As I went over backwards, I yanked his head down into the mud beside me and he never touched me. He leapt to his feet ran to the 49er that blocked him and said, "You so-and-so, you didn't have to grab me by the face mask." I jumped in between them and said, "Come on Mike, cut it out, He didn't mean it." Bill Schleibaum was the line judge, he came running up and said, "Art, if I knew which way to walk I'd throw the flag on you." *Problem solving; thinking fast.*

Number four. Do you know where *teamwork* fits into a professional operation? *Teamwork means respect for the dignity of difference in people.* In a time when there are those in our society who would like to put us all into one big bucket, shake us up and have us come out as average Americans—divide the wealth, divide the brains, divide everything; I am proud to be part of a sport that does not pay off on averages. We don't play average teams in the Super Bowl. We play the best and we don't care who knows it.

But a part of that team work, a part of responsibility in that team work, is to look for your weakest link. I can't tell you how many times I've looked at films where 10 guys on offense did it right but one guy blew a signal on what should have been a touchdown and went for a three yard loss. A part of the responsibility of a pro is to look not only for your own weaknesses but for those around you in order to strengthen them or get rid of them.

Next question. Do you understand *successful failure*? Football is a game of failure. A guy learns to get knocked down and then get right back up. If he keeps getting up maybe he blocks the punt and wins the ball game. It takes a mature attitude toward failure. I have a deal with the preachers, priests and rabbis, I don't monkey with the first 10 commandments. I leave that to the pros. But I handle the 11th.

The 11th commandment is, *"Thou shalt not take thyself too seriously."* Can you laugh at yourself? It's the second greatest God-given gift. The first one is the ability to think creatively—to be able to respond to change or cause change, to solve problems. Then secondly—we are the only animal with the ability to laugh. I guess He figured that when reason failed if we couldn't laugh, we'd all end up in a looney bin. And in this game of the most violent competition you'll ever see, right under that veneer of competition lies a sense of humor.

I spoke at the Cleveland Browns' Touchdown Banquet a few years ago and Art Modell, the owner of the Cleveland Browns, a great sportsman and owner, was sitting next to me and told me this story. "Brian Sipe was our quarterback a couple of years ago and he was having a terrible year. He was leading the league in interceptions—we were 2 and 12. We were playing Dallas and we were down 40 to 10 with two games left to go in the season—the season is gone. Sipe has thrown five interceptions in the game, then he threw his sixth. As he's coming off the field, with his helmet in his hand and his head down, Sam Rutigliano (the Browns' Coach)—reached out and grabbed him by the arm and said, 'Brian, why are you throwing the ball to them?' And Sipe said, 'Because they're the only ones open!'" The ability to laugh at yourself.

You see, you don't close every sale. Creative sales people lose sales. But they know the two "L's" of failure; to learn and laugh at failure. When we're creative—when we try to meet tomorrow in a creative way, sometimes it doesn't work. And sometimes even when we respond to something today it doesn't work. To be nice I sent flowers to a friend of mine who opened a new branch of his business. I went out to call on him and look for my flowers. There's a big wreath with a sash on it that said 'Rest In Peace.' I went out of there and called the florist. I said, "What in the devil are you doing? I send the guy flowers to wish him well in business, and you send him a wreath that says Rest In Peace!" He says, "I'm not worried about you, Art. Somewhere in this town there's a man being buried, and he's got a big bouquet of roses with a sash on it that says 'Good Luck in Your New Location.'"

Part of the challenge of excellence is to wear a smile on your face. One of the greatest sales tools ever given to man or woman is hung between the point of the nose and the tip of the chin. It's called a big friendly smile that says, "I like you, I want to help you. I am quality. I represent quality in my service, quality in my product and most of all, I care about you." Because people don't care how much you know until they know how much you care.

Last question. Do you believe in the *principle of added value*? When iron ore comes out of the Mesabi range in Minnesota it's a red dust. It'll get your shoes dirty, it's worthless.

We add value to it, spend money on it and ship it across the Great Lakes to Pittsburgh. We put it through a blast furnace, add more value, spend more money. It comes out as various kinds of steel. We ship it back to Detroit and pickle it, tool it, paint it, put rubber on it, wrap glass around it and advertise it. That worthless red dust shows up in your driveway and mine as a ten, fifteen, twenty thousand dollar automobile. Value has been added all along the way.

But—there is a similar principle of added value in human beings. The professional not only knows about added value in products, the professional knows about adding value to human beings. He gives those people around him the opportunity to live up to their potential.

So, I want to close with a poem, an old one that's a favorite of mine.

'Twas battered and scarred and the auctioneer
Thought it barely worth his while
To spend much time with the old violin,
But he held it up with a smile:
"What am I bidden, good folks," he cried,
"Who'll start the bidding for me?"
"A dollar? A dollar"; then, "Two! Only two?
Two dollars, who'll make it three?
Three dollars, once; three dollars, twice;
Going for three—" But no,
From the room, far back, a gray-haired man
Came forward and picked up the bow;
Then, wiping the dust from the old violin,
And tightening the loose strings,
He played a melody pure and sweet
As a caroling angel sings.

The music ceased, and the auctioneer,
With a voice that was quiet and low,
Said: "What am I bid for the old violin?"

And he held it up with the bow.
"A thousand dollars, and who'll make it two?
Two thousand! And who'll make it three?
Three thousand, once, three thousand, twice,
And going, and gone," said he.
The people cheered, but some of them cried,
"We do not quite understand.
What changed its worth?" Swift came the reply:
"The touch of a master's hand."

And many a man with life out of tune,
And battered and scarred with sin,
Is auctioned cheap to the thoughtless crowd,
Much like the old violin.
A "mess of pottage," a glass of wine;
A game—and he travels on.
He is "going" once, and "going" twice,
He's "going" and almost "gone."
But the Master comes, and the foolish crowd
Never can quite understand
The worth of a soul and the change that's wrought
By the touch of the Master's hand.

Myra Brooks Welch

You are good—I know you are—but the question is not "how good are you?" The question is, "how good can you be?" Because you see, no matter how good you are, you are never, never so good that you can't be better. That's the challenge of a professional. That's what excellence is all about. Go for it, good luck and God bless you.

"Excellence is dealing with that which you find ... It is the ability then to do what's to your intelligent self-interest, to be patient and tolerant with people who have skills and interests that are different from yours, and finally to treat different people differently."
A.J.H.

MANAGEMENT TECHNIQUES THAT WORK OR LEADERSHIP IN ACTION!

Allan J. Hurst
45-175 Panorama Drive, Suite D
Palm Desert, CA 92260
800/367-4873
619/779-1300

Allan J. Hurst, C.M.C., is President of Quorum, Ltd., a practice limited to professional presentations and specialized consulting. He has a broad background in sales, management and marketing. He has experience in the grain industry, the printing industry, and in the financial arena.

In 1965, he entered management consulting and has handled assignments in sales, marketing, organization and motivation for industrial and commercial organizations. Recently he has given particular attention to specialized counsel and education programs for professional selling and sales motivation. He was responsible for the design, development and presentation of specialized education programs for sales, management and professional groups.

Allan is best known and recognized nationally for his motivational training programs for sales, management, professional and financial groups. He meets with over 100 groups annually throughout North America and Canada and has received numerous awards from sales, marketing, trade and professional groups for his dynamic presentations.

The challenge of excellence makes certain demands on you as a human being and as a business person. It places that responsibility squarely on your shoulders to do that which may not be popular at the time, but is finally seen as very sound. Whenever I think of excellence and leadership, which I consider to be synonymous, I think of the challenge that we face each day to do something more right than wrong.

How much better do you have to be in the decisions that you make each day? I don't think a whole lot. Here are two dimensions of excellence. One is the "Hair's Breadth of Difference," the difference between good and really great. I find that it's really just a very small difference, the "tremendous trifles" that make a big difference in results.

The second is "part-way success." You're good already or you wouldn't be reading this book. You're "part-way" toward the success you are capable of being. So how much better do you have to be? I think just a hair's breadth.

Let me give you an example. A big game hunter who had an absolute skill. He was the epitome of big game hunters. He had an absolutely crackerjack eye to bag an animal at a hundred yards. He could put the cross hairs on an animal and drop him, making it appear as though the animal just fainted. While his trophy room was full of game taken at a hundred yards or more, he had never acquired a big Bengal tiger.

He and a hunting party of three went on a safari in India to hunt the Bengal tiger. First morning out of the compound, they drove 20-30 miles, until the jungle was so dense that they could drive no farther. One of the men hopped out with his machete and started chopping through the underbrush. As they proceeded into the jungle, they came to a clearing not a hundred yards across, where his skill was absolute, but just 30 yards across. As they got to the center of the clearing, they heard the pre-kill growl of a big Bengal over in the brush. All the men except the big game hunter ran back through the cut in the jungle and got to the jeep just as fast as they could. Seizing the opportunity, as leaders do, the big game hunter whirled around to bag the Bengal, but the tiger wasn't a hundred yards away, he was only 10 and closing fast and the big game hunter only got the gun to his hip. He shot too quickly and missed. He hit the ground on the butt of the gun and got just as close to the ground as he possibly could. Luckily, the overzealous tiger jumped over his head and landed in the brambles, giving the hunter just enough time to make it back to the jeep...very shaken! Here was the best big game hunter in the business and he almost lost his license permanently!

They all went back to the compound and had what we call a "3-martini lunch!" After his nap, the big game hunter became concerned with his technical skill with a firearm, went outside the compound and put some cans on top of a log and moved back 10 yards. Because he had a natural skill with the firearm, it wasn't long until he could hit every can at 10 yards. He sat them back up and moved back 20, then 40, then 60, then 80 yards...and practiced shooting at each distance. By mid-afternoon he was not only the best long shot at 100 years or more, he was also the best short shot. As he started back to the compound, what do you think he saw? *It was the tiger practicing short jumps!*

There are four keys to leadership in management techniques. The first key of excellence and leadership is that *you do what is to your own intelligent self-interest.*

Abraham Lincoln demonstrated in all his writings an ability to think through the chaff right through to the grain. One example, was when Abraham Lincoln was in the afternoon courtroom representing the defense. Earlier that same day he had been in the same courtroom in front of the same judge on the same point of law and had been awarded the verdict as the plaintiff attorney.

The judge stopped the proceeding, called Lincoln to the bench and said, "Mr. Lincoln, I'm confused. How can you be so sure this afternoon, when this morning you were equally sure on the other side of the same issue?"

Mr. Lincoln said, *"Your honor, this morning I may have been wrong but this afternoon I know I'm right."*

That's the ability to think through to what is to your intelligent self-interest. Ask yourself this question—not, what action is justified—but what action will lead me to do what is to my intelligent self-interest? The ability to see through the emotional fabric is the first key of excellence and leadership.

The second key is that *we must make decisions.* Research has proven that there are two kinds of people in the world. There are people who say, "If I do not try, there is no way I can fail."...and failure is to be avoided at all cost. But there is another group who say, "If I don't try there is no way I can succeed. If I try, I have a chance for both success or failure."

It is like the fellow in Pecos, Texas, who walked into the smithy shop where the smithy had his foot on the forge pedal, pumping the coals white hot. The smithy picked up a horseshoe with the tines, shook the coals off and tossed it to the sod buster. He reached up involuntarily and grabbed it then quickly tossed it down. The Smithy said, without missing a pump, "Hot, ain't it?" The sod buster said, "No, just don't take me long to look at a horseshoe." Decision making, the ability to make a decision, to jump in and say, "I'm going to give it a go," is a key part of excellence and leadership.

The third key is *we must learn to be patient and tolerant.* How patient must you be? I think Job had something to say about that in the Bible. "The patience you must exhibit is that which transcends all frustrations."

You must be patient in managing the skills of others. *Never set standards for others that you set for yourself!* Set a standard for others that's based on their capabilities, not yours. You see, if you are to teach and transfer, to give to others the benefit of what you've learned, you must give it willingly, completely, without any expectation of a refund of value. If you do this, you will be a true coach and sponsor.

It's like the parents, Cy and Mary, at the dinner table. Mary says to Cy, "How come you tell Junior 20 times how to hold his fork?" Cy says, "Because 19 isn't enough."

In my junior year in high school, my father was not patient. It's Saturday evening, I'm broke, and I have a date with a young lady. All I have left to get is $5.00 and the family car from my father. When I asked him for it, you can imagine how many times I heard, "Boy it's sure different than when I courted your Mom! A buck and a half took us both to the movie, we each had a cheese sandwich and a Coke on the way to the movie...and another thing, we used to walk 8 1/2 miles from the farm into Yukon, Oklahoma and back! What do you think of that?" I had nothing to do with coming along in 1935. I'm there late for a date needing two things, five bucks and wheels! Finally, in my senior year, my father got very brilliant. Maybe he always had it and I just discovered it! He finally set standards for me in terms I could understand. Can Allan operate the car safely? Does he have a driver's license? Can Allan spend within the $5 budget or is he going to charge the coke and cheese sandwiches on our Visa card? Can he show enough personal discipline to come home at a reasonable hour and not wake his mother and me or the neighbors next door or the whole community at 3 a.m. driving across their lawns singing "When the Saints Come Marching In?" Can Allan show the discipline and tolerance to sometimes say "No?"

And key number four, as managers, *you must recognize the differences in people.* I maintain that there are three general types of employees. The first group I will speak about is a group I call *the Hermans and the Marthas.*

You recognize them by what they do, not what they look like. You soon learn to know what they look like by what they do. Here are their traits.

Number one, and clearly the most beneficial is that they set a standard of performance higher than you, their boss, would set for them. You find you seldom have to talk to them about performance. They are already one step ahead of you. They may even come early to get a jump on the day, and they do it without making you, the supervisor, feel guilty. The standard they work toward is understood and clear...and if they don't understand, they are secure enough to ask.

You ever notice how the Hermans and the Marthas are very gentle with those people who let them down? They say, "It was my responsibility to check with you." They also are loyal to a fault. They don't want to transfer or move. They won't even think about a job offer from another firm. They tend to respect authority. If you call a meeting at 3 a.m. on Sunday morning, they'll ask which door they should come in. That's the Hermans and the Marthas.

Another thing I notice about them is that they never talk long at coffee breaks and certainly not about gossip. The minute you start to talk about somebody who isn't there they demonstrate excellence by getting up and leaving quietly. They don't want to be in an arena in which they may contribute to something that does not build.

The Hermans and the Marthas are delights to manage. You seldom have to tell them anything; you only present the situation and they see things they could do. The "Herman and Martha" group generally represent 15-20% of your employees.

The other end of the scale is a group I call the *Red Ants* or *"Ormiga Kojas."* A Red Ant has the goal each day to have as much work to do at the end of eight hours of pay as there was in the beginning. The "Red Ant Emeritus" wants to have *more* work to do at the end of eight hours of pay as there was at the beginning. In order to accomplish this they will even undo their own work or the work of others.

They are a bane on corporate life. They're there to tear up and confuse and serve selfish interest. They're against everything you're for. They argue on every issue; they'll take the devil's advocate position, not to add clarity to thinking but to add confusion and take away focus. They tend to not relate at all to the Hermans and the Marthas. They stay away from and are not comfortable with the Hermans and the Marthas. They create havoc in the company. The Red Ants are 10 to 15% of the work force.

When Red Ants get into the computer world, you've really got problems as they carry their own "virus." A computer can be a very excellent decision-making tool, but it is also a device that can do more wrong in less time than anything ever designed. In fact, it can bring you bad information quick enough for you to take action on it. You're able, therefore, to go in the wrong direction with a greater degree of certainty! However, it also can do more correctly and bring you good data on which to base a sound decision.

The third group is called the *Vanillas*. They're the ones who go into a Baskin-Robbins store that has 92 flavors and ask for vanilla. If they want to stretch quantum leaps into the future they say, "I'll have french vanilla with marshmallow topping." In paint terms, they're a tint base...waiting for the color of the day.

I'm certain that when I go home at the end of this week on the front of our fridge door, held by a magnet, will be something for me to accomplish on the home front. We've got so many magnets on the front of our fridge door that a steel can of pineapple juice from Dole came from the back of that fridge to the front door the other day. On our fridge door is a BEMAR List—Backlog Of Essential Maintenance and Repair. Some know it as the "Honey Do" list.

There will be some things there that I have to paint on Saturday. I'll go down to the paint store and talk with the paint expert. We'll pick a color and the expert will put the pigment into the can of tint base.

That is the employee that occupies 60-80% of your time. They are the ones who have no color. They believe that if they show up and are clean, scrubbed, and dressed, they have done 100% of their job description. They come to work on Wednesday morning and say to you, "I'm here, now what do you want me to do?" You say, "Well, why don't you just continue doing what you did yesterday?" They say, "Well, could you go over that again? You see I bowl on Tuesday evenings and yesterday I had to concentrate on that! I've sort of put it out of my mind."

You would evaluate them as people who do not have the same interest in your business that you do. I suggest that you look at them in a different way, as raw material. Raw material is something that needs to be upgraded, to be given a bigger horizon. Someone you stretch so that they have a chance to grow with the opportunity that you create. Vanillas are something to behold because they tend to put out of their mind those things that they've done well in the past. They are afraid to make a mistake...but they represent the most potential for the company's future. You see, the Hermans and Marthas are already giving 100-110% and the Red Ants work hard at "not working" or ruining the work environment for all. Therefore, from a "pay-off standpoint," the Vanillas contain the greatest growth potential.

Now, in managing these three types of behavior, we get to the decision process, we need to do something that's to our intelligent self-interest in being a manager. *The Hermans and the Marthas, for example, you manage as peers.* You share with them: Here's what we're after, what do you think you might contribute? When do you think it can be done? They tend to respond with a realistic answers.

How do you deal with the Vanillas? *The Vanillas need constant positive direction every day.* They are 60-80% of the people in the work force and need the reinforcement of what is to be done next so you must put the *emphasis on the expectation.* The Vanillas tend to respond to that.

They tend to only then say "no" when they don't understand. They'll want you to go over it a little bit more in detail. Whenever a Vanilla asks for detail, take a book and open it up and write down exactly the things that you want him to do. Then give him that sheet of paper. Give them the next step to do.

The Red Ant is quite different. We must call upon a skill that is not with us at birth. To handle a Red Ant, there are three things you do. *Number one, load them up with work!* Give them *more* work than many people could do in a reasonable amount of time and expect them to do it.

Number two, isolate them. Give them work in the proverbial Siberia so that nothing they do is dependent on anyone else or no one is waiting for the output of their labor. Isolate them, get them totally out of the system and let them do their work. Remember, if you must keep them around, it is better to pay them to not work than to have an expectation of productive work and not have them do it.

Number three, fire with honor. This is a true art of management. There are three phrases that I would like you to commit to memory. Firing with honor must possess all three of these ideas expressed in these phrases. First, "I choose no longer to purchase the skills you bring to work." Second, "Inside you is a heck of a worker that on occasion has come out, but has not come out often enough nor stayed out long enough for me to continue to add you to our overhead." Third, "I share a part of the responsibility—not enough to keep you, but enough to tell you that I did not manage you correctly."

You see, firing with honor says that you must leave them with some true shreds of self-esteem and self-regard. Because inside every Red Ant is a Herman or a Martha who is just uncomfortable at coming out. You are the hard-nosed manager, but you will be the respected manager because they will come back and thank you for demanding more from them than anyone they had ever worked for.

The ability to deal with these three different types says that you must not have just one skill. *Excellence is dealing with that which you find.* It's dealing with that hot horseshoe. It is the ability then to do what's to your intelligent self-interest, to be patient and tolerant with people who have skills and interests that are different from yours, and finally to treat different people differently.

The last demand of excellence is that we must *dismiss personal grudges promptly*. We cannot let that anger, that vanity, hang on and be a sea anchor to our forward progress. We must look to the future and dismiss personal grudges immediately. They keep you from moving forward and clearing the air.

Tact is that invaluable ingredient. Tact, by definition, is the personal ingredient that smooths out the rough spots of life. It's the lubricant that eases the friction that's going to occur any time you put people together. I know someone's gone too far when I hear them say, "Well, I can tell you one thing or, to be perfectly frank..." Well, don't be. Be tactful. The ability to apply your knowledge and skill to the next moment is the first step in that quantum movement to the great expectation that you have of yourself.

I close with a story. It's the story of a wise old man. He was so wise that he astounded everyone in the community with the correctness of his counsel. In the town was a "Red Ant" who belittled and talked down to the old man constantly. He thought the old man was an fool and publicly said so.

He thought, "I must devise a scheme to disgrace the old man in front of his peers. I'll catch a bird from the field and gather everyone into the town square. I'll hold the bird in my hand and I will ask the old man, 'If you are wise, tell me is the bird alive or is it dead?' No matter how he answers I will cause the other to happen and therefore make him be thought of as a fool."

So the day came, and the legions came and sat upon the hillside. The old man was there in his robes. The young man placed a bird in his hands and said to him, "Old man, be ye so wise, tell me is this bird alive or is it dead?" The old man said, with the wisdom of his ages, "It is in your hands my son. It is in your hands." And so it is with your pursuit, your challenge and your acceptance of excellence. It is in your hands!

"I would like to suggest to you that today and in the future, you think about the fact that we create and control our own level of motivation. We can be productive to the extent that we arm ourselves with the skills and that we motivate ourselves to put forth the effort."

D.H.

PRODUCTIVITY THROUGH MOTIVATION

13

Don Hutson
P.O. Box 172181
Memphis, TN 38187-2181
800/647-9166

Don Hutson's record-setting careers in sales, management and speaking have brought him many honors. He successfully worked his way through college, graduating at the age of twenty-one with a major in Sales. He was the number one salesman in a national organization at twenty-three and was President of his own training firm at twenty-four.

Don mastered the skills of public speaking and results-oriented training early, and at age 30 was elected by his peers to the Presidency of the National Speakers Association. He has now given over 4,000 presentations. Corporations throughout the free world now invest more than one million dollars a year for exposure to his spoken, written, and recorded programs. Additionally, Don has addressed over two hundred Positive Thinking Rallies with audiences of up to 18,000 people. He has been awarded the C.P.A.E. from the National Speakers Association.

He has been featured in over thirty training films for American Industry and addressed over half of the Fortune 500 Companies. In addition to making some one hundred fifty speaking appearances per year, Don is Founder and Chairman of U.S. Learning, Inc.

Have you noticed that you never see a mule running in the Kentucky Derby? A stringent task is for a stringent achiever, isn't it? What about our level of personal motivation? What about our level of personal productivity? We need to stop and think about the way we have our minds set on what we want to accomplish in our given period of time on God's green earth. Sometimes we need to erase our barriers and see things in a more positive and vibrant perspective. What is your mind set? Whatever we think we're going to accomplish is what we're usually going to accomplish! Isn't that true? It's all a matter of perspective.

On his death bed J. Paul Getty was asked in an interview, "Mr. Getty, you're one of the richest men in the world, but I must ask you at this moment just one question. If you had your life to live over, what would you do differently?" And J. Paul Getty, without even a pause, said, "Oh, that's an easy question to answer. I'd go for bigger deals." A billionaire at his death. It's a matter of our mind set. So often the perspective that we have is going to influence our level of motivation.

I happen to believe there's a correlation between the commitment we have to a cause and the achievement we experience; between the motivation that we have and the energy that we enjoy. The greater and the deeper our level of commitment, the more energy we will have. It will become internalized for us. It becomes a natural thing. Have you ever heard about the kamikaze pilot who flew 188 missions? He was busy but he wasn't committed. There are a lot of people who are *busy* but are *not committed.* They are simply not getting the job done.

In working with organizations throughout the world, I've had the privilege of working with some very high achievers who are very motivated people. I've also looked at some people who, with all their potential, weren't doing very well. Have you seen people like that? Maybe you even know some in your very own organizations or families. You know who I'm talking about—the kind of person who projects an image that he just likes to arrive without having made the trip. Our great challenge is to understand motivation and productivity. The late Bob Bale was a master of understanding motivation, especially as applied to the concepts of achievement. I was with Bob at our National Speakers Association convention in Phoenix many years ago. We were chatting and I said, "Bob, I've got to get your opinion on something I'm curious about. You're recognized as one of the true experts on human motivation. Bob, I want your definition of motivation. Would you share it with me?" He said, "Don, I'd be glad to give you my definition of motivation and you're welcome to use it until you find a better one." That was many years ago and I've never heard one half as good, much less any better. Bob Bale said motivation is *"an idea, emotion, or need from within a person which incites or compels that person to act or not to act."* The key words in that definition are the words *"from within."* All motivation is self-motivation. I'm convinced of that.

Years ago I was doing a management seminar for about 500 people in Atlanta in the ballroom of the Downtown Marriott. I was down front in the room preparing my visuals and getting ready for my presentation. I thought I was in the room by myself and all of a sudden, out of the corner of my eye, I spied a man walking down the center aisle toward me. This individual had on tennis shorts, tennis shirt, sweatbands around the forehead and wrists and a tennis racket in his hand. I couldn't imagine where he was going! He walked up to me and said, "You must be Don Hutson who's going to conduct the seminar for our company this morning." I said that was correct. He said, "Don, I don't know if you're aware of it or not, but at your management seminar this morning, attendance is not mandatory; it is voluntary and I'm not coming." I told him that was fine. But he was here for some reason and I was curious what it was. I asked if there was something I could do for him. He said, "As a matter of fact there is, Don. You see, I'm running my branch and I'm doing a pretty good job. We're well ahead of last year and we're pleased and proud of our performance and our productivity so far, but we're not number one. I only wanted to ask you a simple question so I thought I'd come down a few minutes, get your answer and still make my tennis date at nine o'clock." I told him I would help him if I could. "All I want to know is," he said, "how can I motivate my people?" I said, "Oh, is that all you want to know?" He said, "Yeah, that's all." I said, "You can't. Have you got any other questions?" That response intrigued him to the extent that he elected to stay for the seminar.

I learned from Bob Bale and my personal experience in sales training that you don't directly motivate another person. Motivation is accomplished through an indirect process. If we're going to motivate a customer to buy, if we're going to motivate our spouse to respond the way we want them to, if we're going to motivate anybody—we don't do it directly, we do it indirectly.

How do we achieve that? We achieve that *by creating an environment and atmosphere around them that will serve as an inducement for them to motivate themselves.* If you get but this one idea, it can be an idea that can change your life and the lives of those people you touch. That one idea is that all motivation is *self-motivation.* Don't wait on somebody else to motivate you. We're all on the periphery of greatness just for living in a free society. We've got to motivate ourselves to get out there and make it happen.

My favorite story on motivation is the one of the boy who was on his way to baseball practice. He had a coach who wouldn't tolerate tardiness. Unfortunately, the little boy was running late. He could see the baseball field some 300 yards away but he couldn't go straight to it because between where he stood and the baseball field was a large fenced pasture that contained the meanest, largest bull in the country. The little boy realized he couldn't go through the pasture; he'd have to go all the way around it. He would undoubtedly be late and be severely disciplined as a result. He was about to start walking around when, all of a sudden, he looked down and saw that the old bull appeared to be sleeping. He thought if he could get over the fence and all the way across to the other side before the old bull woke up, he'd be on time for the game. He knew if he went for it he'd have to make it all the way across the pasture because there was nothing in the center of that pasture for protection but one very large tree with its lowest branch 18 feet off the ground. He was a gambler so he thought he'd go for it.

He sneaked over the fence and took off. Have you ever tried to run and tiptoe simultaneously? Well, that's what he was doing, running and tiptoeing. He looked back to check his progress and the bull was not only awake but it was chasing him! Needless to say, he was motivated. He looked back and saw that bull charging after him like a locomotive. As the boy sprinted across the pasture, he could feel the ground rattling. He looked back again and there was that bull not 15 feet behind him and gaining. Perspiration was pouring off the young boy's forehead. He looked back one more time and there was that bull now not 18 inches behind him. He could feel that bull's breath right on the back of his neck. He knew he was never going to make it to the other side of that pasture but he was almost to the tree with the 18 foot limb. He looked at that 18 foot limb with apprehension but with motivation. He could still feel that bull right behind him. Even though that limb was way up there he knew he had to go for it. With all the motivation he could muster, the kid leaped up in the air for that 18 foot limb. He missed it...but he caught it coming down! It just goes to show that with the proper intensity of motivation we can reach incredible heights!

If we're going to motivate ourselves sufficiently, we need to clarify the objective of motivation. The obvious object of motivation is for us *to achieve something productive* as a result of that inner energy and desire we feel. You see, to feel motivation and not to take action is the greatest waste in the whole world. I've always heard that the average human being functions on 16 to 18% of his or her brain power. That tells me that we have incredibly powerful, untapped resources of talent and abilities within the minds and bodies of each of us. What is our job? To tie into that source of power and motivation and not to look for it externally. Let's do it to ourselves. We are at the helm of our own ship.

People often say things like, "Don, you know motivation's fine and good, but motivation doesn't last." I have an interesting rebuttal to that. A bath doesn't last either, but it's a good idea to take one once in a while. It doesn't have to last forever. When we experience that process, that feeling of motivation, it can energize us and make us get out there and make positive things happen.

What is a deterrent to motivation and productivity? Often times one deterrent is yourself. You say, "Well, it's easy for all those other people to be motivated and fired up, but for me it's tough. For me things don't always go just right." Things don't go just right for anybody. You see, our success is not determined by how much crow we can eloquently dish out. Our success is determined by how much crow we're willing to eat! How much rejection can you experience?

Perhaps you experience a situation where you interact with somebody and it doesn't go very well. When you have that experience, when you get rejected by another individual, what does it do to you? Does it ruin the rest of the day, the week, a month or two or your career maybe? There are some people who handle rejection very poorly. *But the real pro in any given situation is the individual who experiences rejection and negative events and in the next split second is as good as he's ever been.* The proverbial water off the duck's back concept...they don't let it get to them; they function from a posture of confidence. They believe in their own ability to get out there and make something happen with an internalized force of motivation. There are some people who handle that motivational process so poorly that they just can't motivate themselves after rejection. Why do you think movies are open in the daytime? They're for people who have just been rejected.

So we're going to motivate ourselves. What is the desired result?

The desired result of that internalized motivation is greater achievement and higher productivity. Have you ever had a slump in production at whatever you do? Everybody has slumps. Everybody's individual productivity is cyclical. We all have peaks and valleys. I hope you never have another slump, but if you ever do, I'm going to give you a couple of tools and techniques that will help you get out of that slump. Can you use that? Maybe you will never have to experience a long term slump for the rest of your life. Maybe you will make more money than you've ever made before.

There's an equation I'd like to share with you called the productivity equation. The equation is *Skill x Effort = Productivity.* Let me give you some examples on how this equation can work. The first example is the person who is relatively unproductive. His production in the last six months would probably best be described by management as underwhelming. He possesses only one half a unit of skill. In other words, when it comes to the required knowledge to be good at what he's doing, he has a deficiency. The interesting thing is that when this deficiency is there, most people know it. Now what does this do to the human psyche? How is he going to feel about himself? A lack of confidence is the most easily detectable negative attribute a person can have. We've got to function from that posture of confidence. This person doesn't muster confidence because he doesn't have the skills. But skills are always available. We can always learn skills. The people who don't have skills are so often the people who have not been diligent enough in their quest for skills. It's out there for us if we want it badly enough.

Predictably, this type of person will possess only one half a degree or unit of effort as well. This is an example of the relatively unproductive person. They're not fired up, so they experience a reluctance to work diligently. So in this equation we're obviously equaling one fourth a unit of productivity. This person is ineffectual. It's tough to get fired up when one doesn't know what he's talking about!

Now let's go to the average producer. We're going to say that the average producer is the person who possesses one unit of skill, puts forth one unit of effort and creates one unit of productivity. He is average across the board. So that's acceptable.

But let's also talk about the superstars. The true achievers. *The true achievers are the people who are most diligently seeking ideas and skill building concepts and techniques.* Extraordinarily high producers, those achievers, the people who have a very high skill factor, usually are a result of the fact that they have a hunger for knowledge and excitement for information that is unparalleled when compared to their peers. These people might well possess two units of skill.

What happens to these people psychologically? They feel good about where they are. *They're confident and they're competent.* So often these are the people who are out there eager to put forth the effort. In fact, they are often putting forth two units of effort, working twice as hard as the average person is working and creating four units of productivity, which is, ironically, 16 times greater than our first example. So this is a geometric and very positive force.

But, these numbers don't have to be the same horizontally. For example, there might be a person in your business, industry or profession who is a true encyclopedia of knowledge. You name it, he knows it. He possesses three units of skill. He's got his proverbial act together in terms of true knowledge and ability to perform. But he's got a problem. You see, in addition to being so skillful, he's also well-intentioned. He goes home at night and sets the alarm for five o'clock the next morning. He jumps out of bed when the alarm goes off, clapping his hands and almost bumping his head on the ceiling because he's so fired up. He possesses vigor and motivation. He goes charging into the bathroom to shower and shave. He catches a glimpse of himself in the mirror and is captivated. He gets in front of the mirror and says, "You are absolutely fantastic; you are a high producer; you can really make it happen." He's got all these great intentions. The only problem is he then goes back to bed.

You see, if the effort factor is zero, we all know that zero times anything is Zero. Isn't that a sad state of events? Here's an individual who has everything in the world going for him or her except a willingness to put forth the effort. It's like dragging a ball and chain around for his entire life. We've got to put forth effort; we've got to implement and utilize our skills. *When the effort is not there, the productivity is not going to be there either. It's a self-imposed limitation.* In training we refer to these people as those who are inflicted with the mineral disease which denotes an excess of lead in certain parts of the anatomy.

The viability of this equation is predicated upon the subject maintaining a reasonably positive mental attitude. A skilled, hard-working individual with a negative attitude is simply not going to be as productive as a skilled, hard-working individual with a positive, wholesome attitude.

The establishment of that productive attitude is vital to our success and must be achieved principally by an energized vision of higher personal accomplishment. This is the reason goal-setting is so important. The more seriously a person takes the goal-setting process, the more likely he is to achieve great things. Experts say that as soon as we reduce our goals and visions to writing that we have not only tripled our commitment to the goals, but also simultaneously tripled the probability of achieving them. Keep in mind, too, that the goal-setting process works best when giving yourself deadlines. The key to higher productivity is getting a given amount done in shorter periods of time. I'm convinced that is an issue of deadlines and discipline!

I vow each year to keep my goals written and my visions for achievement defined. One way I am energized into this process is through a hunger for new and reinforcing positive input which I know I can gain from books and tapes. I love to read—especially old books by great people—in fact, I collect these books and have taken great pride in the assembly of a personal library of these materials through the years.

One such positive force for me has been Orison Swett Marden. Here's a sample of his great work and how the right ideas can keep us focused positively instead of negatively...

> The habit of dwelling on difficulties and magnifying them weakens the character and paralyzes the initiative in such a way as to hinder one from ever daring to undertake great things. One who sees the obstacles more clearly than anything else is not the one to attempt or do any great thing. The one who does things is the one who sees the end and defies the obstacles. If the Alps had looked so formidable to Napoleon as they did to his advisors and other people, he would never have crossed them in midwinter. It is the one who persists in seeing his ideal, who ignores obstacles, absolutely refuses to see failure; who clings to his confidence in victory, success, that wins out.

That inspiring copy from *The Miracle of Right Thought* was published in 1910. Marden wrote almost 30 books—some still findable in old bookstores—all of great inspiration and insight. Legendary author and good friend, Og Mandino, credits Marden with much positive influence on his life.

Yes, if your attitudes and expectations are uncompromised, you will simply have a more productive life.

May I put everything in capsule form for you? May I suggest to you that in terms of motivation we've got to accept the fact that *it's an emotion, idea, or need from within us which incites us to act or not to act.* We've got to take *responsibility* and accept the fact that we are accountable for our own productivity. It's not an external thing; we can't rely on others; it's up to us individually. That's one of the greatest benefits of living in a free society, but it's also your responsibility as a member of that free society, is it not?

I would like to suggest to you that today and in the future, you think about the fact that we create and control our own level of motivation. *We can be productive to the extent that we arm ourselves with the skills and that we motivate ourselves to put forth the effort.* If you do that, and do that consistently, I promise you a highly productive future.

"...If, however, you are seeking excellence, the key will not be found in pointing the finger, but rather will be found in identifying with people, helping others see where they are wrong with a genuine concern and a good laugh, and how they can do something about it."
C.J.

EXCELLENCE THROUGH HUMOR OR LAUGHTER, THINKING AND BOOKS

Charlie "T" Jones
206 West Allen Street
Mechanicsburg, PA 17055
800/233-2665
717/691-0400

For more than a quarter of a century, over 5000 audiences throughout the world have laughed while listening to Charlie Jones share his ideas about life's most challenging situations in business and at home. Known by his *"Tremendous"* nickname and humor, he is a recipient of the C.P.A.E. from the National Speakers Association.

Charles Jones entered the insurance business at age 22, with M.O.N.Y. At age 23 he was awarded his agency's most valuable associate award. Ten years later, Charles received his company's management award for recruiting and business management. At age 37 his organization exceeded $100,000,000 in force, at which time he founded Life Management Services, Inc. to share his experiences through seminars and consulting services.

He is the author of *Life is Tremendous*, which has over 1,000,000 copies in print.

Did you know that it is possible for someone to look you right in the eye and not hear a word you've said? I made this discovery early in life thanks to the help of my six kids. I knew they were not listening because their eyelids would be struggling to stay up. Often I would catch myself wondering why they weren't listening before I finally figured out that it was my fault. My six kids did not hear a word I said because I had developed a bad habit of talking to people's ears. And although everybody knows that you hear with your ears and you see with your eyes, because I had only been talking to their ears, their eyes decided they had nothing to do so they would close for a while.

If you are going to enjoy excellence in your life, you had better *be learning the technique of not only speaking to the ear, but of going to the heart as well.* One of the greatest lessons you will ever learn in communication is to go first to the ear with the point, and then to the heart with an illustration. Watching their eyes light up, you know that you have helped them see with their hearts what they have just heard with their ears.

Their lips curl up as they smile in recognition, as you rush back to the ear again. This is the art of successful communication–learning to speak to the heart–learning to paint pictures with words that speak to a person's feelings, needs and fears.

To some, however, it is a lost art. Some teachers don't teach because they spend years drilling rules and regulations into the students' ears and not the heart. Some clergymen never touch the hearts of their congregation because they are content to pour proverbs and psalms into the ears. Some managers and sales people never reach their potential because they set dreams and goals that program the ears, but not the heart. And, yet, there is a simple key in speaking to the heart that many people forget to use–*humor.*

When you come to the realization that most people love to laugh, humor can be used to pave the way to excellence in life's communication with others. Hearing a truth with the ear can be boring, but discovering a truth with the heart produces the warmth of recognition complete with a smile and sometimes even laughter.

As I stated before, once you make a point, you then need a good illustration to help others mentally see what you have said. Have you ever heard the old saying, "You brought it on yourself?" If you're married, you probably hear it every day.

Suppose we work together and you come to me with a problem, perhaps asking for advice. And suppose I say to you, "What do you expect? You brought it on yourself." How would you react?

The problem is that for the most part you already know you brought it on yourself, and I already know you know you brought it on yourself. Why should we dwell on it if you already know it. It's too discouraging to keep repeating it, and we need to move forward.

Sometimes you'll hear someone take pride in the fact that they "tell them to their faces like it is." But if you are going to confront someone with something directly to their face, you are involving their feelings. If you don't go to their heart, identify with them, and help them see the problem in a humorous perspective, barriers will go up and the words will be too hard to bear. Some confrontation is necessary to wake people up, but if they are already awake, confrontation won't speak to a person's heart.

Like most people, I like to see where I'm wrong or where I'm about to make a mistake. The constructive criticism of others can save us valuable dollars and time. But to like to actually hear that you're wrong is entirely another matter. If I approached you, pointed the finger and said, "you brought it on yourself," there would be a confrontation. We have seen this happen hundreds of times in our day-to-day lives. When confronted, your mind automatically says, "I don't have to take this! I'm going to ignore you." You would become defensive and maybe even want to fight. If, however, you are seeking excellence, the key will not be found in pointing the finger, but rather will be found *in identifying with people, helping others see where they are wrong with a genuine concern and a good laugh, and how they can do something about it.* Here is what I mean:

Every day Pat and Mike sit down to eat their lunch. While

Mike would quietly begin to eat his sandwiches, every day Pat would go through the same thing. Opening his lunch, he would take a quick glance, and begin to scream, "Oh No! Not this again! PEANUT BUTTER SANDWICHES! I hate peanut butter sandwiches!" Each day Pat was louder and wilder. Finally Mike couldn't take it any more. He yelled over Pat's ranting, "If you hate peanut butter sandwiches so much, why don't you tell your wife you don't like peanut butter sandwiches?" Grabbing Mike by the throat, Pat yelled back, "YOU LEAVE MY WIFE OUT OF THIS! I PACK MY OWN LUNCH!" You may think this is humorous now, but wait until next week when you find yourself eating some of your peanut butter sandwiches again!

Speak to the Heart. Don't rely on confrontation. If they brought it on themselves, identify with them. Part of communication is helping people see things in perspective and laugh at themselves. Problems take time to work through. Humor lightens the burden and gives us the patience to keep at it another day.

Now I would like to share with you one of the greatest ideas you will ever hear. How would you like an idea that will guarantee you'll never hear another poor speaker; you'll never hear another colorless lecture; you'll never hear another dry sermon as long as you live? Wouldn't you like an idea like that? Like so many others, all my life I had sat through countless meetings, conferences, workshops and all I've heard is LISTEN, LISTEN, LISTEN. Unfortunately, the more I listened, the more confused I became. Finally, I caught on. I wasn't only supposed to listen–I was supposed to THINK.

There is a world of difference *between listening and thinking, between memorizing and realizing*, between listening to a great speaker by memorizing and improving yourself simply to project a better image, and actually thinking with speakers as you realize and become better without actually trying to be better. If you are going to be learning to *speak to the heart*, you have to be learning to listen to the heart. And listening to the heart involves *thinking*.

So what should we be trying to do? A few simple changes in our daily routine can improve the quality of our lives. From now on when you read a book, hear a speaker, or listen to a sermon, always take your pen. As you get used to reading or listening with a pen in your hand, you begin to cultivate the habit of making notes of things you actually think in addition to what you thought you heard. We must learn to listen, but only enough to get our own minds in motion and start our individual thought processes. When we are gathering the facts, we need to listen. When we are trying to identify with someone, we need to listen. But when we are listening to someone preach on what works for them and what they believe we need to do, we need to *think.*

I try to practice this in church. When the pastor starts to preach, I take out my pen and start making notes of things I think. This excites the pastor because he thinks I'm writing out his sermon. Sometimes I think he should throw away his sermon and use my notes. As I leave church I get a smile or laugh when I say, "Pastor, you were really good this morning. You interrupted my train of thought a half dozen times." Whether it is selling, preaching, or teaching, interrupting their train of thought to help them see what they know will always bring a smile or a laugh.

The highest compliment you can pay me is to say, "Charlie, I don't remember a word you said, but I can't remember a time when I so enjoyed laughing at my problems and seeing more clearly things I already knew." Sometimes I'll hear, "You talk so fast I can't remember what you were saying." That's why I talk fast, because when you leave my meeting at least you're going to leave even. One of my objectives in communication is stimulating the mind to think by a rapid bombardment of old truths. There are many factors that can lead to excellence, but none are more important than humor—seeing life in perspective and being able to laugh at yourself—and the discovery of thinking from the heart.

Everyone who knows me knows my trademark is books. As a salesman it was books; as a manager it was books; in my home it's books; in my friends' lives it's books. Years ago I had a habit of giving everybody a book. I hoped they were read, but if not, they were there to be read.

Some time ago I attended a lecture. I don't remember much of what the speaker said, but he had me laugh for an hour at my problems as I identified with many principles that convinced me that even though we had never met we were very much alike. As he closed his talk he said, *"You are the same today that you will be five years from now except for two things–the people you meet and the books you read."* If you hang around achievers, you will be a better achiever; hang around thinkers and you will be a better thinker; hang around givers and you will be a better giver; but hang around a bunch of thumb-sucking complaining boneheads, and you will be a better thumb-sucking complaining bonehead. The "people you meet" and people you surround yourself with are a key influence in your life. We need heroes and positive role models as much as we need positive goals.

But the trouble with our heroes is that we can't take them home. We have got to grow and experience the lessons of life *alone*. But don't mistake aloneness for loneliness. Some people think they're lonely because they're young, while some people think they're lonely because they're old. Some people think they're lonely because they're poor, and yet some people think they're lonely because they're rich. Some discover that everybody is lonely to some degree and that's the way it's supposed to be. You discover out of loneliness comes aloneness when you decide to live and grow. You alone decide to live your life and do your growing. No woman grows for a man. No man grows for a woman. No parent grows for a child. *When you grow, you grow alone.* Growing brings growing pains but the laughs come too if humor is a part of your growing.

How else can we deal with the aloneness of growth? We've talked about "thinking with and listening and speaking to the heart." We've talked about seeing things in perspective and learning to laugh at our growing pains, using humor to break down barriers in our own heart and between other people. But you will never realize these points in your everyday experience without the stimulus of reading that broadens your perspective and pulls you out of the negative circles that can develop in your own thinking.

Here are some examples of heroes and reading.

General Patton made his troops mad and glad. He made them think and laugh when he wasn't around. General Patton once said, "If we're all thinking alike, somebody isn't thinking." When you're thinking, you're constantly discovering new dimensions to everything; when you're the wisest you know the least; and when you're aware of your ignorance, you're the wisest. How good it is to realize my ignorance. General Patton said not to be afraid of fear, "Fear is like taking a cold shower. When the water is ice cold, don't tip-toe in—leap in and spread the pain around. *Success isn't how high you reach, success is how high you bounce every day when you hit bottom.*" Patton almost always helped his listeners see with their hearts what he was saying.

Abraham Lincoln is one of the most revered names in the world today. His life has served as an inspiration to people from all walks of life. Many people will tell you that one of the secrets of excellence is education, yet Lincoln had little formal education. His family was so backward that for a period in Lincoln's childhood, they didn't have a door to their cabin. The year after his mother died, eight people tried to live in a small one-room log cabin. Many believe if you're raised in poverty or a broken home, you don't have much of a chance of growing beyond your past.

There's a lot of emphasis on self-esteem today, yet Lincoln had little reason to believe in himself. His mother died when he was a boy. He had little time with his hard working father. His sister died when she was in her teens. The woman he married didn't make his life a bowl of cherries. There were very few people in Lincoln's life who were there to stand by him and always offer him positive encouragement of what he could and should do.

So how does a man who lacks most of the things that we say

you should have to be a successful leader, become one of the
most revered heroes of world history? Two of the many great
assets of Lincoln were his ability to tell stories in order to illustrate a point and while doing so get people to laugh with him.
Much of this was stored in his mind and heart through the books
he loved to read as a boy. Lincoln was a great thinker because
he learned to *read and laugh.*

I would be remiss if I talked about excellence and my philosophy, and I didn't mention Oswald Chambers. Nearly every
word I have spoken for 30 years has been flavored by this man.
Yet it's no small wonder that many have never heard his name
because Chambers died in 1917 at age 43. He never wrote a
book. How can I have thirty of his books if he never wrote a
book? He married the Prime Minister of England's secretary
and when he went to work with the YMCA in Egypt during the
war, she went with him and made shorthand notes of his talks.
When he died in 1917, she lived on for years and wrote all the
books from the notes she'd made.

Let me tell you why I love Chambers. He's my favorite
writer because he challenges my everyday thinking with a
warmth that has grown out of the struggles of his own heart. He
helps me see how wrong I am in a way that lets me laugh at
myself. Chambers says, "You can determine how lazy you are
*by how much inspiration and motivation you need to do some-
thing.* If you're for real, you do it whether you feel like it or not.
The best way to avoid work is to talk about it."

Get people to think with you and you'll get them thinking
better. Get them laughing, but don't let them laugh *at you.*
Some comedians get people to laugh *at them.* And sometimes
being a clown is necessary to loosen things up. But good managers, teachers, and salespeople learn how to get people to laugh
at themselves. You begin by seeing things in perspective and
learning to laugh at your own heart.

I urge you to read and motivate others to read. *Never read
to be smart, read to be real; never read to memorize, read to
realize. And never read in order to learn more, as much as you*

read to re-evaluate what you already know. Never read a lot, but read just enough to keep hungry and curious, getting younger as you get older.

The heart of excellence for me is one word–*thankfulness*, learning to be thankful. The first mark of greatness is thankfulness; the first sign of smallness is thanklessness. An attitude of gratitude flavors everything you do. Once in a while some young tiger will say to me, "Did you feel this way years ago when you didn't have anything?" I used to go home and say, "Honey, look at me, 'Man of the Month.'" Look at this, "Man of the Year." She would say, "Where's the cash?" I'd say, "Honey, if we don't start learning to be happy when we have nothing, we won't be happy when we have everything." Well, I don't know if I ever sold her, but I finally bought it myself. I'm not trying to sell you, I'm buying it myself and sharing it. The one great thought, more than any other, is to be more grateful and thankful.

When you are in the game and wrestling with problems and achieving goals, the natural tendency is to focus on what you don't have. But if you don't balance this with a perspective that realizes where other people are relative to you, with their needs and goals, and realizes the simple joy of just living and growing through the stages of life, then all your goals and involvement, whether they are successful or not, will only lead to bitterness. At the heart of excellence is thankfulness. When your heart is in a thankless state, it can laugh, but not at itself.

When my family sits down to eat, our giving thanks goes something like this, "Dear God, we thank you for our food, but if we had no food we would want to thank you just the same. Because, God, we want you to know we're not thankful for just what you give us, we're thankful most of all for the privilege of just learning to be thankful."

Thank you for reading my thoughts. I hope you were thinking with me and that someday we'll meet and you'll tell me I interrupted your train of thought several times.

"The human system is primarily an emotional system. Oh, the intellect is terribly important to be sure. The knowledge that you have acquired through educational and training programs is vital to your success. But ...It turns out that how you feel about yourself, your job, your relationships and your future is even more important than what you know about them."

J.N.

FIVE KEYS TO EXCELLENCE

Jim Newman
P.O. Box 1378
Studio City, CA 91614
818/769-5100

One of America's highly regarded authorities in the field of high performance behavior, Jim Newman is a pioneer in the study of individual and organizational excellence. Jim is author of the best-selling personal development book, *Release Your Brakes!*

He is the founder and President of The PACE Organization. Since he created the PACE Seminar in 1961, hundreds of thousands of men, women and teenagers have demonstrated the practical value of the concepts and methods he has developed for enhancing success and personal fulfillment.

In addition to an active speaking schedule, he consults with top corporate executives across the country in the field of effective use of human resources. His daily radio feature, "You Make a Difference!" is heard on stations across the country. Jim is a recipient of the C.P.A.E. from the National Speakers Association.

How do you feel about the idea that people have a lot of potential that they don't use? That's pretty easy to see, isn't it? Especially in other people!

For most of us it is not as comfortable to look at the areas in which *we* have untapped potential. Yet that is just as true for you and me as it is for the people with whom we live and work.

"I know how to do that! How come I blew it?"

You're not the only person who ever had that thought!

William James, the famous American psychologist and philosopher, said that he thought the average person uses about 10% of their potential. I think he was probably high in his estimate. Now you are probably not an "average" person. You probably use a lot more than 10% of your abilities and talents— but can you see that there is a gap between *potential* and *performance* in your life?

That may be difficult to confront, frustrating to think about, but it is a giant first step to increased excellence and success. I'd like to explore some of the reasons people don't use all of the potential they have. Even more important, I'd like to tell you about five keys that can open the door to much greater success in every sector of your life.

Can you get excited about the idea of being the best you can be? Not necessarily being better, or more successful, than someone else—being better than *you* have ever been! What I am going to share with you is based on the idea that one of the most thrilling opportunities any of us has is the chance to become what we can be.

First, let's define some terms and take a look at a simple "model" of what makes people behave as we do.

I'm going to be using the word "potential" to mean the present time accumulation in your system of inborn talent, acquired knowledge and skills and whatever motivation you have to make productive use of those inborn and acquired abilities. I believe that everyone is born "motivated" to grow and become. When people do not act as though they are motivated it's because there's something else going on in the system that is squelching or limiting that natural, inborn desire to excel.

Well then, if everyone really does *want* to use their abilities, why doesn't it happen? Why does the salesperson sit and look at the telephone for 30 minutes and not pick it up to call a prospect? Why does a parent who really loves a child and wants the best for that young person explode, scream and perhaps even become physically violent? The answer to that may seem too simple, but it is just this: The human system is primarily an *emotional* system.

Oh, the intellect is terribly important to be sure. The knowledge that you have acquired through educational and training programs is vital to your success. But you can have a lot of knowledge and information about something and still perform very badly. Or sometimes a person has only a little bit of potential in a particular area and handles the situation very well.

It turns out that how you *feel* about yourself, your job, your relationships and your future is even more important than what you *know* about them. Positive emotions tend to enhance the flow of whatever potential a person has—negative emotions block that flow.

If you will identify some areas of your life that are really "working" it is almost a certainty that those will be areas in which you have some very positive feelings. Joy, enthusiasm, excitement, fulfillment are some examples. You may be tempted to think that you have positive emotions because that area of your life is on track and I am inviting you to look at the possibility that the reason those areas are working so well is because of the positive emotions!

The other side of the coin is even easier to observe. What was the negative emotion that kept the salesperson from lifting up the telephone? Sure! It was fear! Fear of failure, fear of rejection or maybe a combination of both! What was the emotion that caused the parent to explode and strike out?   Anger, frustration?

Now all of those are "normal" human emotions. I am suggesting that to the degree that they build up in your system and virtually "take over" control of your behavior, you are likely to handle that situation less well than you are capable of handling it. Negative emotions block the flow of potential.

Have you ever driven a car with the brakes on?

Not too bright! Not good for the car—or for the miles per gallon! Yet most of us who drive very much have probably occasionally found ourselves driving with the hand-brake partly set. And if that has ever happened to you, see if you can recall how it felt when you reached down and *released* the brakes, a sort of surging, "that's more like it" feeling.

Of course, you could have just pressed harder on the accelerator! That would probably have made the car go a little faster, but it would have wasted a lot of energy. Better by far to release the brakes and allow the horsepower to get to the wheels!

Do you see the parallel? We all drive through life with our emotional brakes partly set! One solution is to grit your teeth, clench your fists and try hard to do things better. I'm sure that you have tried that system. The tragedy is that "will power" often has a backlash effect. It is actually hazardous to your health! What works better is to get acquainted with the braking mechanisms and then release those brakes to allow your potential to flow!

Let's look at some releasing mechanisms. I'd like to invite you to consider five specific positive attitudes which will enhance excellence in your life—at home and on the job. As you allow these patterns to develop in your thought/feeling system you will see some dramatic changes happening in your ability to achieve your goals quickly, easily and with a lot more joy in the journey!

One of the fascinating attitudes that seems to be a common denominator of high-performance people is a pattern I call "growth-orientation." People who excel are excited about learning, growing and becoming.

I recall a program that I conducted several years ago for a national meeting of the Young Presidents Organization. YPO is made up of young, dynamic, successful men and women and their conventions are called "Universities For Presidents." They do have some social activities, to be sure, but the primary purpose of their meetings is to provide the members with a unique opportunity to learn from expert "resources" who are brought in to share their ideas and experiences with the YPOers.

I was scheduled to conduct a class at 8:45 one morning. I went to the meeting room a little before 8:00 to be sure everything was properly set up and was surprised to find that there were already about a dozen people there, ready and waiting. It was impressive to me that people had come early, but what really got my attention was the fact that they were all sitting in the front row! As more people arrived, the room filled up from the front. The price of arriving late was that you had to sit in the back! And when the chairs were all full, latecomers didn't stand in the back of the room, they came down front and sat on the floor—as close as they could get to the speaker.

I must tell you that I have worked with other groups in which the exact opposite happened. The room filled up from the back, the price of being late was that you had to sit down front, and if there weren't chairs, latecomers would stand against the back wall.

Different behavior because of a different attitude!

How do you feel about the learning process? Do you have a personal library of self-improvement books? Do you listen to educational cassettes as you drive in your car or as you jog? When you attend a training program or class do you head for the front row so that you can get the best possible return on the time you are going to invest?

When people stop learning, they've started dying. Decide right now that one of your most important qualities is your vital interest in learning and growing and becoming what you can be!

Here's key number two. Certainly not in order of importance, because this next attitude is probably the foundation of excellence in a human system. It's called "self-esteem."

My definition of self-esteem is your feeling of worthiness, value and significance as a human being. It's different from self-confidence—knowing that you can do something. Self-esteem is the degree to which you are in the habit of acknowledging the fact that you really are a very worthwhile person.

Your self-esteem got started when you were a small child. You got a lot of messages from Mommy and Daddy (and other experts) about what kind of person you were. Some were positive messages—probably there were some negative ones too. What really counted, in terms of your present level of self-esteem, was how you received those messages. Since they were coming from very important "experts," you probably accepted them as "the truth." So, if most of the signals and messages were positive, encouraging and loving, they probably led to the development of a pretty high level of self-respect and acceptance. If most of the messages you received as a child were negative, then you may have made up your mind that you aren't worth much and it is perfectly normal for others to treat you badly.

Whatever your present level of self-esteem, there is a direct relationship between that *attitude* and the flow of your potential.

Here are some suggestions for ways in which you can reinforce and enhance your self-esteem. Whatever your present level might be, test these ideas and see what happens as your feelings of personal worth increase.

One way to enhance your self-esteem is by recalling—and re-experiencing, in your imagination—times when you have felt a sense of pride and value. Another is to give up the habit of "wallowing" in errors and failures. Instead of reliving (and thus reinforcing) events that were negative, think about how you might handle similar situations more effectively "next time" they occur.

You can also build your self-esteem by strengthening the self-esteem of the various groups of which you are a part. Your family, the department in which you work, your company or any other team that you play on.

And, last but by no means least, you can build your self-esteem by giving some to another person. In fact, the more you give, the more you get! See if you can find some simple, direct ways of helping the people with whom you live and work to feel better about themselves. You will be enhancing your environment (people who feel good about themselves are easier to live with) and your own personal self-esteem will be strengthened in the process.

Ready for another key to excellence? Take a look at how you feel about pressure!

One of the very interesting patterns that we can see in top athletes, surgeons, executives—people at the top in every walk of life—is their positive attitude about pressure. They love it! See if you can learn to lean into the demands that come your way. Deadlines, financial demands, the need to adapt to changing situations, all can be seen as stimulating and positive requirements. People who have formed the habit of perceiving pressure as a positive force in their lives are in great demand and command high salaries.

Another key to excellence is the ability to find the joy in life. People who excel have an optimistic outlook, bounce out of bed in the morning with high energy and make it through each day with a good sense of humor. As a result, not only are they more fun to be around, but they are also more healthy. Positive emotions contribute to abundant physical health—negative emotions allow illness to develop.

And, last but by no means least, is the key to excellence that I like to call personal responsibility. It's defined as the degree to which a person is comfortable (or even excited) about the fact that he/she is accountable for the consequences of his/her behavior. People who excel know that to be the case, and wouldn't have it any other way. As a direct result of that attitude, the high-performer is in the habit of reinforcing what works—and correcting for what doesn't.

People who are low on this scale do neither of those. When things go well, the non-responsible person "thanks his lucky stars." And when things go badly that person looks for someone to blame. Neither of those actions has any chance of making subsequent behavior more productive. Notice how this quality applies to the productive people you know—and to the failures, too. Whenever possible, remind yourself that life is a series of choices. All choices and decisions have consequences and success in life is largely a matter of anticipating the positive and negative consequences of any decision and thus increasing the probability that a decision or choice will, in fact, take you in the direction that you really want to go.

Try this idea...

For the next week focus your attention each day on one of the five keys to excellence that we have reviewed. Start the day with the determination that you are going to expand yourself today in this one specific area. As the day progresses, look for opportunities to practice the positive attitude. Observe it in other people to see what effect it is having on their success. At the end of the day, check your progress. Were you able to put that releasing idea to work and let your potential flow more easily and more productively? Then, before you go to sleep, remind yourself of what you are going to be focusing on tomorrow.

At the end of the week you'll see the beginning of some important changes, then start back with number one and work on the five keys for another week.

I believe that you will find the process very exciting and rewarding as you become more and more able to get out of the way and let yourself grow!

"So the philosophical question is 'Who's packing your parachute?' Everybody needs someone to pack their parachute. We all need that kind of support in time of need."
C.P.

PACKING PARACHUTES

Charles Plumb
1200 N. San Marcos Rd.
Santa Barbara, CA 93111
805/683-1969

J. Charles Plumb is a common man with an uncommon story. Raised in America's heartland, he graduated from the United States Naval Academy and became a jet fighter pilot. After seventy-five combat missions over North Vietnam, his plane was destroyed by a surface-to-air missile. He ejected and parachuted into enemy hands. He was captured and spent the next six years in a Communist prison undergoing degradation, humiliation, brutality and torture. Charles describes that experience as "a proving ground for basic psychological principles."

He was repatriated to the United States and began a series of lectures taking him to every state in the nation and many foreign countries. He has appeared on CBS Morning News, The Today Show, Larry King Live, and many others. He retained his Navy affiliation and he holds the rank of Captain in the Reserves.

My first prison cell in Vietnam was eight feet long and eight feet wide. I could pace three steps one way and three steps the other. Inside the cell there were no books to read, no window to look out; no TV, telephone or radio. I didn't have a real pencil or a piece of paper for 2,103 days. I didn't have a roommate for several months.

What I had was three steps one way and three steps the other. I was going stir crazy in that cell. I finally decided, "Charlie, you must come up with something to do or you're going to go nuts in here." So I made a little game to play. I constructed a little deck of playing cards about the size of postage stamps. I tore these cards from 52 strips of toilet paper. I can tell you this with authority; it's tough to shuffle toilet paper!

Recently, my wife Cathy and I were sitting in a restaurant. A man about two tables away kept looking at me. I didn't recognize him. A few minutes into our meal he stood up and walked over to our table, looked down at me, pointed his finger in my face and said, "You're Plumb." I looked up and I said, "Yes, sir, I'm Plumb." He said, "You flew jet fighters in Vietnam. You were on the aircraft carrier *Kitty Hawk*. You were shot down. You parachuted into enemy hands and spent six years as a prisoner of war."

I said, "How in the world did you know that?" He replied, "I packed your parachute."

I staggered to my feet and held out a very grateful hand of thanks. I was speechless. This guy came up with just the proper words. He grabbed my hand, pumped my arm and said, "I guess it worked." "Yes, sir, indeed it did," I said, "and I must tell you I've said a lot of prayers of thanks for your nimble fingers, but I never thought I'd have the opportunity to express my gratitude in person."

He said, "Were all the panels there?"

"Well, sir, I must shoot straight with you," I said, "of the 18 panels, that were supposed to be in that parachute, I had 15 good ones. Three were torn, but it wasn't your fault, it was mine. I jumped out of that jet fighter at a high rate of speed, close to the ground. That's what tore the panels in the parachute, it wasn't the way you packed it."

I didn't get much sleep that night. I kept thinking about that man. I kept wondering what he might have looked like in a navy uniform—a dixie cup hat, a bib in the back and bell bottom trousers. I wondered how many times I might have passed him on board the *Kitty Hawk*. I wondered how many times I might have seen him and not even said good morning, how are you or anything because, you see, I was a fighter pilot and he was just a sailor. How many hours did he spend on that long wooden table in the bowels of that ship weaving the shrouds and folding the silks of those chutes, doing a standard (or even mediocre) job? I could have cared less...until one day *my* parachute came along and he packed mine for me.

So the philosophical question is "Who's packing your parachute?" Everybody needs someone to pack their parachute. We all need that kind of support in time of need. We all need those who step out in front and say, "Yes, I'll help."

My parachute was well packed when I was shot down over enemy territory. My physical parachute, my mental parachute, my emotional parachute and my spiritual parachute were pretty well in place.

All that parachute packing began in a very small town in Kansas. I loved that town. My parachute was packed by my Dad, my Mom, my big sister, my two little brothers and a coach named Smith.

Clancy Smith was a 65-year-old World War I veteran. He was a tough hombre who still had some shrapnel in one leg. He walked with a limp. We were the last team he ever coached and unfortunately, we didn't have a very good season. Our record was one and seven. We wanted to win that last game for him, but we lost. I'll never forget walking back to the locker room and Coach Smith came up and put his arm over my sweaty shoulder. I looked up at him and said, "I'm sorry coach, I guess we're just a bunch of losers." He squeezed my shoulder, sunk his fingers into my flesh and said, "Son, whether you think you're a loser or whether you think you're a winner...you're right."

The next day at school I said, "Coach, I don't understand what you meant. Would you explain it to me?"

He said, "Son, I don't want you to come back here in four or five years and tell me the reason you failed in high school and college was because you didn't learn anything in this little county school. I don't want you coming back here in six or eight years and telling me that the reason you couldn't get a job was because you weren't educated. I don't want you telling me in 12 or 14 years you failed was because you married the wrong girl." He said, "What makes the difference between your success or failure is *you*. It's a choice. You can choose success, you can choose failure, or you can *choose to give away the choice.*"

I graduated from that little grade school and I went away to Annapolis, the Naval Academy, where I was held prisoner! They let me go after four years, but I got my parachute packed there too. Admiral Charles Kirkpatrick was the Commandant of Midshipmen. He would stand up in front of the big pep rallies and clench his fists so tight you could see the veins run in his brow, and he'd say, "You guys can do anything you set your mind to do." That became our motto. For four years we didn't know how to lose. And we didn't very often. We were the number two and number one team in the nation. Best of all, Navy beat Army four times straight!

Uncle Charlie was right. We *could* do anything we set our minds to do!

I graduated from Annapolis, married my high school sweetheart and was sent to Flight Training. Two and a half years later I was qualified to pilot the F-4B Phantom jet, the hottest fighter plane in the world, and set sail on the aircraft carrier *Kitty Hawk* for Vietnam.

After 75 combat missions, on the 19th of May, my jet fighter was hit by a surface-to-air missile. The radar interceptor officer in my back seat and I started to tumble through the sky.

We found ourselves upside down going down at 500 miles per hour—a screaming fireball headed for the ground. My co-pilot was getting a little concerned! He said, "You want to get out, Charlie?" "Wait a minute," I said. "We have this extra special problem." The way you normally get out of a jet fighter is with an ejection seat. It's like a rocket under your chair. Set off the rocket and it shoots the chair out the top of the airplane. We were upside down. To eject from that altitude upside down would have planted us about six and a half feet below the level of the rice paddy.

I had to turn the airplane upright. I grabbed the stick but it was frozen. I'd lost all my hydraulics. The only control I had left was a manual rudder. I hit that rudder as hard as I could. The airplane shuddered, rolled back upright and we ejected. We came floating down in our parachutes over enemy territory.

Ever been in one of those parachutes? I don't mean the silk and nylon kind, I'm talking about those parachutes of life. I'm talking about those times when your gut is twisted and wrenched with a decision you have to make and none of the decisions seem quite right. I'm talking about those fender benders, the hang nails, the little things that get to us.

The parachute opened. I looked at my co-pilot, he was in good shape, and then I bowed my head and said a prayer. I asked for strength from above.

We drifted down to the ground and were captured immediately and hauled into the prison camp. I was tortured for military information and political propaganda. After two days of that they put me in the cell, the one I described to you at the beginning. It was in fact eight feet long and eight feet wide. Now, I was moved around to several cells during my captivity—some were larger, some were smaller, but the first cell and the average cell was 8x8. I could, in fact, take three steps one way and three steps the other. I was afraid. I feared not only for my life but for the lives of my buddies. I feared for those who were at home waiting for me; my wife, my family and friends.

I was pacing along back and forth across that cell. I was well into my 200th mile when I heard, in the far corner, the chirping noise of a cricket. I paid no attention at first. Yet the longer I listened to the cricket the more rhythmic it became.

"Now, that's a pretty educated little critter." I thought to myself, "Maybe I can teach that dude to sing." So I walked over to the corner and found it wasn't a cricket at all but a piece of wire. It was about four inches long and was coming out of a hole at the base of the cell wall and scratching on my concrete floor making a chirping noise like a cricket. I watched the wire bobbing in and out of the wall for quite a while.

I figured the wire had to be connected to an American on the other end, maybe on the other side of the storeroom next to my cell. I needed to communicate with another American. By that time in my experience I was losing track of what was a real memory and what was just a hallucination. I needed to tug on the wire.

But, the overriding emotion was fear. I was afraid to tug on the wire. I was sure that on the other end there was going to be another macho fighter pilot who was stronger than I and who wouldn't understand the condition I was in (and he probably didn't cry when they tortured him). I was 24 years old, a jet fighter pilot, the guy who was supposed to have "the right stuff."

I was a graduate from the Naval Academy, an Officer in the greatest Navy in the world. But, I had 27 boils on my front side and a bunch more on my back. I was bleeding from four open wounds from the torture. I was in the prime of my youth, but I was down to 115 pounds, rotting away in a communist prison camp. My sole possession in life, was a rag I had knotted around my waist to hide my nudity. I didn't want anyone else, least of all one of my peers, to see me the way I saw myself.

Ever had that kind of fear? I guess we all do some times. We're all afraid once in a while to tug on a wire. We're all afraid once in a while to offer to pack that parachute.

Finally, I got the guts up to do it. I knelt down in the prison cell and reached for the wire. I tugged on it three times and it tugged back three times. I tugged again and it tugged again. I tugged four times and it disappeared. Well, I stepped back in the cell wondering what would happen next. The little wire came back an hour later. Wrapped around the end of the wire was a little note. It was made of toilet paper. Just blobs of ashes on this wadded up piece of toilet paper. It said, "Memorize this code, then eat this note." I did. I memorized the code, ate the note. I knelt down again at the hole in the wall and started tugging on the little wire. On the other end of the wire was Lieutenant Commander Bob Schumacher, fighter pilot and astronaut candidate and best of all, a "Parachute Packer." He'd been there two years when I arrived. His first words were, "How you doing, buddy?"

That was my cue. I'd been looking for someone to tell my troubles to so I said, "I'm doing terrible, buddy." I said, "My president sent me over here and I got shot down in his beautiful little war. Then some idiot mechanic didn't put a transistor in the airplane. Get Congress over here. They're the ones who appropriated all the money. Let them sit in this prison camp. I am the victim of circumstances beyond my control. I'm going to rot away and die in here because of someone else's mistake. Help me!"

He said, "You want to know your biggest problem?"

I thought, "You mean I got problems bigger than the ones I can see?"

"It sure sounds like it," he said. "It sounds like you're suffering from a fairly common disease that can kill you if you don't catch it in time."

I said, "What's the name of this disease, maybe I know something about it."

He said, "Around here we call it 'prison thinking.'"

I said, "Prison thinking?"

He said, "Roger. You *think* you're a prisoner."

I thought, what kind of nut did they put me next to? This

guy's in space somewhere. He doesn't know how badly I hurt. But, I had to keep communicating, I had to keep tugging on the wire. I said, "Tell me about 'prison thinking.'"

He said, "Well, when a guy gets shot down, the very normal red-blooded American thing for him to do is start feeling sorry for himself and blaming everybody else." He said, "You go into the 'woe is me' mode of life. 'Woe is me, poor mama Plumb's little boy Charlie is a long way from home in a communist prison camp.' You get a bushel of pity and then just wallow in it. Then you start blaming everybody you can think of. Blame your president for sending you over here, blame Congress for appropriating the money, blame your mechanic for putting your airplane together, blame your mother for giving you birth. The problem with this, of course, is that when you start blaming other people for your misfortune you suddenly give them control over your life." And it hit me, that's what the coach was saying years before. I do have the choice. I control my own destiny.

I must admit, it took me a long time to validate that principle. I'm still working on it today. I get out here on the highway, I'm driving down the road minding my own business doing 55 right on the double nickel. Some idiot comes around me and cuts me off. I hit my horn, I hit my brake, I wave my fist, I yell some obscenity and all day long I'm stirring up those cholesterols, see, getting ready for a good old heart attack. While the guy that cut me off is just driving right on down the road. Doesn't even know my name and yet he's got control of my life.

I said, "Okay, Schumacher. You've got my attention. Now tell me, what's the antidote for this disease?"

He said, "Well, the first thing you need to break down the walls of 'prison thinking' is faith. Not just spiritual faith, you also have to have faith in your country and faith in your roots. The second thing you need while you're here is commitment. You've got to be committed to a set of standards you can't be afraid to stand up and tell the world what you think is right. The third thing you need is PRIDE."

I said, "Pride." I looked at my poor wretched body again.

"That's right, pride. You've got to be proud of yourself. You've got to believe you're a good enough person, you can overcome all the problems and, one of these days, march out of here a proud American, with your head held high."

I said, "Okay, I think I've got those things—faith, commitment, pride."

I found during the next six years that those three factors were more important than the rice we ate or the water we drank. Schumacher sure packed my parachute that day. He gave me the panels which allowed me to overcome the adversity of prison life, but he certainly wasn't the only one to do it. If we hadn't been involved in a fellowship of prisoners of war I don't think I'd be alive today.

One of the greatest parachute packers of all in that camp was an enlisted man. Most of us, as you know, were officers and pilots, we had very few enlisted men in the prison camps in Vietnam, and yet, one guy was there. He was a Navy sailor. How did a Navy sailor get into a prison camp in an air war in Asia? He fell off his ship and got washed ashore! Try to explain that to your commanding officer.

"Seaman Douglas Hegdahl from Clark, South Dakota." He had enlisted in the Navy when he was 17 and they sent him off to a place that he couldn't even pronounce. Late one night he fell off the back of his ship. He floated around for six hours, finally washed ashore, was captured and put into a prison camp 10,000 miles away from home in a communist country where he had to live with 200 macho fighter pilots—which may have been the worst part of all.

Young Hegdahl could take a joke. He was the Radar O'Reilly kind of a kid. What a parachute packer! We'd have these contests. We'd tug on the wire and tap on the wall in our secret code. We'd say, "Who's the oldest in the prison camp," or "Who's been here the longest," or "Who's got the most children back home?" One time we had what we called the "High Fast—Low Slow" contest to determine what pilot had ejected from his airplane highest and fastest, who had gone out lowest

and slowest. Well, High Fast was won by some Air Force jock
who punched out of his F-105 at 52,000 feet at 1,000 miles an
hour. The Low Slow contest was won by Seaman Hegdahl—12
feet at 15 knots.

About three years into my stay, the North Vietnamese were
getting a lot of flak from the World press about their treatment
of prisoners and their torture techniques. So they decided to
release some guys early as proof of their good will. Most of us
were given an opportunity to go home early. But we had a code:
the Code of Conduct. It's not a military regulation, it's only a
code. You can't be court-martialed for violating it. And yet, we
knew the strength of our unity, so we elected not to accept early
release. Our senior man selected Seaman Hegdahl to go home.
Why? Hegdahl was the youngest person there, and an enlisted
man; but more importantly, Hegdahl had developed a photo-
graphic memory in that prison camp. He'd gone through the list
of 200 prisoners and memorized their first, middle and last
names. He memorized our next of kin and then each hometown
of each of the relatives. Finally, he memorized the telephone
numbers of each of the relatives of each of the 200 prisoners of
war.

Well, Seaman Hegdahl came home. Here's a nineteen year
old lad, a sailor with two years back pay in his pocket, hadn't
seen a girl in two years and he's free on the streets of San Diego.
Remember, he's a parachute packer. He started to travel. He
went from the West Coast to the East Coast. He spent his own
time and a lot of his own money. He went North to South. He
went through each of the hometowns he'd memorized. He
spoke to each of the relatives he'd memorized and told them that
their prisoner was alive. Doug Hegdahl wasn't looking for a
great kudo or accolade. No achievement medals were given for
what he was doing.

We wondered for six years how we'd find out we were
going home. Finally they told us. A peace treaty was signed
and a POW exchange was underway. We launched out of there
on an Air Force C-141. What a sight that was—I had a big lump

in my throat—the American flag on the side of the airplane. Wow! Our first stop was Clark Air Force Base in the Philippines. I made a telephone call I'd been wanting to make for six years—to my wife in Kansas. And she had gone. I called my Dad. "Dad, what's happened to my wife?"

He said, "Come on home son, and we'll talk about that face to face."

I said, "Dad, it's going to take me three days to get back. Tell me now, will you? What's happened?" My father couldn't do it so he passed the telephone to my mother. I'll never forget her words.

She said, "Son, I'd give ten years of my life if I didn't have to tell you this. Your wife filed for divorce...just three months ago. She's engaged to another man."

I returned to Kansas City and found lots of well-meaning people giving me advice. The legal advisors were all saying, "Sue her and her boyfriend. We've got the papers all written out (which they did). Just sign right here. We're going to put him in jail. We're going to take them for all they're worth. That'll fix them." Psychiatrists and psychologists had some pretty good ideas too. They were saying, "Charlie, you've got to get angry about this. You've got to get all this stuff out of your system. If anybody has the right to be bitter, you do."

Imagine that. Somebody telling me I have the right to be bitter. I'm saying to myself, "Now wait a minute. I fully admit I am a Rip Van Winkle awakened after six years. I really don't know exactly what's going on here, but I have been through six years of the 'University of Hanoi.' And I got a degree in hard knocks. But, if there's one single thing I validated in that communist prison camp it's this: Coach Smith was right. It is my choice. I can choose to be bitter, and maybe that's the easiest choice. I can choose to sue everybody I can think of. I can choose to be really angry. I can choose to crawl over in the corner and die and I *know* I can do that. I have that capability, I've seen men do it. Or, I have another choice. Pick up the pieces of this great jigsaw puzzle, press on with my life with the confidence and the commitment that it's going to take and live every day to the fullest, regardless of the price." That's what I've done, and that's what the other men have done too. You know who we are, you read about us in the papers. The ex-POW's from Vietnam are alive and well.

We had a POW reunion recently in Washington. We're setting records. So far we've produced two U.S. Senators. We have state legislators all over the country. We have bishops, judges, teachers, doctors, lawyers, professional pilots and public speakers. The medical community tells us we're healthier today, mentally and physically, than the men who didn't get shot down. Schumacher, the guy on the end of the wire, is a three star Admiral today. Doug Hegdahl, the kid who memorized the names, has a masters degree and is teaching. My ex-wife went ahead and married the fellow she was engaged to. I bounced around the Country as a bachelor for a lot of years. I married a gal from Memphis, Tennessee. We have a handsome son and a beautiful daughter.

But what's the connection? You'll never be a prisoner of war, you'll never have to pace three steps one direction and then turn around and pace three steps the other. You'll never have to learn all of those codes. But, don't you see the similarity? Each of us has a choice. We have the choice to stand up and be counted for what we think is right. We have the choice to give of ourselves and pack those parachutes. We have a choice to be part of the team. When you get older and look back on your life, you don't count dollars, you count the parachutes you packed.

Six years is a long time to pace three steps one direction and three steps the other. I wouldn't wish it on anyone. And yet, I would tell you it's the most valuable six years of my life. Amazing what a little adversity can teach a person. It gives a man a pause to think, "How will I survive? What are the techniques of survival, what are the properties of a winner?" There's no bed of roses. You'll have some mountains to climb and some parachutes to pack and you'll have to tug on some wires along the way. You'll have to apply the faith, the commitment and the personal pride.   But if you can put those basic principles together as part of your daily discipline you truly can "do anything you set your mind to do."

"But none of our commitments can stand up to the pressures of daily life unless they are firmly rooted in an all-consuming passion—a purpose that we feel is worthy of our very best efforts."
N.Q.

POSITION YOURSELF FOR SUCCESS

Nido Qubein
806 Westchester Drive
P. O. Box 6008
High Point, NC 27262
919/889-3010

Qubein is chief executive officer of Creative Services, Inc., an international consulting firm whose client list includes many successful corporations. He is also director of Southern National Bank Corporation, a four-billion dollar bank holding company with over 200 offices. He serves on the board of Harvard University's Institute for Social and Economic Policy and the international board of American Humanics Foundation.

He is author of many books and numerous audio cassette programs, distributed worldwide by Berkley Publishers and Nightingale-Conant. He holds a master's degree in business from the University of North Carolina at Greensboro.

As a professional Speaker, Qubein has addressed more than 3,000 corporate and professional groups from coast to coast and in 20 foreign countries. He is a past president of the National Speakers Association and is the youngest person ever to receive its most coveted award, "The Cavett." He has also been awarded the CPAE distinction for speaking excellence and has been inducted in the International Speakers Hall of Fame.

He is also a trustee of Mount Olive College, and Westchester Academy, a member of the board of McNeil Lehman public relations firm, a member of the Piedmont Entrepreneurs Roundtable and founder of the Qubein Scholarship Fund which has, since 1972, awarded more than 200 scholarships to deserving young people in North Carolina.

Have you ever wondered why some people always seem to get ahead, while others always just get by?

Is it because those who get ahead were born with more money, or talent, or brains? Is it because success begets more success? Is it because they always happen to be at the right place at the right time?

The fact is that some people do get ahead for those reasons. After all, it's a lot easier to climb the ladder of success when your parents are holding the ladder. Some people do seem to have highly marketable talents or brainpower. And, others seem to constantly be blessed with incredible opportunities.

If you look more deeply at the facts, though, you'll discover something that can change your life, forever. Most of the people we call truly successful are ordinary people, with average abilities and with routine opportunities.

So, what makes life's real winners different from the masses of average, hard-working people?

Simply stated, they position themselves for success ...

The real winners have a system that consistently positions them for success. They don't wait for success to come to them —they systematically show up at the right places, at the right times, with the right plans and actions to make their own success.

Some of the best advice I ever received was, if you want to be successful, you must first walk side-by-side and hand-in-hand with successful people. Another very wise person once told me, if you want to be successful study everything that successful people do and learn from them.

My staff and I have spent years researching some of the success systems of the most successful people of history. We've studied the lives of great statesmen and successful business leaders from all generations to determine the success strategies that made them so great.

One of the first things we noticed was that not all people define success in the same way. Success to one person means making a lot of money. To another, it means as serving the needs of the human race.

So, let me ask you: How do you define success? What does it mean for you to become really a successful person? The best definition I have ever found for success is simply this: *Success is achieving what matters most to you in every area of your life and in all your relationships.*

Now, that's a big order!

Yet, many people in every generation have proved it could be done. They have achieved what they wanted most in every area of their lives and in all their relationships.

Let's begin with the master strategy for all success—Position yourself for success in your own mind. The real winners in life are successful because they have a winner's attitude.

"Life is difficult," says Dr. Scott Peck. "But, once you face up to the fact that life is difficult, it doesn't seem so difficult anymore." He's right.

We live in the age of instant everything. We have instant coffee, instant foods and instant pain relief. Masses of people sit around wishing they could find instant success. "If only I could win a lottery..." they dream. "Or if only I could win a multi-million sweepstakes, all my problems would be over." And, a few...a very few...do find themselves suddenly wealthy by a stroke of luck or maybe a stroke of genius.

Yet, even those who beat the overwhelming odds and become suddenly wealthy, often find that they are no more successful than they had been when they were poor. In fact, history is filled with stories of people who suddenly became wealthy only to become miserable with all their money.

Remember that success in life is achieving what matters most to you in every area of your life and in all your relationships.

Truly successful people recognize that there is no instant success. Real success comes only to those who are willing to face the challenges of life day after day with a winner's attitude.

There are four vital ingredients that go into developing a winner's attitude:

Ingredient #1: *A strong sense of purpose.*

It is what some people call vision. Others refer to it as a dream. Whatever you call it, a sense of purpose is absolutely essential if you want to become a real winner in the game of life.

Purpose is like a guiding light that gives meaning and direction to our lives. It enables us to separate what is important from what only seems urgent at the moment. Nothing helps you focus your energies and concentrate all your resources like a strong sense of purpose.

We may talk about commitment as a critical factor in achieving any goal. And certainly, we have to make commitments if we expect to succeed. *But none of our commitments can stand up to the pressures of daily life unless they are firmly rooted in an all-consuming passion—a purpose that we feel is worthy of our very best efforts.*

Sometimes success in any venture demands a great deal of courage. We have to be willing to risk everything we hold dear to achieve something we believe in. Nothing short of a strong purpose can create within us that kind of courage.

For example, two centuries ago the founders of this country declared their independence from all foreign powers, and established their own government. They were well aware that in taking that action, they were risking their fortunes, their homes, their families—even their own lives.

History reports that many of them lost everything they owned. Some even lost their lives because of the stand that they took. But those men and women had a purpose. They dreamed of establishing a new nation in which individual freedom could flourish as never before in history. So, they were willing to make the total commitment and exhibit the great courage that was necessary to create that kind of freedom.

The great writer William Faulkner focused very clearly how important purpose is. He said, "I have found that the greatest help in meeting any problem with decency and self-respect...and whatever courage is demanded...is to know where you yourself stand. That is to have in words what you believe and are acting from."

Think about that statement. Do you have, in writing, a simple statement of your purpose for life? Can you tell someone in a few words what you consider to be your vision of success?

If so, you already have in place one of the ingredients of the will to win—you have found a purpose that is worthy of your best efforts. To achieve great things, you have to believe in a purpose that is bigger than yourself.

Ingredient #2: *A strong, positive self-image.*

In short, you have to believe in your worth, your value, as a human being.

Our self-image is the mental picture we have of ourselves. Dr. Joyce Brothers, psychologist and syndicated author, says, "An individual's self-concept is the core of his personality. It affects every aspect of human behavior, the ability to learn, the capacity to grow and change, the choice of friends, mates and careers."

It's no exaggeration to say that a positive self-image is the best possible preparation for success in life. One reason many people never reach their full potential is that they have so little self-esteem. For some reason, they may feel that they don't deserve to succeed.

Maybe it's because they feel so guilty for their past mistakes and failures. Or, perhaps, they have been put down by others for so long, that they have begun to believe the worst about themselves.

Whatever the reason for low self-esteem, it can be devastating to a person's will to win. It may show up as a paralyzing fear of rejection, or fear of failure. Psychologists have found that some people actually sabotage their own efforts because they feel a need for having an excuse for not measuring up to their own expectations of themselves.

Remember, a winner's attitude grows out of a deep-seated belief that you can, and deserve to achieve whatever matters most to you.

But let's get one thing straight. There is a big difference between having a healthy, positive self-image and being self-centered or egotistical. People who have a positive self-image value themselves, but self-centered people only demand that others hold them in high esteem. *High self-esteem is believing that you have a rightful place in the universe. But, egotism is believing that you are the center of the universe.*

The problem with low self-esteem is that it robs us of our will to win at the times when we need it most desperately. Someone once said that the battles of life are all fought uphill, and people who have achieved great things know that it's really true. The circumstances and problems of life can close in on us with a brutal fury, but the real winners in life always say to themselves, "I will not be defeated."

So, if you want to be a real winner, start by accepting yourself as you are—starting right now. Stop putting yourself down. And, cultivate the habit of paying yourself compliments. You'll find you like yourself a lot better.

Next, *hold others in high esteem.* It is a mark of personal maturity to accept others exactly as they are, and to hold other people in high esteem. Helen Keller said very wisely, "Tolerance is the first principle of community. It is the spirit that brings out the best in all human beings." If you want to feel good about yourself, learn to look for the good in others.

Then, *learn to be self-reliant.* You don't know what you can do until you do it. If you want to really see your self-esteem soar, start standing on your own two feet, and look for ways that you can be helpful to other people.

And, finally, to build a positive self-image, *cultivate a sense of gratitude.* Low self-esteem forces us to grumble about how bad things are. But, a sense of gratitude focuses our attention upon the many things we have to be thankful for.

For example, think about some person who spoke an encouraging word when you were near despair, or think about a person who believed in you when you needed a job. Or think about the person who befriended you when others were unkind to you. In all of our lives there are those special people who have given so much to us.

To help you think about and remember things to be grateful for, let me share with you a list of things that I constantly give thanks for in my own life.

I am thankful for the people who love me, for health, for my physical abilities, for mental abilities, for good food, for shelter and clothing, for God's love and care, for people who have been helpful to me, for opportunities to learn and grow, for the struggles which helped me mature, for a free country where I can live and work, for laughter, and for all the beauties of nature.

So, if you want to build a strong self-image, accept yourself as you are, stop putting yourself down, hold others in high esteem, learn to stand on your own two feet, and cultivate a sense of gratitude.

Ingredient #3: *Personal confidence.*

Plutarch, the great Greek philosopher, said, "A herd of deer, led by one lion is more formidable than a herd of lions led by one deer."

And, Henry Ford said, "Whether you say you can or you can't, you're right." The fact is *you will never rise above your expectations of yourself.* Personal confidence goes a long way toward increasing your enjoyment of life, your effectiveness in dealing with people, and your ability to achieve your goals.

The challenge to achieve does not simply ask, "What do you think?" or "What do you feel inside?" It asks, "What can you do?"

In fact, the only way to be an extraordinary person is to do the things ordinary people can't, or won't, do. Real achievers are not fool-hardy, but they are willing to take whatever risks are necessary to accomplish their goals. That kind of risk-taking requires a great deal of personal confidence.

Personal confidence is not making a lot of noise about who you are or what you can do or even what you have done. Personal confidence is taking charge of your life, believing in your abilities, and being willing to pay the price for success.

It is only when we believe we can tackle the challenges of life that we can turn all of our potential into reality. The more we believe in ourselves, the greater will be our achievements.

How can you cultivate personal confidence?

(a) *Rid your vocabulary of expressions like, "I'll try" or "I can't."* Promising to "try" something only commits you to make the effort. And, it leaves an open door for a quick retreat if you fail in that effort. It's like setting yourself up to fail.

Those who want to build their self-confidence promise themselves and others they will do it! Not that they will simply try to do it. The second self-defeating expression is "I can't." People who want to boost their self-confidence learn to take on challenges that stretch their abilities to their full potential, and then to meet those challenges head on.

"Do something," said Franklin D. Roosevelt. "If it works, do more of it. If it doesn't work, do something else."

I like that attitude. It's the outlook of a self-confident person who knows that not everything can be done, but is willing to take on new challenges and risk failure, rather than sit around and feel timid.

So, if you want to build up your self-confidence, say goodbye forever to those self-defeating expressions "I'll try" and "I can't."

(b) *Concentrate on the task at hand.* When we are worried about all the many challenges that lie ahead of us, we can become overwhelmed and not be able to accomplish anything.

"A journey of a thousand miles begins with a single step," is a wise old proverb from the Orient. The real achievers have learned to break their challenges down into bite-sized tasks and to take them on one at a time. Even the most complex of jobs becomes simple when it is broken down into smaller jobs that you can get your teeth into.

(c) *Prepare yourself for whatever you plan to do.* Anything worth doing is worth preparing for.

(d) *Build on your greatest strengths.* We usually enjoy doing those things that we are good at doing. And, we don't like doing those things that we are not good at doing. The really self-confident people have learned to spot the things that they do best and to build on those things.

(e) *Learn from your setbacks.* Many of the great success stories of history came after years of failing. People who ultimately succeed do so because they are willing to learn from their failures and mistakes. Life's losers are the ones who keep making the same mistakes over and over again.

(f) *Surround yourself with people who believe in you.* Critics can severely damage your feelings of self-confidence. There are some people who always try to belittle your abilities and put down your ideas.

What's the solution? Seek out those people who are positive about their own abilities and about the abilities of others. You will find they are a great boost to your self-confidence.

(g) *Feed positive thoughts into your mind.* What Earl Nightingale said is really true: "We become what we think about most of the time." If we think about positive and up-building ideas, we have a positive outlook on life. But, if we are always looking for the worst in every situation, we are sure to find something bad in everything that happens to us.

Most people can only concentrate on one thing at a time. If we choose to concentrate on positive thoughts, we have little time or energy for worrying about our shortcomings and the calamities that might come our way.

(h) *Compliment yourself frequently.* When you've done something well, don't be afraid to pay yourself a nice compliment.

(i) *Compliment others frequently.* Everybody likes to be complimented. When you pay honest compliments, it sets in motion a pattern of being complimentary, instead of critical. As a result, your self-confidence will soar.

(j) *Reward yourself for your victories.* Really capable people tend to be harder on themselves than anyone else. No matter what they accomplish or how well they do something, there is this little voice inside them that says, "That's not quite good enough."

If we listen too much to that little voice that drives us on toward perfection, and never find a way to balance it, it can make us feel like we never do anything right. One of the best ways to offset that feeling is to celebrate our victories by rewarding ourselves.

If we reward ourselves for our victories, we will find it more pleasant to give every effort our best shot. So, always make an effort to reward yourself. You find it helps tremendously to boost your self-confidence.

Self-confidence is a vital part of a winner's attitude, but it doesn't come easily to most of us. Remember, the more you boost your self-confidence, the more you will be able to stand up to whatever challenge life brings your way.

Ingredient #4: *A commitment to excellence.*

Most people are satisfied with simply getting by, but the real winners in life insist on being the best they can be—at whatever they do.

Watch the Olympics, or the Word Series, or the Super Bowl, or the master chess tournament, or even a game show. The faces always tell the story long before the scoreboard flashes the final tally. All you have to do is watch the faces of the contestants.

With some you can spot the signs of victory or defeat as early as the first stages of victory or defeat as early as the first stages of training. The winners show determination, commitment to excellence, and mastery. They have the will to win. It's clear that they are in it to win it! When the odds are against them, and everyone in the arena believes they arc going to lose, the look in their eyes tells they believe they can win.

It is that commitment to personal and professional excellence that keeps them going—when everything within them cries out for them to quit.

Winners learn to put forth their best efforts when it counts—before and during the contest. They expend their greatest energies when they are preparing and actually competing.

But the losers hold back part of themselves. They have to save something because they know it will be emotionally draining and physically exhausting to carry around the disappointment of defeat.

The fact is: it is easier to win than it is to cope with all the agony of defeat.

So, what makes life's real winners different from the masses of average, hard-working people? The real winners position themselves for success... They have a system that consistently positions them for high achievement.

The master strategy for all success is: *Cultivate a winner's attitude.*

"Let's look at our ticket again. If we have a definite destination, if we are willing to start now, if we don't look for the easy route but for one that will make us stronger, an optimistic route, a route of service and finally, if we are willing to pay the price, then we can, with certainty, know that our little ticket can take us anywhere in life we want to go."
C.R.

A TICKET TO ANYWHERE

Cavett Robert
1284 E. Edgemont
Phoenix, AZ 85006
602/266-2508

The unique ability of Cavett Robert to add "People Knowledge" has earned him the reputation of the number one speaker in America in the field of Human Engineering and Motivation.

Cavett received the coveted Golden Gavel Award by Toastmasters International for the nation's outstanding speaker in the field of leadership and Communication. Walter Cronkite and Lowell Thomas were former winners. He was selected by United Airlines and International Speakers Network as Speaker of the Year from a canvass of over 10,000 associations, convention planners and corporations. Cavett has earned numerous other awards for his speaking skills.

Cavett's vast knowledge in Sales and Human Relations is drawn from a wide background of experience. He sold insurance and real estate for over twenty years, held sales schools and conducted courses in Sales, Human Engineering, Personal Development and Management for many of the nation's outstanding companies.

One of the mysteries of mankind is that we find 20% of the people in practically every line of endeavor responsible for 80% of the constructive activities and the other 80% responsible for the remaining 20%

Why are some people creators of circumstances and others, with equal opportunity, only creatures of circumstances? Why do things happen to some people and why is it that others cause things to happen?

I hope this chapter will assist you in understanding this great mystery of life. I hope you will better realize why some people find their opportunity rather than their problem—why, to them, life is magic, not mystery; logic, not luck.

Let's Take An Imaginary Journey

One Saturday night a businessman found himself in a little town in the territory he served. His car needed repairs and he couldn't drive to his home town.

The streets were bare; there was no entertainment to be found. Very bored and somewhat cynical, he walked up to a stranger on main street and sarcastically asked, "What is this town noted for anyway?"

The local member of the chamber of commerce straightened himself up and proudly said, "My friend, you can start from this town and go anywhere in the world you want to go."

I'm not sure that he was not telling the stranger off, but in any event, it gives me a cue to invite you to take a little imaginary journey with me. Imagine that you have a little card in front of you. I suppose a card is made up of pulp, rags or wood and a few chemicals, but if you will just for a few minutes fill in this card mentally with me, I'll guarantee it can take you anywhere in the word you want to go—that is, if you really want to make the trip.

If you sincerely and voluntarily fill it out, it can be a ticket to take you anywhere in life; it can be a magic carpet that will take you to the great city of your dreams, aspirations and ambitions; it can be a key to open the door to the miracle of life with its wondrous possibilities. All of this is possible, however, only if you really want to make the trip.

Now let's examine this card and fill it out carefully.

First—What Is Our Destination?

What is the first thing we see on any ticket? Yes, it's our destination, isn't it? Where do we really want to go in life?

Some people just don't want to go anywhere. They are bogged down in complacency and are satisfied to remain there. About all we can say for these people is that we hope they vegetate silently, unobtrusively and don't affect the lives of those around them.

Just a Short Trip

Then we have those people who want to take just a little trip, they don't want to go very far. They want to hurry back to the status quo. They have built-in limitations. They want a life of quiet desperation. They flit from mediocrity to mediocrity with enthusiasm and optimism.

As for this second group of people, all we can say is that they were born in inertia and had a relapse. They don't even burn the candle at one end. They are suffering from the scientific disease that's known in technical circles as laziness.

They Advise Others in their Travels

Also, we have those people who don't want to take the trip, but they pose as experts on criticizing the travels of others. It's a "dog in the manger" situation. They are like the man who didn't kiss his wife for 30 years and finally shot the guy who did. They don't want to take the trip and they don't want anyone else to take the trip either.

The only thing we can say about these critics is that they were born in the objective case and have been walking around in the subjunctive mood ever since.

As Far as the Ticket Will Take Them

Finally, we have those people who want to go as far as the ticket will take them. They truly have the gift of dissatisfaction and divine discontent. They have hitched their hearts to a task they love—their souls are blazing with purpose and they know where they want to go.

These people are not afraid to reach for the stars. They know that even should they miss, they'll at least not come up with a handful of mud. They'd rather shoot at something and miss than shoot at nothing and hit. They are ever conscious of the fact that there is no such thing as a trip without a destination, no such thing as success without a purpose. Ever mindful are they that obstacles are only those things we see when we take our eyes off our goal. Long ago they learned that people do not fail in life because they plan to fail—they fail because they fail to plan.

Your Destination Must Be Specific

Nothing clutters up the landscape of understanding and congeals confusion as do generalities. Specifics alone give a directional compass to life.

Do you really have a specific goal in life? What is it? Is it that you want to put your kids through college? Is it to be head of your firm—President of your company? You must have something specific you desire. If your desire is great enough, this one quality brings into focus all the other qualities within you which enable you to accomplish your specific goal.

It's a tragic fact that in our country, the greatest country in the world, if I went out and stopped the next two dozen people on the street, there would not be six who could recite a specific desire which governs their lives. And I am afraid there wouldn't be a dozen who could tell with certainty just why they went to work this morning.

And so the first thing we must write on our ticket is our destination. Without this, there is no trip at all. Just as it's impossible to come back from some places we have never been, it's altogether preposterous to suppose that we can arrive anywhere without a place to go!

Second—What Is Our Time Schedule?

What's the next thing we see on a ticket? It's the time schedule. When do we want to go? And more important still, when do we want to arrive at our destination? Do we want to go now, from this very room, today—this moment? Or do we want to join those disenchanted people who are always putting something off until tomorrow and consequently never take the trip?

One of the unhappy circumstances of this life is that the world is full of well-meaning but misguided people who want to prepare for the future. In fact, they periodically vow emphatically that they want success enough to do something about it, and yet somehow they never get around to it. How many of these people do you know who are always about ready to commence to begin to start to do something pretty soon?

Unless you decide to go now, I guarantee you'll never take the journey. Why? I'll tell you why. There is no tomorrow. Yesterday does not exist. We live only today, right now, this very hour. Our only existence is the present.

The Magic and Miracle Of Time

Does time really have a meaning to us? Each day we have the opportunity to watch the magic and miracle of time. Time— life's most priceless tool, that which cannot be weighed in the balance or tested in the crucible. But we know it's the only ingredient that we use to transform our dreams into realities and our hopes into success.

A New Gift Each Day

Did it ever occur to you that God, in his infinite wisdom, gives time to us in such small doses that we can't too easily squander it? Every morning, when I wake up, my pocketbook is

magically filled with 24 hours of this precious, priceless substance we call time. And when tomorrow comes and I know
that I have given up a whole day of my life for it, I want it to be
something that's good, not bad, some gain, not loss—something
I can be proud of. And yet, nature is so forgiving. Even if I
waste it, "each night I burn the records of the day. At sunrise
every soul is born again." Again I wake up—24 more of those
non-refundable fragments of eternity that are magically in my
pocketbook—just as valuable and unused as if I had not thrown
the others away.

Did you ever hear a person say, "I just don't have time."
What he is really saying is that there are other things more
important to him. We all have a lot of time. We have all the
time there is. The hands of the clock go around at the same rate
of speed for everyone of us. The main thing is that sometimes
we don't put importance on those things that are important. We
give inconsequential matters disproportionate importance. We
major in the minors and we minor in the majors.

The Trip is Now or Never

Just how valuable is your time to you? Can you afford not
to start the trip today? Our time is too valuable to waste and
since we know there is no tomorrow, then unless we fill in
today's date on our ticket, I'm afraid that next week, next
month, next year, ten years from now, honest as may be our
intentions, we shall find ourselves in the wilderness of procrastination, still responding to the siren songs of complacency.

Why can't we realize that there is no other way except by
starting today? Don't we feel honestly that we are worth the
investment?

Starting Now is Our Only Insurance

Most people wouldn't drive their car from the garage unless
it were fully covered by insurance. Practically everyone has
insurance on their house. Very few people would dare to subject

themselves to the dangers of everyday living without life insurance.

And yet, insurance-minded as these people may be, many of them are not insuring their futures against constant changes by starting now to prepare themselves to cope with those changes.

The world owes us nothing, but we owe ourselves, our loved ones and the entire world the duty to develop our God-given qualities to the ultimate. It is a great challenge and not an easy one to meet. But it's also up to us and us alone to make our dreams come true, our plans come alive.

And so, look at your ticket again. Let's make the date today—this very moment. It's the only way we can be sure to get our just share of the tasks and rewards of this life. If we don't start now, we'll never reach the great city of our ambitions and aspirations.

Third—What is Our Route?

What's next on our ticket? It's the route, isn't it? Let's not be seduced by the temptation to try the easy paths of life. Some people say that the great focal point of life is where the two highways of preparation and opportunity cross. Others call it luck. I won't argue the point but this I do know. Strength always flows from adversity. Troubles, trials and sacrifices have always constituted the fertile soil for growth.

If you will take time carefully to review your life, you will realize that you make your greatest progress in life during times of discouragement and challenge. You will find that the lasting qualities of life are usually forged on the anvil of disappointment.

While no one seeks hardships, we know that they can't be avoided along the highway leading to success. Our only choice is to meet them squarely and rise above them. The road will never be easier—it is up to us to become stronger.

An Optimistic Route

Be sure that you take an optimistic route. We read so much about positive thinking these days that we are tempted to be casual in considering its importance. But please, never forget, the sweet magic of a cheerful disposition. Everyone enjoys being around an optimist.

On the other hand, a pessimist takes such a toll on us. I'd much prefer that a man steal my money than steal my optimism. The reason a pessimist is so dangerous is due to the law of emotional gravity. One pessimist can pull six optimists down with less effort than six optimists can lift up one pessimist.

Yes, we want to be kind and helpful to everyone possible, but to expose ourselves to a person with the smallpox of pessimism is a calculated risk too grave to take.

A Route of Happiness

We cannot be successful in our work or undertaking in life unless we enjoy what we are doing and feel a sense of fulfillment. Unless we are happy in what we are doing, we are a job hazard, a professional malcontent.

Years ago I was attending a convention on salesmanship. There were six or eight small meetings going on simultaneously. One that attracted my attention was labeled "The Greatest Sale I Ever Made." I was intrigued and could hardly wait to get to the meeting. I was sure that the speaker would relate his experiences on difficult persuasion. I thought perhaps I would hear that a man 90 years old had bought a 20 year endowment life insurance policy. Maybe the speaker would relate the old cliche about selling two milking machines to a farmer with just one cow and then taking the cow in as a down payment.

What I really heard was this, "The greatest sale I ever made in my life was the day I finally bought what I was doing—the day I saw the big picture, the day I had the great concept, the great passion—when I truly began believing in what I was doing."

The Route Of Service

We can believe in what we are doing and feel a permanent sense of fulfillment only if we know we are rendering a service to others. Any undertaking divorced from this feature has no lasting attraction. Never forget that service is the only rent we pay for the space we occupy while we are here on earth.

A person who desires to become rich should certainly not be criticized, provided he desires to become rich for the proper reason. There is nothing wrong with a desire to prosper. We can do so much more for our loved ones and contribute so much more to worthwhile programs in life if we are financially able. But if you are to be successful in such an undertaking, you must never lose sight of this cardinal principle: you can never become truly rich except by enriching the lives of others; you will never truly prosper unless you bring prosperity to others.

So, in filling out our ticket let's not look for the easy route, but for the one that will make ourselves stronger. Also, it should be an optimistic route and a happy route. Never lose sight of the fact that unless it is a route of service it will lead only up a blind alley. Man is so constituted that he must feel a sense of fulfillment if life is to have any permanent meaning. Some people feel that an undertaking must be monumental and world shaking to offer a challenge. This should not be. The size of the project is of minor importance—of major importance is the unselfish effort and dedication with which we tackle the job. Remember that any place of duty, however small, is a shrine wherein we can glorify our lives with the blessings of service.

Fourth—Are We Willing To Pay The Price?

And finally, at the bottom of any ticket is—the price. So many want to take the trip, but how few are willing to pay the price of the ticket. All of us want to improve our circumstances but how few of us are willing to make the sacrifices to improve

ourselves. I get enthusiastic over the idea of building a greater
future but do I have that same enthusiasm for the slow tedious
task of building myself?

I was attending a college in Greenville, South Carolina,
called Furman University. A professor by the name of F. P.
Gaines taught me English my freshman year. He later became
president of Washington and Lee University.

Dr. Gaines called on us in alphabetical order. I can repeat
the entire roll call even to this day. It was important to commit
the roster to memory because if you always knew just when you
would be called on, there was no need to prepare for recitation
except about once every two months—at least that was my feeling during those green years of my life.

Furthermore, good sportsmanship demanded that if a person was sick or absent for any other reason, he was duty bound
to protect those students whose names followed his by notifying
them in ample time to fortify themselves for recitation.

On a certain day, when my name was fairly well up the list,
a very embarrassing situation presented itself. Raleigh and
Riley didn't show up at class and neither one had pressed the
panic button. I was unprepared, a rather normal condition under
the circumstances. I had been over to a neighboring girls' college the night before to see the girl who is now the mother of
my five kids.

Fortunately, Dr. Gaines, as he so often did, had departed
from the subject of the day and was giving one of his little informal talks on some phase of personal development. I have long
ago forgotten the definition of a nominative predicate or the
subjunctive mood. But I shall never forget some of the great
inspirational ideas of life he gave us, nor will any who attended
his classes ever cease to feel forever the impact of his great personality.

On this particular day, Dr. Gaines had been discussing character. Finally he picked up his roster and I knew that I was to be
called on next. I glanced up at the clock and suddenly realized
that the dismissal bell would ring in five minutes.

Frantically, as I grabbed a pen and looked for a piece of paper, I blurted out, "Dr. Gaines, could you give us a definition of character that we could write down?"

He looked at me and then up at the clock. I realized how transparent my improvised scheme had turned out to be. But he was the essence of kindness and gentleness. He looked at me and smiled. He realized, of course, that I couldn't have cared less about the definition of character.

Dr. Gaines walked around the room in silence for about a minute with his hands behind him and his chin tilted slightly upward, which was a favorite pose of his. Finally he stopped in front of me, put his left hand on my shoulder and pointed his finger in my face.

"Young fellow," he said, "I'm not sure, but I'm going to give you a definition that I want you to keep until you can find a better one." It was many years ago and I have never heard one half as good. "Character," he said slowly, "Is the ability to carry out a good resolution long after the mood in which it was made has left you." He continued, "Now I didn't say just the ability to carry out a good resolution. We all have our moments of supreme dedication—whether it be fidelity to a person or loyalty to an ideal. But how few of us carry out that resolution when the mood has left us and the tides of temptation come sweeping in."

"Tomorrow morning you are going to have a test on the material we have covered over the past few days. Tonight you will perhaps decide that you are going to get up at six o'clock in the morning and study for this test. And actually you are going to get up in the morning—that is, tonight you are, because you are in the mood. But tomorrow morning when you stick your foot out and it touches the cold floor, you don't have that mood any longer. I say character is that which causes you to exercise the self-discipline to get up anyway."

The bell had rung but none of us had heard it. We knew it must have rung because the room was invaded by the next class. Those five minutes have burned brightly for me over the years.

I would not exchange them for an entire semester of my college career.

Since that time I've committed myself to a project or assignment many times while I was in an enthusiastic mood. After the mood was gone, the picture was different. The task seemed drab and difficult and without glamour or attraction. The price to pay seemed too high. On such occasions I have tried to remember this definition of character—that which we have within us to substitute for the mood after it is gone.

It's so easy to accept all parts of the ticket except the price. This is where real character and self-discipline enter the picture.

Don't Settle For a Limited Trip

Let's look at our ticket again. If we have a definite destination, if we are willing to start now, if we don't look for the easy route but for one that will make us stronger, an optimistic route, a route of service and finally, if we are willing to pay the price, then we can, with certainty, know that our little ticket can take us anywhere in life we want to go.

I repeat. It can be a magic carpet that will take us to the great city of our dreams, our ambitions and our aspirations. Yes, it can be a key that will open the door to the miracle of life with its limitless possibilities.

This journey is certainly not an easy trip. It's not for little people with little minds. It's not for people who are afraid the sun won't rise tomorrow. It belongs only to those brave and courageous people who dare to dream, have faith and expect the best. If you really want to take the trip, you must be willing to be baptized by immersion in some of the tougher aspects of life.

It was about 2,000 years ago that a great Greek philosopher and mathematician, Archimedes, was asked if he could perform a certain task.

This is what he said, "Give me a lever that is long enough, give me a fulcrum that is strong enough and give me a place to stand and single-handed I will move the world."

Our lever is our goal in life. Our fulcrum is our self-discipline and willingness to pay the price. Furthermore, we must stand upon the firm ground of dedication and belief in our pursuits and activities in this life. If we have these qualities, we too can move the world.

Read and re-read this chapter, over and over. It has tools of greatness you can't afford to ignore. Practice its principles and resolve to start your trip today.

> *"I believe that everyone has a Sahara to cross—perhaps more than one. Many people are crossing their own Sahara right now. Everyone eventually goes through periods of great difficulty, their own private hell, their 'dark night of the soul.'"*
>
> *B.T.*

SUCCESS
IS A JOURNEY

Brian Tracy
462 Stevens Ave., Suite #202
Solana Beach, CA 92075-2065
619/481-2977

Brian Tracy is one of America's leading authorities on the development of human potential and personal effectiveness. He is a dynamic and inspiring speaker who addresses more than 100,000 men and women each year on the subjects of leadership, strategic planning, organizational development, creativity, self-esteem, goal setting, success psychology and time management.

Brian has an M.B.A. and C.P.A.E. and is the President of Brian Tracy Learning Systems Inc., a human resource company based in San Diego, California. He served as Chief Operating Officer of a development company with $265 million in assets and $75 million in annual sales. He has had successful careers in sales, marketing, advertising, investments, real estate development and syndication, importation, distribution and management consulting for a broad spectrum of industries. As a consultant, Brian has trained key executives of more than 1000 corporations in the U.S., Canada, Mexico, the Far East, Australia and Europe.

Brian has traveled and worked in over 80 countries on six continents and speaks four languages. He is a voracious reader in management, psychology, economics, metaphysics, history and philosophy. He has a wonderful ability to translate his knowledge and experience into practical ideas that get immediate results.

He is the author/narrator of several best selling audio and video-based training programs. These programs are in worldwide distribution through Nightingale-Conant Corporation, Peak Performance Training Inc., and Brian Tracy Learning Systems Inc.

Did you ever stop and ask yourself, "Why is it that some people are more successful than others? Why do some people make more money, live longer, have better relationships—while the great mass of people, as Thoreau said, 'Live lives of quiet desperation'?"

When I was 15, I set out on a lifelong journey to find the answer to that key question, "Why are some people more successful than others?" I wanted to know.

You see, when I was growing up, my family never seemed to have enough money. My parents grew up during the depression and I heard the same thing over and over throughout my childhood, "We can't afford it." "We can't afford it." "We can't afford it." Repeated over and over.

I was not a great student. I passed out of high school when I was 18. I say "passed out" rather than "graduated" because that's what happened. I passed out in the half of the class that made the top half possible. The person in front of me on the stage and the person in back of me received diplomas. I got a "leaving certificate." When I opened it up and read it, all it said was, "good-bye."

Since then, I've traveled or worked in more than 80 countries on 6 continents. I've sailed on all the great oceans, and became fluent in French, German and Spanish, as well as learning to get along in Greek, Portuguese, Swahili, Thai and Hindi.

I started off as poor as I could be, searching for the secrets of success. Over the years, I've read and studied for more than 30,000 hours in business, economics, psychology, philosophy, religion, metaphysics and history. And, I'm happy to say, I eventually found the answers I was looking for.

Today, I live in a beautiful house on a golf course in Southern California and have business interests in nine countries. Today I know that I've proven that success in any field is as predictable as the sun rising in the east and setting in the west.

My purpose in writing this is to share with you some of the most important things I've ever learned. However, as Aristotle once said, you can't teach a person something he or she doesn't already know. That's why you probably already know what we're going to talk about. If not, you will recognize these principles as soon as you hear them.

About five years ago, I met a wise and wealthy man who had spent his entire life studying success. He had reached a clear conclusion concerning the primary reason for success in life and in business.

He's dead now but I'll never forget what he told me because I immediately recognized that he had put the finger on my reason for success, and yours, as I'll come to in a minute.

He said the key to success was to set a goal and stay with it until you achieve success at one important thing. He said that your subconscious mind will then accept that success experience and store it as a pattern of success. From then on, your subconscious mind will drive and direct you to repeat the pattern of success in other things that you attempt.

Another way of saying it is that, "Nothing succeeds like success." Psychologists have demonstrated that achievement gives you a natural high. Once you've experienced your first great success, not only are you unconsciously programmed to repeat it, but nothing else will ever give you the same wonderful feeling of satisfaction.

I learned the truth of this idea many years ago when I first started traveling. In many ways, a trip or a journey is a metaphor for life. My first big trip was that and more, much more.

It had such an enormous impact on me that I've never really gotten over it. My whole life has been different as a result of what I call, "The Sahara Crossing."

When I was 19, three friends and I decided to go off to see the world. We were well out of high school and laboring in saw mills on the West Coast. This was in 1963 and a lot of our friends were heading for Europe to travel around with backpacks. We decided to do something different. Nobody was going to Africa, so we decided we'd go to Africa.

It never occurred to us to ask why it was that no one else

was going to Africa. That was our first mistake. We were to find out for ourselves the hard way soon enough.

After working and saving for a year, the four of us piled into an old 1946 Chevy and drove out of Vancouver bound for Montreal. It was late at night, it was pouring rain, we were all 20 years old and we were off to see the world.

I learned later that almost every great venture begins with an act of faith, like driving into the dark, the unknown. In a way, nature protects us by shielding us from knowledge of the difficulties and obstacles that lie ahead.

If we really knew all the problems we would face, the setbacks, the suffering, the temporary failure and the disappointments, many of us would hesitate about starting out at all. I think this applies to getting married, having children, starting a career or setting out for any distant goal.

Our plan was to drive across country to Montreal, get jobs on ships to cross the Atlantic and then head south across Europe for Africa.

However, as it happened, in Montreal one of the guys decided to give up and go home and left us. The other two, after one day of looking for work on the waterfront, decided to quit trying and spent their limited savings to pay their way across the Atlantic.

I tried to talk them out of it. I told them that quitting is a habit. If you quit the first time you run into difficulties, you'll always quit when the going gets rough. You will, in fact, establish a pattern for failure rather than success.

But their minds were made up. So we split our savings, and they took a ship to England. I worked on a construction site in Montreal for the winter, then got a job on a Norwegian freighter out of Halifax in late February and arrived in England in mid-April.

As I had predicted, my friends had quit and stayed in England working at odd jobs. However, we made up and once more headed for Africa.

At this time, the only map we had was an 8-1/2 x 11 inch page from a school atlas that showed both Europe and Africa on one page. It seemed to be a very simple thing to go from London, a dot at the top of the map, to Johannesburg, a dot towards the bottom.

Oh yes, there was this orange part on the map of Africa called the Sahara Desert, but that would be no problem. We'd just "whip over it" to the green part below.

It never occurred to us that the total distance was about 8,000 miles. We were "big picture" people. We didn't let ourselves get bogged down with details.

We took a train to London and there we bought bicycles. We had never heard of anyone riding from London to Johannesburg on bicycles and we decided we would do it first and become famous.

This was a big mistake. We soon learned that when you ride bicycles across France in the springtime, you find that the hills are all uphill and the wind is always in your face.

Likewise, when you embark on any new venture, you often find the same thing—everything seems to go wrong, usually at the worst possible time and in the worst possible and most expensive way.

After two weeks of grinding along on bicycles, we said, "The heck with this," loaded them on a train and rode across France and Spain to Gibraltar. There, we sold the bicycles, and bought a Land Rover. We had definitely learned why no one had ever crossed Africa on bicycles.

Now we had a little problem. We were out of money. We had exhausted our meager finances buying the Land Rover and we didn't have enough money left for fuel and equipment. So we all sat down and wrote letters to everyone we knew, pleading for money. We got a few dollars here and there and one big score. An uncle of Geoff's, my buddy, sent us 100 pounds, $300 at that time, or the equivalent of more than $1000 today. We were ecstatic.

And this was another lesson. Nobody makes it on their own. We all need help from others to get over the rough spots on the journey of life.

With the influx of funds, we loaded up with food and supplies and took the ferry over to Tangiers, in Morocco. We headed out of Tangiers toward the Atlas Mountains and the Sahara full of excitement, singing as we drove down the road.

Twenty miles out, the radiator blew up. The old Land Rover had never been driven on open road. It had spent its working life tooling around the narrow streets of Gibraltar. Once on the open road however, it began to fall apart.

The radiator was just the beginning. Over the next 10 days, the steering rods bent and threw the front wheels out of alignment. The tires blew one by one.

We were so poorly equipped, we didn't even have a jack or a lug wrench. When we got a flat tire we had to wait by the side of the road, sometimes for hours, until someone came along with the proper tools to help us change the tire. But we pressed on anyway.

As we drove deeper into Morocco, over the Atlas Mountains, and onto the Sahara escarpment, we entered into a world that had changed very little in a thousand years. There were long stretches of barren country roads and an occasional oasis surrounded by primitive farms irrigated from wells and underground rivers.

It was the beginning of an experience that I still remember quite clearly. By this time, I was speaking French fairly well. We could converse with the natives in the occasional small town we passed through.

In one town, early in our slow, halting trek across Morocco, someone asked where we were headed. We told them we were going across the Sahara and into Africa.

He said, "Oh no, you can't do that. You will die in the desert." The French words were, "Vous allez mourir dans le wuste." We began to hear this on a regular basis, everywhere we went.

We'd stop in a small town and people would bring their friends up to us and introduce us as the young men who were going off to die in the desert. They seemed quite cheerful about it but after a while it became quite irritating.

By the way, these were not your average Arabs. These were Bedouin, and Taureq, people of the desert, members of tribes that had lived in the Sahara for a thousand years. They were in a position to know what they were talking about.

I learned a valuable lesson from this. I learned then, and for the rest of your life, whenever you try to do something out of the ordinary, people will line up to tell you that you can't do it, why you can't do it, that you will lose your time, lose your money, that you will, in effect "die in the desert." Even people who should know better will try to discourage you. To achieve anything great or worthwhile, you must train yourself to rise above these people, ignoring them and pressing on toward your goal regardless.

We crossed from Morocco into Algeria and drove south to the town of Adrar, on the edge of the Sahara. By this time our vehicle was falling apart and with the cost of repairs, gasoline and food, we had almost run out of money.

One of the guys, sick from dysentery, decided to give up. He took his belongings and hitchhiked to the Mediterranean, 500 miles north, and then back to England. That left two of us.

We began wondering, "What are we doing here?" We were two young men, both 20 years of age, thousands of miles from home, sick, tired and almost broke, with thousands of miles ahead of us. We couldn't even remember why we started out in the first place.

But one of the things that kept us going was a book of poetry by Robert W. Service. He had driven an ambulance in World War I and had written poetry to cheer up the soldiers in the trenches on the Western Front.

There was one poem we read over and over. It always gave us a boost and the determination to go forward. It was called "Carry On" and it started like this:

It's easy to fight when everything's right,
And you're mad with the thrill and the glory;
It's easy to cheer when victory's near
And wallow in fields that are gory.
It's a different song when everything's wrong.
When you're feeling infernally mortal;
When it's ten against one, and hope there is none
Buckle up, little soldier, and chortle:
Carry on! Carry on!
There isn't much punch in your blow.
You're glaring and staring and hitting out blind;
You're muddy and bloody, but never you mind.
Carry on! Carry on!
You haven't the ghost of a show.
It's looking like death, but while you've a breath;
Carry on! My Son, Carry on!

We were now in the Sahara, the largest desert in the world. It stretches across the Tropic of Capricorn from the Atlantic Ocean to the Red Sea, more than 5,000 miles.

The part we faced was the Tenezeruft, the emptiest single stretch of the Sahara, 500 miles of nothing—not a fly, not a blade of grass—flat as a table top.

The enormity of what we had embarked upon finally began to sink in. We learned that over 1300 people had perished in the Tenezeruft in the last 20 years. Forty-two vehicles had broken down in the desert, and many of their drivers were never seen again alive.

By this time, Geoff and I were out of money. All our tires were scraped bald and needed to be replaced. We needed additional tanks so we could carry enough gas and water for the crossing. We needed tools, a jack and a lug wrench so we could do repairs.

For three weeks, we stayed in Adrar. Geoff hitchhiked north to Algiers to wire for more money. I sold all our supplies except for a bare minimum. By stripping abandoned vehicles, I got the Land Rover repaired and properly outfitted with good tires, a reserve gas tank, proper tools and supplies for the crossing. It's amazing how enterprising you become when your survival is at stake.

The Sahara Desert in June is hot—very hot! At midday, it reaches 140 F. An exposed man can die of dehydration in as little as 20 minutes. When the French ran Algeria, they required travelers to carry five gallons of water per person per day for the crossing.

Because of the heat, you can only travel before 10:00 a.m. and after 4:00 p.m. The midday sun is so hot that if you drive, your engine oil boils as thin as water and your vehicle will seize up and never run again.

Six weeks after crossing from Gibraltar, we were ready. Geoff came back with some money from his parents and the vehicle was in perfect condition for the crossing. We realized that if anything went wrong and we couldn't fix it we would most certainly "die in the desert."

Three days before the "big push," the crossing, we met five Germans in a Volkswagen bus who were waiting for a truck convoy that would cross in a few days.

They were going to play it safe and cross with a convoy, safety in numbers. We told them we were going, convoy or no convoy, and they decided to cross with us. The Algerian government stamps your passport out of Algeria 500 miles north of the border. From there onward, you are on your own and they don't want to know what happens to you.

We set out at sunset on a Thursday, following "le piste," which is a French word for "track" that led straight south across the desert. As we drove through the night, our troubles began. The Germans' vehicle sank in and got bogged down in the fine sand that had blown over the track. It also began to break down mechanically and delay us hour by hour.

We had to get across the 500 miles in two days or we would be out of water. We pressed on as fast as we could, but over and over, the Germans' vehicle got stuck and we had to stop and drag it out, losing time and using precious fuel.

Geoff and I alternated driving the Land Rover while the German vehicle drove parallel with us across the flat waste-land.

We kept ourselves motivated by quoting the poem "Carry On" back and forth.

> And so in the strife of the battle of life
> It's easy to fight when you're winning;
> It's easy to slave, and starve and be brave,
> When the dawn of success is beginning,
> But the man who can meet despair and defeat
> With a cheer, there's a man of God's choosing;
> The man who can fight to Heaven's own height
> Is the man who can fight when he's losing.
> Carry on! Carry on!
> Things never were looming so black.
> But show that you haven't a cowardly streak
> And though you're unlucky you never are weak.
> Carry on! Carry on!
> Brace up for another attack
> It's looking like hell, but—you never can tell;
> Carry on, old man! Carry on!

By morning, we had made only 150 miles and we were all exhausted and a bit tense. There was an abandoned army fort, Poste Weygand, in the middle of the desert and we had hoped to shelter there from the midday sun in one of the empty buildings. Now it was almost too late. The sun had begun its implacable climb in the eastern sky. Still, we hurried on. Fortunately, you couldn't get lost crossing the Sahara in the daytime. The track across the desert is marked by black 55-gallon oil drums located every five kilometers. As you drive, you can always see two oil barrels, the one you've just passed and the one you're heading for.

All you have to do to cross the biggest desert on earth is to take it one oil barrel at a time. Of course, traveling at night, if you wander from "le poste", the track, you can get lost in the desert and drive until you run out of gas. Many people had died that way.

As we would approach each oil barrel, the next barrel would pop up on the horizon five kilometers ahead and the barrel behind us would fall off of the horizon, as though it had been in a shooting gallery.

In the years since then, I've found that you can achieve almost any goal you set for yourself if you simply take it one step, one "oil barrel" at a time.

Now the sun really became the enemy; it sat on the horizon like a big evil yellow cat and then began to rise inexorably as we raced south. The temperature grew hotter and hotter. Finally, at 9:30 a.m. it reached 100 degrees F. We signalled between the two vehicles, and agreed to stop and wait out the heat—in the middle of that 25,000 square mile parking lot.

I'll never forget that day. Hour after hour we sat in our vehicles, prostrate from the pounding heat of the sun, that reached 140 degrees F by noon and seemed to stay there forever.

We drank quart after quart of water, our throats going bone dry minutes after gulping down a full canteen. It was worse outside so we just stayed in the vehicles and suffered—hour after hour. Finally, as the afternoon wore on, the temperature slowly began to fall. By 4:00 p.m. it was down to 105 degrees F. When it finally got below 100 degrees F at 5:00 p.m. we started on.

Now, we were racing the clock. We had only made about 200 miles and we had 300 still to go. There was a small oasis and army post on the other side of the Tenezeruft and we knew we had to get there before the midday sun caught us again.

We hadn't slept since Thursday morning and it was now Friday evening. We pushed on over the desert but the Germans' vehicle kept breaking down. All night, exhausted, we worked to get the Volkswagen bus, with the Germans, across to the other side. We were both desperate and scared. We knew we could not last another day. Our water was almost gone.

When the sun rose slowly on Saturday morning, we were still struggling with the Germans' vehicle. Finally, at 9:00 a.m. with 20 miles to go, their vehicle broke down for the last time. We quickly abandoned it, loaded the five Germans in the back of the Land Rover and headed for the oasis.

It was farther than we thought but we made it just before the heat forced us to stop. We all realized how close we had come to actually "dying in the desert." We sat out the heat in a native hut near the fort and then went back and towed the Volkswagen bus into the army post that evening. We had done it. We were over the Sahara. We hadn't slept for 2-1/2 days but we had made it.

I won't go into details of what happened on the rest of our trip across Africa. I won't trouble you with how we had to cross two countries illegally with the police and army on orders to shoot to kill if they saw us. I won't go into how we were almost killed under the boots and riflebutts of a mob of soldiers in the Congo. And I won't talk here about meeting and working with Dr. Albert Schweitzer, in his village at Lambarene.

No, I'll wrap up this story here by telling you what I learned about life and success in the Sahara Crossing. Here are seven rules you can apply to any challenge you face in achieving anything you desire:

Number One: The most important key to achieving great success is to decide upon your goal and then LAUNCH. Get started. Take action. A 12-year study at Babson College concluded that the act of taking the first step is what separates winners from losers.

We set out at the age of 20 to cross three continents and travel 17,000 miles from Vancouver on the West Coast to Capetown on the tip of Africa. And we made it in just under 12 months. But the most important step was the first one. All the rest followed from that.

Number Two: Once you have launched toward your goal, never consider the possibility of failure. The Germans have a saying, "Immer forne, nie zuruck." Always forward, never backward.

Every person who succeeds, succeeds because he or she refused to quit when the going got rough. Your ability to persist in the face of setbacks and disappointment is vital to all great achievement. And it is always a decision that you make.

Number Three: The biggest goal in the world can be accomplished if you just take it "one oil barrel at a time." Thomas Carlyle once wrote, "our great business is not to see what lies dimly at a distance but to do what lies clearly at hand."

The only time you will ever have is NOW. If you live every day, every hour, the best you can, the rest will take care of itself. "Sufficient unto the day are the cares thereof."

Number Four: Watch out for the nay-sayers, the negative people around you who are always telling you that, "You'll die in the desert."

Get around positive people, winners. Fly with the eagles and refuse to listen to objections and reasons why you can't succeed. Someone once said that if every possible objection must first be overcome, nothing will ever get done.

Number Five: Welcome obstacles and difficulties as valuable and inevitable steps on the ladder of success. Remember that difficulties come not to obstruct but to instruct.

Our trip to Africa was one problem after another. We ran out of money over and over. We strained every muscle of our bodies trying to ride bicycles across France and Spain.

Our Land Rover broke down again and again. We suffered from dysentery, heat stroke and exhaustion.

But when it was time, we were ready for the Sahara Crossing. In retrospect we saw clearly that without the lessons we learned from our mistakes, we would have surely died in the desert.

When you look back on any achievement, you will find that it was preceded by many difficulties and many lessons. They are the price that you pay for your success, and no success is possible without them.

Number Six: Be clear about your goal; be flexible about the process of achieving it. Be willing to change, to try something new. Keep your mind open, fluid, flexible.

Be willing to accept feedback from your environment and correct your course. This is a key quality of peak performers. Remember, it's not what you have, but what you do with what you have that separates winners from losers.

It's not what happens to you, but how you respond to what happens to you that counts. In the final analysis, your response to the adversity of life is the real measure of who you are and what you're made of. The Greek philosopher Epictetus said, "Circumstances do not make the man, they merely reveal him to himself."

And finally, **Number Seven:** Remember, no one does it alone. At every step on our journey across Africa, people helped us with advice, with food, with assistance, with money, and especially with warmth, kindness and generosity.

When life is over, it will be the people we lived and laughed and loved with that we remember more than anything else.

Don't be afraid to ask for help from others. It's a mark of strength and courage and character. Don't be reluctant to give of yourself to others generously. It's the mark of caring and compassion and personal greatness.

The reason the Sahara story was so relevant to me was because after the Sahara, I never felt that there was anything I couldn't do. I felt programmed for success for life although it took me many years to understand it.

The reason for this story may be of interest to you because I believe that everyone has a Sahara to cross—perhaps more than one. Many people are crossing their own Sahara right now.

Everyone eventually goes through periods of great difficulty, their own private hell, their "dark night of the soul."

But it is by facing whatever life gives us, with courage and determination, that we grow more surely toward the stars.

Let me conclude with the last verse of "Carry On."

> There are some who drift out in the deserts of doubt.
> And some who in negativity wallow;
> There are others I know, who in piety go
> Because of a Heaven to follow.
> But to labour with zest, and to give of your best,
> For the sweetness and joy of the giving;
> To help folks along with a hand and a song;
> Why, there's the real sunshine of living.
> Carry on! Carry on!
> Fight the good fight and true;
> Believe in your mission, greet life with a cheer;
> There's big work to do, and that's why you are here.
> Carry on! Carry on!
> Let the world be the better for you;
> Carry on, my soul! Carry on!

Dear readers, whatever life hands you, make the decision that you will "Carry On" and if you do, nothing can stop you from achieving the greatness for which you were created.

"What is the environment in the U.S.? We have a dictator and we call it change...The death and the life of the environment is your reaction to it... don't let the environment turn you off. Say...'I see some opportunity there that I wouldn't see anywhere else.' Your life has a special purpose regardless of what the environment is."

H.T.

A PSYCHOLOGIST'S PERSPECTIVE ON EXCELLENCE

Herb True
1717 E. Colfax
South Bend, IN 46617
219/234-2340

Herb True is best known and recognized for his unique ability to direct an entertaining, thought-provoking program. His extensive background, continuing research, and zest for living give an extra dash of purpose, meaning and fun to his presentations. Herb has presented programs to most of Fortune's top 500 companies, thousands of small businesses, civic organizations and youth groups.

He is a valued consultant to businesses, associations, government and educational institutions on management, motivation, creativity, communications, leadership, sales and human behavior.

Herb is currently President of TEAM International, Inc., a company dedicated to the release of human potentials and the development of interpersonal effectiveness. He has also been President of the National Labor Management Foundation; Senior Partner of the True-Klemp Organization; Chief Executive Officer for Sterling Guild of America.

He is an Adjunct Professor of Management at the University of Notre Dame and Saint Mary's College. He has also guest lectured for the American Management Association as well as many of the Major universities in the United States. Dr. True is a recipient of the C.P.A.E. from the National Speakers Association.

One statement that can be made about everybody everywhere is that we're different weights. We can say that people have different I.Q.s. We can say that people are different heights, but, the one statement that we can make about everybody is...no one has reached his potential.

Human potential is the least understood and the most squandered source on the face of this earth. Let's take women... we've squandered tremendous female talent when we really could learn so much from women. For example, what is man's best friend? A dog. What's woman's best friend? Diamonds. Have you ever tried to hock a dog?

What can we do to increase the quality of our performance? How can we get closer to reaching our potential? Think of your performance not as a square, not as a triangle, but as a circle. Think of half of that circle being your desire and half being your capability. So half your performance is desire and half of your performance is capability. *It's one's desire times his capability that gives him his performance.*

Your *desire* is influenced by your *environment*. Suppose your friends call and invite you to play a game of golf. If it's a beautiful day, you may feel a strong desire to go play. However, if it's raining, you may not wish to go. *Your desire is a combination of the environment multiplied by your attitude toward that environment.*

I grew up in Oklahoma where I was poor and had no toys. I used to slide down the hill on my cousin. I look at my kids and they've got their own environment. They have their own hi-fi stereo and ten speed bike. If they wanted to run away from home they would have to call Mayflower van lines. They've got their own bedrooms and their own beds. Since I had two brothers, I never had either my own room or my own bed. I never even slept alone, until I got married.

What is the environment in the U.S.? We have a dictator and we call it *change*. Think about it, that's our dictator. If there is magic in being a human being, the magic is the sensitivity to recognize that moment in passing—that little increment of time just before what you're doing is old and obsolete and the new becomes necessary for survival.

Take, for example, the change in our approach to women. Look at the research. We're finding all kinds of exciting things that women can do better.

What are we finding out about Chicanos? By the year 2000, more people in the U.S. will speak Spanish than speak English.

To talk about change means talking about forecasting. What's going to happen in the 21st century? There are people who forecast and then there are people who like *Megatrends* say, "It's already happening."

We've already changed from an industrial society to an information society. We've already changed from a hierarchy where we have an organization chart with one man at the top who walks around saying, "I am the boss, just think of me as a friend who is always right." Now we're finding out there are different kinds of organizational charts that are more like a wheel. They're called networks. In the 1960's the big concern was discrimination against the blacks. In the 70's we almost forgot about the blacks because we were concerned about discrimination against women. Now, it's the 1990's.

In the 1990's we will have discrimination against older people. My mentor, Bill Gove, is thirteen years older than I am— biologically and chronologically. But in terms of his dreams, in terms of his hopes and in terms of his ability to give, he is the youngest, most playful man you'll ever know.

So what is success? What is excellence? You can read at a thousand words a minute, but you can't think at a thousand words a minute. How fast can you feel? Is it best to do a thousand things one percent better, or, to do one thing a thousand times better? The most successful organizations have a reputation for doing the little things well. Excellence is made up of a thousand little things all being done well.

You're in the business to make a profit. The customer's the boss, and you're in business to serve the customer's need. If you don't serve that customer's need, you'll be like the guy who started a tall man shop in Tokyo. You may sell lots of suits and lots of clothes, but you're going to lose it on alterations. Nobody is immune to this.

The people who are excellent are continually asking me, "What's the big need?" How do we meet other people's needs? I would say consider the customer to be the boss. Also, remember that *environment* is a variable over which you have no control—it *changes*. And if your performance, if your excellence is going to be better or worse, it's affected one way or another by something we call *attitude*.

Your *desire* is a combination of your *attitude* multiplied by the *environment*. The most powerful force that you and I have is what we tell ourselves and believe. I believe in positive thinking; it's the positive talkers that bug me. If you read the book on positive thinking, you probably realize the key word is thinking, not positive.

I play golf with a positive talker. He's gonna drive this water hole. He didn't drive it last year, but he's gonna do it this time. So he gets some new boots and some new clubs. But he gets up there and he puts down an old ball. He's going to do it with old ideas and old attitudes.

I am judged on the number of times that I succeed; I'm not judged on the number of times I fail. And the number of times I succeed is in direct proportion to the number of times I can fail and keep on trying. What do I tell myself? I made a mistake. I made a big mistake but did I fail? No, I made a mistake. Many people succeed when nobody else believes in them, *but never does a person succeed when they don't believe in themselves.*

I have a 118 IQ. You can't even get into Notre Dame with a 118 IQ, but you can teach there. I was told in grade school and in high school that I was dumb. I can show you at the top of my college transcript 15 hours of F. Then I went into the Marine Corps. I found out that I'm not dumb, I'm different. I learn fast, but I forget quick. Then I earned a bachelors degree from the University of Oklahoma. I took all those tough courses like oral penmanship. I married in my junior year of college and we had a child the same month my wife and I graduated. My point in bringing this up is that I've been blessed. I've had great teachers.

My mother is 88. Her recall is down to about fifteen minutes but she still teaches. My new teachers are my own children and my daughters-in-law. Since the beginning of time, before we even knew about the right brain or the left brain, the sages of the ages said, "You do not control your thoughts but you can influence your thoughts."

It always terrifies me when I see pornography. When I was a kid we didn't have as much pornography. It wasn't slicked up and made to look like something really great. People are brilliant; they don't eat rancid food. Why? Because it makes you sick. Aren't there things that you can put in your head that can make you sicker than anything you can put in your belly? Watch your thoughts; they become your words.

Say words enough, program them, and the right brain picks them up. *Your words become your actions and your actions become your habits.* In working with young adults, I try to explain child abuse to them. Every parent who has ever beaten a child learned to beat children, but you can choose to change. So I explain to young gals that if they want to know what a guy is going to be like before they marry him, they should go to his home. Go see how his father treats his spouse. A young man can change, but you should know what he's been taught. One girl said, "I don't have time for that. When I get serious about someone I just explain to him that there will be no pushing

around. Three hundred and sixty-five days after you hit me the
first time, you will have been dead a year."

The death and the life of the *environment is your reaction to
it.* It's your *attitude times your environment that gives you your
desires.* What's the other part? How capable are you? Your
capability is a combination of your knowledge times your skill.
When someone says they want to earn more money, they want
to earn more love or they want to earn more respect, one letter
can change it. Just write down "To Earn More," and the answer
is "Learn More." Maybe you can learn more about yourself,
about your environment and about your competition.

The area of knowledge is overwhelming. In many pseudo
sciences we don't really have many new ideas, so we keep
renaming the old ones. That's great. What is it that makes a
difference? I try to say to myself when I meet somebody, "People want to know how much you care before they care how
much you know."

I know how to kill so beautifully but do I know how to create? One day I killed my son's joy in the victory of his team
by complaining about his dirty clothes ripped at the seams.
The day before, I killed my daughter's pride in the dress she
made by pointing out every fault, then adding my faint praise.
One day I killed a friendship and turned affection into hate. I
misunderstood, but I said it too late. I've killed my spouse's
love, not with a mighty blow, but bit by bit, year by year.
"Where have you been?" "I've been to the beauty parlor."
"What's the matter, was it closed?" I find myself saying things
in a tone and in a manner to my wife I wouldn't say to a clerk at
the Hutson's.

People want to know how much you care. God does not
expect great things from me. He expects love from me, because
I've had love. Expecting some people to love may be expecting
too much. I can't give piano lessons; I can give forgiveness. It
ain't tough for me, I've been forgiven. Bishop Sheen spoke at
the prison in Minnesota. He went in and his first words were,

"We have so much in common. We've all sinned, but you've been caught."

I kill or I create. What am I going to give? Am I going to give joy? Am I going to give hope? What are the options that I have?

Let's go to knowledge. There are things in knowledge I have that I don't like, I don't want it to be true. I wish I could change it. We now know that there is empirical evidence that people make decisions about other people based upon what the person is wearing. We make decisions about other people based on their grooming. We make big decisions about their economic level and their trustworthiness just by what they wear. Go into a store. Wear old jeans, wear worn out tennis shoes, wear an old Marine jacket and nobody even wants to see you. Dress up and even the customers come to see you. I wish it weren't that way.

So in this great technological world what kind of knowledge could I give you that I would want you to remember more than anything else? Something I want to remember myself.

The hardest lesson I have to learn is the affect that I do have on other people. They call it bank balance. If I give somebody respect, esteem, the time of day, I'm making a deposit in the bank. If I give them a quick shuffle or a little twist, I'm making a withdrawal.

I have children in whose bank I am overdrawn. We got one son that's for sale. He ain't a bad kid. He went to college and he did poorly. Couldn't make that 8 o'clock class—and he was going to night school!

The first stage of life is *Leave Me Alone*. That comes at about 14. Anybody who has 12, 13, or 14 year old kids know that it's Leave Me Alone time! That stage lasts for some people till they are 50. We have 50 year old people saying, "Leave me alone. I don't need any help."

The second stage of life, with your children and maybe with

you, is at 25 when they say, *"Help me."* You know this type if you have kids 25…this is a kid who wants help with the insurance on his car or buying a home.

Then at about 35 this marvelous thing happens. The third stage of life is *Let Me Help You.* This is a trap for some fathers. "I've got to help my daughter. I've got to give her a better car because I can't have her driving that kind of car." "Now wait a minute Dad. I don't want a better car. I bought that car. You want to do something with that money? Buy a microwave oven for Mom."

The fourth stage is awkward. *"I Don't Have To Help You, But If You Ever Want Or Need Help, Call Me."* I warn you that if you say this to anybody and you really mean it, they're gonna call you. They're gonna catch that feeling. As Marilyn Monroe said, "I can't just learn the words. I have to learn the feelings." If they ever feel that, they'll call you. But, I warn you it may be the most inopportune moment of your life.

What about all of these skills that we have—the management skills, the marketing skills, the finance skill, the human skills, the entrepreneurial skills, all these skills? Why is the listening skill so important? Why do some therapists charge you $150 an hour to listen?

The planning skill is also important. The will to win isn't everything, but the will to prepare to win is. If you listen to the excellent things you will find over and over the requirement of having a plan.

What are your priorities? I have Jewish friends whose number one priority is to say an "Our Father" before they get out of bed. I have teachers whose number one priority is to touch every student. Our families should be a top priority. "No other success can compensate for failure at home." Notice the critical word there is failure. We all make mistakes. Marriage is the only war in which you sleep with the enemy. My wife and I married for better or worse. I couldn't do any better and she couldn't do any worse.

What have we said? Number one, don't let the environment turn you off. Say, "That really turns me on. I see some opportunity there that I wouldn't see anywhere else." Your life has a special purpose regardless of what the environment is. You were not an accident. You may have been a surprise to your parents, but you're not an accident. You'd be impossible to replace, and there will never be another you.

We all have to make very difficult decisions in life. Art Holst said, "You make a decision, it's gonna be good, or bad, or happy or sad." Immanuel Kant said, "You make the difference." He also said, "To be is to do." Sigmund Freud said, "To do is to be." And Frank Sinatra said, "Do be do be do."

Lord, I ain't what I ought to be. With my potential I ought to be more loving and more open. I ain't what I want to be. I want to be more sensitive; I want to be more patient and more tolerant. Lord, I ain't what I'm gonna be. Thank you, Lord. I ain't what I used to be.

"Position power comes from a title and hierarchy. Personal power, on the other hand, has nothing to do with what other people say you are. It has nothing to do with what you say you are. It has everything to do with who you know you are. Personal power comes from the strength of your choices and the steadiness of your belief in yourself."
J.T.

THE WINNING EDGE OF EXCELLENCE

Jim Tunney
P.O. Box 1500
Carmel-By-The-Sea
CA 93921
408/659-3200

Jim Tunney, Ed. D., began his career as a high school teacher and progressively advanced until he was Superintendent of Schools for a school district in southern California. This career gave him the opportunity to be in the classroom as an instructor, have administrative responsibilities as a Vice Principal and Principal and serve as an Assistant Superintendent.

Parallel to his career in education, Jim also has an outstanding career as a sports official. This career began at the same time he started teaching. Like his education career, Jim's sports official career also was successful, culminating with his involvement with the National Football League. Jim joined the NFL in 1960 and is still active as a referee. He was selected to referee three Super Bowl games. He is the only NFL Referee to officiate two consecutive Super Bowls.

In addition to his education and sports career, Jim is actively involved as a professional speaker and is President of his own company. He makes professional presentations, lecturers, and seminars.

Jim's professional peers have recognized his leadership by electing him to the Presidency of the National Speakers Association as well as the Professional Football Referees Association. He has received numerous professional awards, including the C.P.A.E. from the National Speakers Association.

"Why do I do it?" This is the question I am asked more often than any other by people who attend the presentations I give for corporations, associations and educational institutions.

Why, with a Doctorate in Education, a former superintendent of a large urban school district, a former high school principal, do I walk out in front of 100,000 screaming people to referee football games. Because I can't think of what else to do on Sundays?

For thirty years I've left home on weekends to referee games for the National Football League. I do this for two distinct reasons.

One. In the NFL I work with the best people in the world at what they do. Nobody plays football better than the coaches and players in the NFL. I love being on the field, in the midst of the action, where skill and guts are combining to make the near-impossible happen. Walter Payton earned the nickname "Sweetness" not only because he is a sweet, gentle person off the field, but because it was "sweet" watching him sweep around any defensive eleven intent upon crushing his body to the ground.

Two. I like to be personally associated with winners—champions and heroes. NFL players routinely set new personal and league records. It keeps me "pumped" to see them go "one level higher" while "just doing their job."   Their dedication keeps me inspired to do my best in the rest of my life.

What makes an O.J., O.J.?   Roger Staubach, Roger Staubach? Walter Payton, Walter Payton? What's behind their drive to consistently achieve excellence? What motivates them to pull more out of themselves than others with similar talents manage to do?

Is it simply more push, more drive than the next guy? Is it focus? Is it vitamins and training? Is it anger? Is it that mysterious stuff called self-esteem?

Then, too, what do we mean by excellence? How do we know if what we've just accomplished is our peak performance, or only a reasonably good job? How do we accelerate ourselves to reach peak performance? Once there, how do we pace ourselves so that we stay "up" long enough to achieve consistent excellence, as Payton, O.J., Staubach, and others have shown us can be done?

What is it that motivates you? What type of circumstances and personalities draw out your best performance? Do you perform best doing work you love? Or is it the competitive edge that triggers your attention? Or do you need both?

Do you seek recognition from your peers? Or is it the need for approval from your boss that gets you to work on time, ready to go? Do you prefer to work alone? Or are you pulled toward serving others or meeting lots of new people?

Whatever your answers to these questions, when was the last time you asked yourself, "Am I demanding excellence from myself?"

Let me tell you what motivates me. June motivates me. Not the woman. The month. Each June, I have the privilege of working the California Special Olympics Summer Games. Each year more than 3,000 mentally and physically handicapped young people compete in the same events that our Olympic champions compete in every four years. It is an opportunity for me to witness courage—pure, raw courage.

The next time you have a tough decision to make, with knots in your stomach and sweat pouring from your brow, think about an eleven-year-old girl, blind since birth, climbing a ladder she cannot see, walking to the end of the three-meter diving board, and diving off, volitionally, in control, gracefully, into a pool of water that her coach has assured her is there. Now, that is courage.

Each of us has that kind of courage within us, when we believe we do. The ability to routinely tap inner resources is one distinction between Special Olympians and most of us. They work their courage every day in order to do ordinary things. For most of us, with all our abundant skills and resources, we can forget our courage and still get along pretty well. Then, when things get tough, as they inevitably do from time to time, we've lost it. Courage, too, is a use it or lose it proposition.

I saw a kid in a wheelchair with cerebral palsy so bad he had no use of either hand and one leg. He could only move one foot. From his wheelchair, he could just barely touch the ground with that one good foot. To compete in his event, he turned the wheelchair around and pushed it backwards. He won. He was ecstatic with his accomplishment.

The next time you feel stymied and can't seem to find a solution to a problem, think about solving that problem or any problem with only one good foot. The exercise may bring on a rash of creativity and courage.

When frustrated and going in circles, it's best to pause, a moment, an hour, a day. Take a deep breath. Write down what is confusing you. Call a friend. Talk it out. There are always avenues out of gridlock, from the very moment you decide to move on.

After another event, I was standing about twenty feet from the victory stand when a 26-year-old mentally, physically and emotionally handicapped man received his award for winning the 100-meter dash. As the judge placed the gold medal around his neck, the young man said "Thanks."

I looked over to his sponsor, who was standing next to me. Tears were rolling down her cheeks.

"That's a marvelous accomplishment for that young man," I said.

"Yes," she said. "That's the first word he's ever spoken."

What compels you to fight for the best from yourself, even against tough odds? Oliver Wendell Holmes was right when he said, "Most of us die with our music still in us."

How do we get the music out?

I believe you have to get familiar with what's inside, to learn to trust your innate courage, and use it every day so that you don't forget it's there. This gumption, this clarity of will, resides within each of us; latent perhaps, but always there. It is our best resource for managing the changes and challenges of life. Whether the change or challenge is one we have sought, as in a new job or a new relationship, or some sort of trouble which lands as unfairly as the conditions these Special Olympians must face, tapping our personal power is our best, most immediate, and strongest ally.

What I call "personal power" is entirely different from power of authority or "position power." You know position power. In the military, generals have it over sergeants, and sergeants over privates. In the school business, superintendents have it over principals, principals have it over teachers, and teachers have it over students. Position power comes from a title and hierarchy.

Personal power, on the other hand, has nothing to do with what other people say you are. It has nothing to do with what you say you are. It has everything to do with who you know you are.

Personal power comes from the strength of your choices and the steadiness of your belief in yourself. You won't have courage until you have found the source of this clarity and confidence within yourself.

One truth I've found in life is that the more personal power you take into any relationship, the less vulnerable you will be to those working from their position power.

There is power present in all relationships. Husband and wife. Mother and daughter. Father and son. Teacher and student. Employer and employee. General and private. Doctor and patient.

As an NFL referee, I have position power, but I'll tell you, I wouldn't last five minutes on the field unless I am working from my personal power and others can sense it. The striped shirt means nothing compared to strength of character displayed. Even with 30 years' experience and three Super Bowls, I could no more survive on the field with the attitude of "I'm the referee so you better pay attention to me" and expect obedience than I could run like O.J. or throw like Staubach.

In addition to being in the midst of great action, being a referee means you are a target for intimidation. Intimidation can get to anyone in any position, except those working from their personal power.

Once you have learned to forcefully use the self-knowledge and courage that I call "personal power," you will be able to ignore the externals and stay focused, immune to taunts, veiled threats, uncertainty, or a sudden change in conditions.

I refuse to be intimidated by any player, any coach, any arena, any spectator, or any fog. I'm going to stay focused and do my job better than I've ever done it before. What others yell at me—good or bad—doesn't matter. Performing to my best level does.

Staying clear on the distinction between personal power and position power is what develops self-confidence. You have to control yourself before you can control the circumstances. It doesn't matter whether those circumstances involve 22 football players intent on winning, two pre-schoolers in the rec room, or a boardroom of bosses with a long agenda. Your level of performance comes from your level of belief in yourself—from tapping that personal power within you which equates to self-confidence and the courage to hold your own.

So what about dealing with the memory of other times when you didn't hold your own, lost your will, or made a mistake? Consider this: If you break your arm, and the bone heals correctly, the healed bone will be stronger than the original bone.

Strength comes from learning from your failures, not from never having failed. The learning is the healing. All of us fail sometimes. The difference is, some of us do not "heal" as well as others.

If we don't "heal," if we do not identify what we learned, we tend to lose confidence. We may become risk-averse and start putting energy into protecting ourselves instead of stretching ourselves. What usually happens then is that our days become filled with less and less instead of more and more.

Sometimes all there is to learn from a bad time is that we can endure a lot and still survive. Ernest Hemingway said, "Man can be destroyed, but never defeated."

You can never be defeated unless you give up your personal power. No one can take it from you, but, just look around you. Some people sure do give it up easily.

Have you? Will you again?

Viktor Frankl came to the same place from a different direction. Frankl, an Austrian psychiatrist, was captured by the Nazis and spent six years at Auschwitz during World War II. He endured that degradation, and yet found a way to maintain his dignity and continue to build a personal identity. While witnessing and being subjected to those horrors and the constant threat of death, Frankl secreted scraps of toilet paper and wrote the now-classic book, *Man's Search for Meaning.*

My favorite insight from Dr. Frankl's book is his statement about man's ultimate freedom: "Of all the freedoms you have, and of all the freedoms that can be taken away from you, the one freedom no one can take away from you is the freedom to choose the attitude with which you approach any problem, task, or opportunity."

Frankl wrote this while he was a prisoner. The guards were in control of what little he could do, when, and where. Yet, the guards could not take from him his freedom to choose his own attitude. He chose to grow and learn in spite of the miserable conditions, ones many found hopeless.

I agree with Frankl. No one can take from you the freedom to choose your attitude, or force you to give up your belief in yourself. Yet, we see it happen all the time. People say, "Well,

I'm not a morning person. In fact, I'm kinda grouchy in the morning until I've had my first cup of coffee. My dad was that way, and his dad. It's sort of a family thing."

Ah, come on. If you want to be grouchy in the morning, that's your right, but don't blame it on the lack of caffeine or your dear old dad.

Who's in charge here, anyway? If you're not, when did you give up your freedom of choice, and why?

I like the story about the boy building a sand castle on the beach near the edge of the surf. The kid was about eight or nine. He had built this marvelous, elaborate castle, complete with turrets and a moat. Something in the Donald Trump style.

What the kid didn't notice was that the tide was coming in. Just as he smoothed out a really neat section, a wave came in and wiped out his castle.

The kid laughed and immediately began to rebuild. Just as he got it looking great, another wave came in and washed it away. The kid laughed, and began building again.

Do you think his resilience is silly—just a dumb kid not knowing enough to move away from the surf line? His good work kept being destroyed, and yet he laughed and went on.

What are the choices? He could cry. He could swear. He could quit. He could pout. He could run to mama. He chose to laugh. Why?

For one thing, he had a reason to be confident. He had made a great castle already. He knew he could do it again.

Second, and more important for the types of challenges and problems we face everyday, the kid was having fun. He liked the process of building great castles. Ending, being done, wasn't the point of his play. Building was. Are you having fun, yet?

If Vince Lombardi, legendary coach of the Green Bay Packers, had met this kid, he would have pulled him off the beach and made him a number one draft choice. Lombardi, a great inspiration for me over the years, was fond of barking, "Failure isn't getting knocked down. Failure is not getting back up after you've been knocked down."

His Packers were expected to rise fast after a hit or a poor execution, ready to try again even harder. Lombardi understood that rising again after momentary failures was a prime ingredient in the process of winning. He worked only with players who were willing to accept this necessity and get up again, eager and joyful, like the kid on the beach.

I had to learn this lesson myself. When I was growing up, I wanted to be a baseball player. I dreamed of pitching for the New York Yankees. I wanted to stand on the mound in Yankee Stadium, in that house that Ruth built.

The trouble was, I couldn't break a pane of glass in a small room. I just didn't have it. I played baseball for four years in high school. Well, I didn't play a lot. I sat on the bench a lot. I was one of those guys who was there everyday. I never missed a day of practice. I figured they couldn't get along without me sitting on that bench.

By the time I was a senior, I was the starting second baseman on the Alhambra High School baseball team. That may not mean much to you, but, boy, I felt good.

I remember a crucial game. It was against El Monte High. El Monte and Alhambra were tied for the league lead. We wanted to win this game bad. I remember the day so well. It was a Friday afternoon. We were at El Monte High School. Bottom of the ninth. Bases loaded. We were ahead 3 to 2. We had two outs on them.

Got the picture? El Monte up and I'm the second baseman. I thought to myself, "Don't hit the ball to me."

I was afraid that if the ball came my way, it would go right between my legs, two runs would score, and who would they blame? Tunney.

I thought about that fear for days, weeks, months afterward. It plagued me. That scared whispering inside me was the voice of a loser. I didn't want to be a loser. I wanted to be a winner. So I decided to turn it around.

The next year in college, when spring brought baseball season, I was the starting first baseman for Occidental College. We were a good team, 23-2. I made it a point during every game, every inning, every pitch, to say to myself, "Hit the ball to me."

I didn't care about being a star or a hero, but I knew I could make the play if I didn't let self-doubt defeat all those hours of practicing and building skills. I knew that if I kept reinforcing in myself the belief that I could handle anything that came my way, I would strengthen my self-confidence and be ready when the play came my way.

How about you? Which voice are you listening to? Are you whispering to yourself, "Don't hit the ball to me," afraid to commit yourself? Or, are you saying, "I know I can do it," willing to risk failure for the chance to succeed?

The only difference between that scared kid at second base and the ready team player at first base was that I had shifted my attitude. I did for myself what Jesse Jackson is trying to get kids in the inner cities to understand. He wants them to see there is a way out of the gridlock that poverty and a pervading lost hope can breed. His famous maxim is true for anyone wanting to tap the inner resource I call personal power: "It's not your aptitude but your attitude that determines your altitude, if you have intestinal fortitude."

Shift your attention and you will shift your attitude. Silence those whispers of self-doubt. Shut them off. Give yourself positive instructions instead. Build the attitude of "I can" and you will.

Success and excellence are not static. They cannot be located in some magical spot where completion and consensus are assured. The best football game has yet to be played. The smartest deal has yet to be envisioned. Your personal best will improve as your dreams and ability to dare and believe in yourself improve.

Walt Disney credited his success to concentrating on four attitudes: "Think, believe, dream, and dare." This is one concise formula for developing courage.

Consistently demand these steps of yourself. Remember, too, that setbacks are as natural as waves coming in from the sea. They can be just as temporary, if you teach yourself to "heal" and get up again, eager to go again.

The skills involved in developing the courage and self-confidence that I call personal power are not mysterious. The techniques I and many others have used to silence negative inner-whispers and focus instead on positive self-management will work for you and everyone, if you are willing to shift your focus and build a new attitude. When you do, you will find yourself more frequently on the winning edge of excellence, where there is more fun, more accomplishment, and no arbitrary end point.

"Unfortunately, many well meaning but ineffective managers are working as hard as they can without the slightest idea of what direction they are moving. One of the greatest voids in American business today is the lack of true leadership. Most organizations are over-managed and under-led."
T.W.

LEADERSHIP—
THE UNFORGED PATH

Thomas J. Winninger
3356 Kimball Avenue, Suite 300
Waterloo, Iowa 50702
319/236-3174

Tom Winninger is founder of the Winninger Resource Group, a company providing independent businesses with marketing, management, sales and innovative service strategy design techniques. He has developed strategies to assist companies market everything from: wholesale distribution services to chain saws, Spam to chili, blenders to medical reference books, hotel services to restaurant desserts, and computers to financial services

Tom is known for his colorful, inspiring, and highly successful coaching strategies. Over 20,000 business, sales and management professionals attend his presentations annually. Tom has addressed over 1,250 organizations in the past 11 years including 50 of the "Fortune 500."

He is one of only 95 professional speakers to have received the C.P.A.E. (Council of Peers' Award of Excellence) of the National Speakers Association. Noted for his own business success, he is a 1990 nominee of America's Entrepreneur of the Year. As a prolific and insightful author Tom has been published in over 50 trade journals and is the subject of many interviews.

Tom is the 1990-91 President of the National Speakers Association, a 3,800 member association.

I find the great thing in this world is not so much where we
stand as in what direction we are moving.
Oliver Wendell Holmes.

Though penned in a day when life was not nearly as hectic, little did Holmes realize how appropriate his words would be for today. Competition and the challenge to be number one causes many businesses to scurry in every which way, eager to get their piece of the pie. Management is under pressure as never before to "perform" while they take their companies to unscaled heights, constantly carving new notches on the gunbarrel of success.

Unfortunately, many well meaning but ineffective managers are working as hard as they can without the slightest idea of what direction they are moving. One of the greatest voids in American business today is the lack of true leadership. Most organizations are over-managed and under-led. Centering on the day to day activities, routine tasks, and hours of organizing and processing, they lose the "magic" of the momentum needed to change their competitive position in the market or strengthen their company through the cumulative reach for their ultimate goal. The organization with true leadership, however, forges a different path, investing the precious hours of the day unlocking the "mysteries" of building a power-packed future.

Management and leadership share the same common goal. Both seek to give instruction and direction to those under their supervision. Question the goals of management in any busy company today and undoubtedly their answer would be "to lead the company to a bigger share of the market and become #1!" Dig a little deeper however, and you'll often find that most of the management family is spending valuable time actually performing the tasks they've hired talented staff to accomplish. They neglect the opportunities to participate in the thrill of leading their companies through quantum leaps on the road to success.

True leadership operates under the same basic principle but the outcome is sure to be a great deal more effective. Leadership accomplishes growth and builds strength by providing the members of the organization with a "vision." The dictionary definition of vision says... "the faculty of sight, that which is or has been seen," and goes on to further elaborate... "unusual competence in discernment or perception, intelligent foresight, like a man of vision." Therein lies the key to unlocking the secrets of leadership.

Where would this world be if it had been without the men of vision like John F. Kennedy, Abraham Lincoln, Winston Churchill, or Benjamin Franklin? Each faced what looked like insurmountable obstacles, yet through a commitment to vision brought freedom and integrity to those sheltered under the umbrella of their leadership. Thanks to those who have gone before us we now have the opportunity to participate in free enterprise, to see our dreams become reality. Each of these men had a vision, laid out in clear, simple terms.

We are still blessed with great leaders today. Doctors and scientists are finding cures to crippling diseases, revolutionaries are crumbling the walls of communism, and every day life in outer space comes a little closer to home. All of this greatness may tempt one to think the art of leadership is reserved for the chosen few. On the contrary, the secret is not really so mysterious at all.

The two facets blended among all great leaders are:

1. Their ability to perceive what could be done and what lies ahead;

2. Their ability to share this with others and encourage them to share in the same vision.

Please understand, there is no complex formula that produces a great leader. There is no school that hands out a certificate after a crash course in Leadership #101. It is a skill that can be learned. Life's experiences, if we are willing to learn from them, are the greatest instructors. Some people may be born with the instinctive desire to "lead" but the true mechanics of leadership must be played out in the arena of life.

Leadership can be likened in some ways to the children's beloved tale of "The Velveteen Rabbit." In this story the toys in a child's nursery are well versed in the fine art of being loved. One of the oldest toys, a bedraggled, one-eyed rocking horse shares a secret with the newest stuffed creature, a beautiful, lush velveteen rabbit. In a few well chosen words he tells the rabbit that "to be really loved, you have to get some of your skin rubbed off…"

So it goes with leaders. They have to be willing to roll up their shirt sleeves and rub elbows with life's hard knocks. Look closely at truly great leaders and you'll no doubt see the scars of real life scuffles. The wounds may have healed but they come from living on the cutting edge, from not being afraid to step out of the comfort zone. Leaders are risk-takers. They are the first ones to grab a new opportunity, to see another path not yet forged, to leave behind the tried and true and take on the new and uncharted course.

There are a few ground rules that leaders operate with. They are simple but essential. Leaders must learn to:

1. Create a vision—then clarify it. The vision must be clear-cut, attainable, and realistic.

2. Sell the vision to the team. The successful leader is eager to share the vision, not cloister it behind boardroom doors. Team members must be able to perceive co-ownership in the vision.

3. Understand power—leadership is not license to trample on people's emotions and self-worth.

4. Identify the motivating force of the individual team members. This means coming out from behind the "iron curtain" of the corporate office and getting to know your people.

5. Encourage the team to join in taking risks. Delegate tasks of considerable importance.

6. Recruit team members who are willing to "buy in" to the vision. (When interviewing be sure to look for people with rolled up sleeves and evidences of scratches with life.)

It is easy to see that the management driven organization is more involved with the "how-to" detail while the leadership driven organization deals with the "why" concept. A manager tends to focus on tasks, while a leader will build a staff that shares the vision, believes in it, and is willing to carry out the steps to realizing the vision. Companies operating under the lack of leadership will eventually begin to show the effects in high turnover, absenteeism, lack of team spirit, flat production, no direction and a perpetual cycle of reward and punishment. On the flip side, companies flourishing under the benefits of leadership experience team spirit, reduced turnover, upward mobility, positive reinforcement and ultimately...increased pro-ductivity.

In keeping with the theory that leadership is a skill, it's important to remember that "organization" is essential. Leaders must make a commitment to effective use of time, effort, and talent, beginning first with themselves. It is safe to assume that great leaders follow a well planned daily agenda. We know for a fact that Abraham Lincoln kept a personal daily journal and Ben Franklin was the premier user of a daily planner. The success of an organization is dependent upon the leadership capabilities of the person behind the vision. That person must be stream-lined and well-tuned. The key to effective personal management is "doing the right thing at the right time." The leader who is bogged down with simple daily tasks will be forced off track and the vision will turn cloudy. A minimum of 10-20 minutes per day should be spent in planning the next day's activities. It is essential in giving the team a sense of direction. It's bringing the future into today! When a leader writes realistic, prioritized, time sequenced goals, that's called "planned achievement." Sadly enough, many managers today are so busy playing catch up ball they have little time to plan for success.

A great leader will gather around him a team of people who are committed to the common goal. Of course not all members of a team will have the same skill level or background experience. They will all possess different personality traits (thank heaven!), physical make-up, and ethnic backgrounds. But a keen leader will seek out those who are best matched with a specific task and groom them to become the "manager" of that particular area. Through the art of sharing the vision, making goals achievable, open communication and praise, the leader creates a fine tuned symphony of players orchestrating success for themselves and the company as well.

A lot of myths surround the great leaders. People have been led to believe that to be a great leader one must be an accomplished orator, a shrewd politician, extroverted, and possess great looks and a powerful physique. How foolish! Franklin D. Roosevelt and John F. Kennedy both were physically impaired. Moses, the beloved leader of the Israelites had a speech impediment. Einstein was extremely homely in looks and never even went to college! Fortunately the myths are being broken down. Leaders can be short, tall, brown eyed or blue, shy or outgoing, or even wheelchair bound. The key lies not in the outward appearance, but in the combination of the skills, strategies and personal commitment that an individual holds inside.

Insights Into Excellence
Speakers Roundtable
Resource Materials

Chapter 1: The Role of the Manager
Ken Blanchard, 125 State Place, Escondido, CA 92025;
(619) 489-5005
Books, Audio and Video Programs:
One Minute Manager Library:
The One Minute Manager (1982).
Putting the One Minute Manager to Work (1984).
Leadership and the One Minute Manager (1985).
The One Minute Manager Gets Fit (1986).
The One Minute Manager Meets the Monkey (1989).
The One Minute Manager Builds High Performing Teams (1990).
Management of Organizational Behavior, Co-author with Dr.
Paul Hersey, textbook, fifth edition.
The Power of Ethical Management (1988) with Dr. Norman
Vincent Peale.

Chapter 2: Quick, Before It's Gone: Grabbing Hold of Tomorrow
Ty Boyd, The Cullen Center, 1727 Garden Terrace, Charlotte, NC
28203;
(704) 333-9999 or (800) 336-2693
Book:
Visions...From the Leaders of Today—For the Leaders of Tomorrow
Audio Cassettes:
Hear It, Feel It, Tell It, Sell It (Communications and time manage-
ment—originally produced as *Skill Builder I*).
Life Planning and Success Achievement (Goal setting, communi-
cation skills, leadership-originally *Skill Builder II*).
Achievement Through Motivation Series.
Encyclopedia of Self-Improvement: 4 Volumes (with M.R.Kop-
meyer, Narrated by Ty Boyd, each volume 12 cassettes).

Chapter 3: Technology Has Dealt Us A New Deck Of Cards
Daniel Burrus, P. O. Box 26413, Milwaukee, WI 53226;
(414)774-7790 or (414) 774-8330 Fax
Books:
The New Tools of Technology
Medical Advances
Environmental Solutions
Advances in Agriculture
Audio Cassettes:
Futureview®: Your Competitive Edge
Futureview®: A Look Ahead
Newsletter:
Technology Futures Newsletter®

Chapter 4: Inner√iewing: Finding "The Natural" In People
Jim Cathcart, PO Box 9075, La Jolla, CA 92038;
(619) 558-8855 or (800) 222-4883 or (619) 558-9677 Fax
Profiles:
Individual *Inner √iew*™ profiles: A computerized narrative
(approximately 16 pages) describing your own unique strengths
and traits. Based on your responses to a 100 question profile
questionnaire.
Art of Choosing Well Executive Skills Training (certification in the
use of Inner√iewing).
Book:
Relationship Selling.
Video Cassettes:
Think Service (An Evening at the Improv, 2 hours).

Chapter 5: Passport to Potential
Danny Cox, 17381 Bonner Drive, Tustin, CA 92680;
(714) 838-3030
Audio Cassettes:
Leadership When The Heat's On (6 cassettes, leadership course).
High Achievement Here and Now (4 cassette, Developing poten-
tial, turn around techniques for business).

Chapter 6: Take Charge of Your Future
Patricia Fripp, 527 Hugo Street, San Francisco, CA 94122,
415/753-6556 or (800) 634-3035 or (800) 553- 6556 (in CA).
Book and Audio:

Get What You Want. (Relationships, habits and thoughts that stop
you from being the person you want to be; Book/6 tapes).
Audio Cassettes:

Creative Thinking for Better Business
(Live Seminar on goals, creativity, and time, 6 tapes).
*Express Yourself With Flair: Increase the Speed With Which You
Succeed* (Communication skills for any situation, 6 tapes).

Chapter 7: You Do It To You
Bill Gove , 250 JFK Drive, Suite 101, Atlantis, FL 33462;
(407)964-5225
Audio Cassettes:

*Excellence is an Inside Job: (Achievement Through Motivation/
Personal Success Series).*
Nightingale Treasury of Humor: Vol. 2.
Video Cassettes:

Addiction to Positive Growth (Part of Ultimate Success Library
Video Series).

Chapter 8: Takin' Up The Slack
Tom Haggai, 209 N. Main St., Suite 203, High Point, NC 27260;
(919) 889-8962
Books:

How the Best Is Won: Lessons in Management from the Old West
(Thomas Nelson Publishers).
Today: Daily readings to encourage your confidence, stimulate
your creativity and inspire you to excellence.

Chapter 9: Stop Hoping and Start Coping
Ira Hayes, 326 Meadowlark Court, Marco Island, FL 33937;
(813) 394-0830

Ira Hayes Continued:
Books:
> *Success: Go For It.*
> *Yak, Yak, Yak* (Public Speaking).

Audio Cassettes:
> *Keeping Pace With Tomorrow* (1 Hour).

Video Cassettes:
> *Keeping Pace With Tomorrow.*

Chapter 10: The Consistently Exceptional Leader
Christopher Hegarty, PO Box 1152, Novato, CA 94948;
(415) 892-2858 (USA)
Books:
> *How to Manage Your Boss.*

Profiles:
> *Consistently Exceptional Leadership* .
> *Stress Analysis* .
> *Recognizing and Redirecting Stress* (Participants Manual for Stress Analysis Profile).
> *Management Effectiveness Survey* .
> *Integrated Management Development System* (Four Part Kit).

Audio Cassettes:
> *How To Manage Your Boss* (4 Audio Cassette Album).
> *Speak Easy To One or One Thousand* (4 Audio Cassette Album).
> *Avoiding Calamities In Public Speaking* (Single Cassette).

Video Cassette:
> *Workaholism...How To Make A Life As Well As A Living* (Single Video Cassette).

Chapter 11: The Challenge of Excellence
Art Holst, 2001 W. Willow Knolls Rd., Suite 206, Peoria, IL 61614;
(309) 691-9339 or (800) 926-9339
Books:
> *Sunday Zebras* (Forrest Publishing).

Audio Cassettes:
> *Challenge of Excellence.*

Challenge of a Pro.
Touchdowns in Selling.
The Challenge of Excellence: Achievement Through Motivation
Series.
Video Cassettes:
Challenge of Excellence.

Chapter 12: Management Techniques that Work
   or Leadership in Action
Allan J. Hurst, C.M.C., Pres., Quorum, Ltd., 45-175 Panorama Drive,
   Suite D, Palm Desert, CA 92260;
(800) 367-4873 or (619) 779-1300
Profile/Checklist:
   What Is Your Management Effectiveness Quotient?
Audio Cassette:
   *What every CEO Should Know: What's the Real Role of You
   Firm's Financial Function.*

Chapter 13: Productivity Through Motivation
Don Hutson, PO Box 172181, Memphis, TN 38187-2181;
(800) 647-9166
Books:
   High Performance Selling (Spring '92).
Audio Cassettes:
   High Performance Selling (50 Skills for Professional Salespeople,
   6 cassettes).
   Mastering Creative Leadership (Workbook, 6 cassettes).
Video Cassettes:
   High Performance Video Series (14 video tapes on management,
   leadership, sales and personal development).
   Ultimate Success Library (A comprehensive cross-referenced and
   indexed product featuring the works of over 150 different speak-
   ers, authors, and trainers; format: books, audio tapes and video
   tapes).
   Insights Into Excellence Video Series (Video tape series with 20
   different titles, produced by U.S.Learning, Inc.).

Chapter 14: Excellence Through Humor or Laughter, Thinking & Books
Charlie "T" Jones, 206 West Allen St., Mechanicsburg, PA 17055;
(800) 233-2665 or (717) 691-0400
Books:
Life is Tremendous.
The Books You Read: Business Edition. (250 leaders share a book
that influenced their life).
The Books You Read: Professional Edition, Vol. 2.
The Books You Read: Devotional Edition, Vol. 3.
Humor Is Tremendous.
Wit & Wisdom.
Audio Cassettes:
Price of Leadership /7 Laws (3 Hours Live).
Managing Your Life (3 Hours Live).
Video Cassettes:
*Decision Making/Laws of Leadership/Communication/ Emotional
Maturity* (Four—25 Minute VHS/Live).

Chapter 15: Five Keys to Excellence
Jim Newman, PO Box 1378, Studio City, CA 91614;
(818) 769-5100
Book:
Release Your Brakes!
Audio Cassettes:
High Performance Behavior (6 cassettes).
Seminar:
PACE (A 4-day resident program for executives and their spouses).
Video Cassettes:
Releasing Human Potential (Fourteen session training program
with Leader's Guide and Student Manuals).

Chapter 16: Packing Parachutes
J. Charles Plumb, 1200 N. San Marcos Rd., Santa Barbara, CA 93111;
(805) 683-1969
Books:
I'm No Hero (Hardback and softcover).
The Last Domino.

Audio Cassettes:
  Packing Parachutes.
Video Cassettes:
  Overcoming Adversity.

Chapter 17: Position Yourself For Success
Nido R. Qubein, Creative Services, Inc., 806 Westchester Drive, P. O.
  Box 6008, High Point, NC 27262; (919)889-3010
Books:
  Communicate Like A Pro
  Get The Best From Yourself
  Nido Qubein's Techniques For Professional Selling
  (Books published by Berkley Publlishers)
Audio Cassettes:
  How to be a Great Communicator
  Positioning
  Selling Savvy
  The 12 Essential Elements to Professional Success
  How to Market Your Professional Expertise
  How to Develop a Winning Image
  how to Market Through Direct mail
  how to Promote Yourself Through Public Speaking
  (All Audio programs produced by Nightingale-Conant)

Chapter 18: A Ticket to Anywhere
Cavett Robert, 1284 East Edgemont, Phoenix AZ 85006;
(602) 266-2508
Books:
  The Fine Art of Doing Better.
  Retire To Fun and Freedom.
Audio Cassettes:
  Success With People (6 cassette).
  Sales, Human Engineering and Motivation (6 cassette).
  The New Real Estate Survival Kit (6 cassette).
  Success With People (6 cassette).
  Sales, Human Engineering and Motivation (6 cassette).
  The New Real Estate Survival Kit (6 cassette).

Cavett Robert Continued:
Video Cassettes:
Sales Pros Speaker Video Series (Four-25 min.VHS Video tapes).

Chapter 19: Success is a Journey
Brian Tracy, 462 Stevens Ave., # 202, Solana Beach, CA 92075;
(800) 542-4252 or (619) 481-2977
Audio Cassette Learning Programs:
   The Psychology of Achievement.
   The Psychology of Selling.
   The Psychology of Success.
   How You Can Start, Build, Manage or Turn Around Any Business.
   How to Master Your Time.
   Getting Rich In America.
   The Peak Performance Woman.
   How to Raise Happy, Healthy, Self-Confident Children.
   Leadership.
Video Learning Programs:
   Phoenix Seminar on the Psychology of Achievement (12 hrs).
   The New Psychology of Selling (7 hrs).
   Time Management for Results (3 hrs).
   How to Start and Build your Own Successful Business (12 hrs).
   A Gift of Self-Esteem (Teenager; 6 hrs).
   Effective Manager Seminar Series (14 hrs).
   Success Secrets of Self-Made Millionaires.
   24 Techniques for Closing the Sale.
   10 Keys to a More Powerful Personality.
Books and Audio Programs:
   Maximum Performance (48 cassettes, 30 hrs, 500 pgs.).

Chapter 20: A Psychologist's Perspective on Excellence
Herb True, Ph. D., 1717 E. Colfax , South Bend, IN 46617;
(219) 234-2340
Books:
   Funny Bone Pocketbook.
   Humor Power (Doubleday).

Audio Cassettes:
   (A) *Selling* (B) *Enthusiasm* (C) *Management* (D) *Motivation* (E) *Love* (F) *Communications* (G) *Humor Power.*
Video Cassettes:
   The Winning Edge.
   Humor Power.
Computer: (IBM compatibles with hard disc)
   Computerized Humor Library.
   Professional Presentation Manager.

Chapter 21: The Winning Edge of Excellence
Jim Tunney, Ed. D., C.P.A.E., P.O. Box 1500, Carmel-By-The-Sea, CA 93921;
(408) 659-3200
Books:
   Impartial Judgment—The "Dean of NFL Referees" Calls Pro Football the Way He Sees It (Franklin Watts Publishing).
Audio Cassettes:
   Here's To The Winners (1 hour).
   A Professional Way to Winning (6 hours).
Video Cassette:
   Here's To The Winners (1 hour).
Reprints:
   The Self-Evolution Series: Essays on Leadership and the Discipline of Optimism.

Chapter 22: Leadership—The Unforged Path
Tom Winninger, C.P.A.E., 3356 Kimball Avenue, Suite 300
Waterloo, Iowa 50702;
319/236-3174 or (800) 833-3464
Audio Cassettes:
   Book–It, Vol. 1 & Vol. 2 (Professional Speaking, both volumes contain 8 cassettes).
   The Persuasive Art of Selling (Sales, 8 cassettes).
   Getting the Right Things Done (Management, 8 cassettes).
   Keeping The Customer #1 (Customer Relations, 4 cassettes).

Insights Into Excellence
Video Series:

New! A collection of twenty-two professional video and audio tapes featuring the members of Speakers Roundtable.

Now you can see and listen to members of Speakers Roundtable in your home, office or car. The program includes individual audio and video tapes, plus a comprehensive *Leader's Guide and Workbook.* Your organization becomes involved in an in-depth learning experience in sales, communication, customer service, leadership, management techniques and more.

This dynamic, comprehensive training program will make your training and motivation challenge easier than ever. In addition to the video tapes you will receive a *Leader's Guide* with the "Excellence Index" for *targeted problem-solving* and focusing on *individual training needs.* Additionally, the learning experience will be supplemented by workbooks for note-taking and audio cassette sound tracks of each video for retention and review.

Produced by U. S. Learning, Inc., Memphis, TN. For more information, call any member of Speakers Roundtable.